Role of Women in Reservation Politics

Role of Women in Reservation Politics

Alka Saxena

ALTAR PUBLISHING HOUSE
NEW DELHI (INDIA)

Published by

ALTAR PUBLISHING HOUSE
L- 9 A, IInd FLOOR, STREET NO.42
SADATPUR EXTENSION
DELHI-110094 (INDIA)
CELL- 0-9899346553, 0-9868990429

Role of Women in Reservation Politics

Edition 2011
ISBN 978-81-910524--9-7

Printed in India
at Asian Offset Printers, Delhi

Preface

Women in India have been endowed with several responsibilities concerned to the household and family circle, nonetheless now with the drift in development and political policies, encumber of decision making is also laid on women. Keeping in mind the importance of women as human resource affecting national development, women's participation in democracy was felt later after Independence. To provide enhanced representation to rural women in political world, specific provision were incorporated in the constitution of India through the 73rd amendment act in 1992. A significant provision of this Act is the reservation of 1/3rd seats for women in all position in the local rural parliament. It was a landmark for women empowerment. Through this amendment, participation of women was encouraged at the village politics. This provision not only addressed the strategic needs of women but also provided her a platform to participate in rural development activities.

However, the Women's Reservation Bill (The Constitution (108th Amendment) Bill) has been a long pending one in India which aims to empower women with 33.3 per cent of seats reserved in the parliament and state legislative assemblies. Although the Upper House Rajya Sabha passed it on 9 Mar 2010, it has yet to present in the Lok Sabha. To certain extent if not largely, opportunities through reservation will assure female involvement and representation in the development and political processes at the grass roots.

In spite of all stumbling blocks, women in India are trying hard to make space for themselves in the political arena. Women elected members in large numbers are emerging well regardless of the social boundaries. Some emphatic changes are already visible. However, a lot more is to be discovered by women as a leader to establish herself in compliance with rural men. Reservation is just means towards equality and not an end in itself. To make it successful both men and women must strive to ensure that the end is achieved.

The present volume aims to provide a detailed account of women's reservation in Indian politics, and the issues associated with it. It carefully analyses the current trends in Indian politics and emphasises the importance of women's participation in politics and the role of reservation policy for the empowerment of women. Designed for courses in women and politics, this book is also an ideal supplement for women's studies and comparative politics courses.

Alka Saxena

Contents

1

Reservation of Women in India

Women represent more than half of the world's population and just less than half of the global electorate. Nevertheless, women constitute a marginal proportion of representatives in the world's legislative bodies. In 2008, the average rate of female representation in national parliaments stands at a meagre 18 per cent.

India has of yet managed notably limited success in rectifying these imbalances, with women currently holding only 8 per cent of parliamentary seats. Although India was one of the first democratic nations to grant women the vote, women are neither represented in the legislative spaces nor contributing towards the formation of national laws.

After twelve years of the Women's Reservation Bill lying in limbo amid intermittent and embarrassingly hot-headed scenes in the House, it was finally introduced in the Rajya Sabha during the last day of the Budget Session, 2008. As it is a Constitutional Amendment Bill, it must now acquire a two-thirds majority to be passed in the Parliament. Parliamentarians have the opportunity to enhance women's representation, strengthen democratic governance and enable access to decision making bodies for India's most sizeable and potentially must subjugated minority. For these reasons, it is essential that the Bill gets passed in the next session of Parliament, with the political will for its implementation during and after the 2009 general election.

The arguments in favour of reserved representation can be simply delineated:

— Women represent half of the population of a country and therefore have the right to half of the seats, since decisions made in parliament have a direct impact on their lives.
— Women have different social and biological experiences which should be represented in institutions of governance.
— Women and men have partly conflicting interests.
— Women in positions of power can inspire more women to place themselves in influential and decision-making roles.

The main provisions of the Bill, as introduced in the Rajya Sabha in May 2008, are:

— Not less than one-third of seats to be reserved in the Lok Sabha and State Legislative Assemblies for women;
— One-third of the total number of seats reserved under clause (2) of article 330 (the existing quota for Schedule Castes and Scheduled Tribes) to be reserved for women belonging to the Scheduled Castes or the Scheduled Tribes;
— Reservation of seats to cease to exist or expire after 15 years of the commencement of the constitutional amendment;
— To select women candidates through a system of rotation, by which one third of the total number of constituencies to be reserved for women candidates will be determined through a draw of lots;
— To consider extending the reservation to Rajya Sabha and the Legislative Councils of States, without making any definite provisions within the scope of the current Bill.

1.1. Women's Rights and Social Development

Taking measures to enhance the status and visibility of women is critical for sustainable progress against the range of human development indicators, both because women are particularly vulnerable to social and economic marginalisation when resources are scarce, and because women are critical agents in the development processes. According to various international reports, development in India is being severely hampered by the breadth of the gender gap and limited female participation in traditionally male dominated institutions and social strata. There are countless studies to demonstrate the effectiveness of women's empowerment as a tool for development. For example, Kerala and Manipur have experienced rapid progress in improving health and reducing mortality and fertility rates—the benefits of which affect men as well as women – and in these states women also play a vital social and economic role. This correlation should not be surprising, given that nutrition and child health generally fall within the remit of the woman's household decisions. Ultimately, healthy, educated and empowered women are more likely to raise healthy, educated and confident children and engage positively with the life of the community.

To eliminate gender discrimination and promote female empowerment, women's decision making capacity must therefore be enhanced within the household, the workplace and the political sphere. Increased political influence should have reverberations for women's equality in the other two realms, which will in turn have implications for India's performance against all milestones for social progress.

Reservation of seats is a basic, consistent and logical step towards both women's emancipation and inclusive development—particularly for a government which promised that the "equal access to participation and decision making of women in the social, political and economic life of the nation" would be at the heart of its agenda.

Whilst there is no universally accepted definition of 'democracy', any functional analysis must include two fundamental principals: all members of the society must have equal access to power, and all members must enjoy universally recognised freedoms and liberties. The Indian model of democracy also prioritises representation so as to avoid the pitfalls of "majority rule". On this basis, there already exists a quota for Scheduled Castes and Scheduled Tribes.

It is clear from the statistics alone that women do not have easy "access" to traditional power structures. Their entry into public spaces is persistently disabled by prevailing historical constructions of gender, created and perpetuated by the dominant institutions such as family, religion, education and the State. Nevertheless, the nature of this relationship also means that the same institutions which created the imbalance can take responsibility for its repair.

The final objective of reservation is to increase women's visibility in all policy decisions on the basis that all policy decisions affect women as well as men, and affect women differently to men. This applies equally to the "harder" issues such as trade, industry, agriculture, defence, employment etc., as it does to those "softer" issues which are traditionally assigned to women politicians.

Political participation of all sections of society is essential for building a functioning and representative democracy. Women must therefore be present in new arenas of decision making, with their experiences, perspectives and visions of the future informing public debate. Reservation will provide elected women with the ability to compliment elected men in making the rules that apply equally to both sexes, and which women are equally expected to abide by.

1.2. Political Participation and Mobilisation

Of those states reported on in the Election Commission's Report, 2004, the average differential between voter turnout for men and voter turnout for women amounts to approximately 7 per cent, and rises to substantially more than this within certain states. In one 1996 study—four years after the adoption of the 73rd Amendment – more than one in three women said that they were not interested in local elections at all, in contrast with one in every 5 men. There are multiple explanations for this discrepancy. For one, women are more likely to be uneducated or illiterate, which has limited the dissemination of political ideas and engagement. For another, women are currently an unrepresented political minority amongst political institutions that have consciously and subconsciously excluded them from their registers. Meanwhile, those policies that were originally designed to protect women's rights and level the playing field have rarely been implemented on the ground, further disillusioning large sections of the female population.

A democracy grants political sovereignty to the people: the people must therefore retain a fundamental belief in its ability to represent their needs and act in their interests. In terms of countering apathy, reservation for a sub-group of the population can open up the system and demonstrate that a democratically elected government works for them, and that is not just an elite bureaucracy functioning solely for the dominant sections of society. Indeed, economic and social empowerment cannot be sustained unless women are politically aware, active participants in all levels of decision making. It is thereby imperative that women are politically mobilised and engaged with political processes, and for this to happen they must believe that their voices are being heard within the legislative spaces. Women's political participation can provide the inspiration for women to take action on a vision of a better and more equal society, and to make meaningful contributions towards inclusive national development. Women are and have been politically active throughout India, and the large and expanding mass of women's groups and advocacy efforts are testament to this. However, their participation has been within movements, not structural politics. The questions of women cannot be asked, certainly not answered, by individual groups, and women's questions need to be seen as matters of public interest not matters of specifically female concern outside of the political sphere. They must be raised and debated at all levels, with "women's issues" becoming public issues.

At the same time, women will become visible as competent individuals capable of holding positions of power, enacting laws and demanding accountability for their implementation within political spaces. There can be no equal society until women help to elect lawmakers and make laws.

The Constitution of India is a progressive document that guarantees equal rights for both sexes, and entitles women to enjoy economic, social, cultural and political rights on an equal footing with men (Article 325). It proceeds to consider the appropriate use of legislation to redress inequality and prevent the further infringement of women's fundamental democratic freedoms and human rights. Under Article 15 (3), the State is thereby empowered to make "special provisions", legislative or otherwise, to secure women's socio-political advancement. Indian case law has already interpreted the Equal Protection provisions to allow for affirmative action for women. In addition, India is a signatory to a number of international agreements that support proactive state measures for women's political development:

The Convention on the Elimination of All Formsof Discrimination against Women (CEDAW) wasratified by India in

1993. Article 3 discussesappropriate measures, including legislation, toensure the full advancement of women. Beyondthis, Article 7 affirms that signatories should takeall appropriate measures to eliminatediscrimination against women in the political andpublic life of the country. It recognises that, unlesscountries take active steps to promote thisintegration, women will never be able to fullyenjoy the basic human rights guaranteed ininternational law.

The Inter Parliamentary Union's (IPU) Universal Declaration on Democracy (1997) asserted that

> "the achievement of genuine democracy presupposes a genuine partnership between men and women in the conduct of the affairs of society in which they work in equality and complementarity, drawing mutual enrichment from their differences."

The Beijing Platform for Action (BPfA), 1995 affirmed that women's persistent exclusion from decision making was substantially hampering the achievement of democratic transformation women's empowerment and achieving the goals of sustainable development. The BPfA therefore endorses affirmative action for women in the political spheres.

Under the Constitution and other national and international Commitments, the State is thereby under an obligation to protect and promote the human rights of women, including the right to political equality, without any discrimination on the basis of sex.

1.3. Reservations in India

Reservation in Indian law provides for a quota system whereby a percentage of posts are reserved in employment in Government and in the public sector units, and in all public and private educational institutions, except in the religious/ linguistic minority educational institutions,in order to mitigate backwardness of the socially and educationally backward communities and the Scheduled Castes and Tribes who do not have adequate representation in these services and institutions. The reservation policy is also extended to the Scheduled Castes and Scheduled Tribes for representation in the Parliament of India. The central government of India reserves 27% of higher education, and individual states may legislate further reservations.

Reservation cannot be exceeded 50%, as per the rulings given by the supreme court, but certain Indian states like Rajasthan have proposed a 68 % reservation which includes a 14% reservation for forward castes.

Reservations are intended to increase the social diversity in campuses and workplaces by lowering the entry criteria for certain identifiable groups that are grossly under-represented in proportion to their numbers in the general population. Caste is the most used criteria to identify under-represented groups. However there are other identifiable criteria for under-representation—gender (women are under represented), state of domicile (North Eastern States, as Bihar and Uttar Pradesh are under-represented), rural people, etc. — as revealed by the Government of India sponsored National Family Health and National Sample surveys.

The underlying theory is that the under-representation of the identifiable groups is a legacy of the Indian caste system. After India gained independence, the Constitution of India listed some erstwhile groups as Scheduled Castes (SC) and Scheduled Tribes (ST). The framers of the Constitution believed that, due to the caste system, SCs and the STs were historically oppressed and denied respect and equal opportunity in Indian society and were thus under-represented in nation-building activities.

The Constitution laid down 15% and 7.5% of vacancies to government aided educational institutes and for jobs in the government/public sector, as reserved quota for the SC and ST candidates respectively for a period of five years, after which the situation was to be reviewed. This period was routinely extended by the succeeding governments.

Later, reservations were introduced for other sections as well. The Supreme Court ruling that reservations cannot exceed 50% (which it judged would violate equal access guaranteed by the Constitution) has put a cap on reservations. However, there are state laws that exceed this 50% limit and these are under litigation in the Supreme Court. For example, the caste-based reservation fraction stands at 69% and is applicable to about 87% of the population in the state of Tamil Nadu.

1.3.1. History of Reservations

Reservations in favour of Backward Classes (BCs) were introduced long before Independence in a large area, comprising the Presidency areas and the Princely States south of the Vindhyas. Chatrapati Sahuji Maharaj, Maharaja of Kolhapur in Maharashtra introduced reservation in favour of backward classes as early as 1902 to eradicate poverty from amongst them and to give them their due share in the State administration. The notification of 1902 created 50% reservation in services for backward classes/communities in the State of Kolhapur. This notification is the first Govt. Order providing for reservation for the welfare of depressed classes in India.

The concept of untouchability was not practiced uniformly throughout the country, the identification of oppressed classes is not an easy task. What is more, the practice of segregation and untouchability prevailed more in the southern parts of India and was more diffused in Northern India. An additional complexity is that there are certain castes/ communities, which are considered as untouchables in one province but not in other provinces. Some castes, based on traditional occupations, find place in both Hindu and non-Hindu communities. Listing of castes has had a long history, starting from the earliest period of our history with Manu. Medieval chronicles contain description of communities located in various parts of the country. During the British colonial period, listings were undertaken after 1806, on an extensive scale. The process gathered momentum in course of the censuses from 1881 to 1931.

India is divided into many endogenious groups, or castes and sub-castes, as a result of centuries of practicing a form of social hierarchy called the caste system. Proponents of reservation policy says that the traditional caste system, as it is practised, leads to severe oppression and segregation of the lower castes and limited their access to various freedoms, including education. Caste, according to ancient scriptures such as "Manu Smriti", is "Varnasrama Dharma", which translates to "offices given according to class or occupation". "Varna" in Varnasrama (Varna + Ashrama)is not to be confused with the same word meaning 'colour'.

Indian Judiciary has pronounced some Judgments upholding reservations and some judgments for fine tuning its implementations. Lot of judgments regarding reservations have been modified subsequently by Indian parliament through constitutional amendments. Some judgments of Indian judiciary has been flouted by state and central Governments. Given below are the major judgments given by Indian courts and its implementation status:

1.3.2. Types of Reservation

Seats in educational institutions and jobs are reserved based on a variety of criteria. The quota system sets aside a proportion of all possible positions for members of a specific group. Those not belonging to the designated communities can compete only for the remaining positions, while members of the designated communities can compete for all positions (reserved and open).

For example, when 2 out of 10 clerical positions in railways are reserved for ex-servicemen, those who have served in the Army can compete both in the General Category as well as in the specific quota.

1.3.1.1. Caste-based

Seats are reserved for Schedules Castes, Scheduled Tribes, and Other Backward Castes (based chiefly on caste at birth) in varying ratio by the central government and state government. This caste is decided based on birth, and can never be changed. While a person can change his religion, and his economic status can fluctuate, the caste is permanent.

In central government funded higher education institutions, 22.5% of available seats are reserved for Scheduled Caste (Dalit)and Scheduled Tribe (Adivasi) students (15% for SCs, 7.5% for STs). This reservation percentage has been raised to 49.5%, by including an additional 27% reservation for OBCs. In AIIMS 14% of seats are reserved for SCs, 8% for STs. In addition, SC/ST students with only 50% scores are eligible. This ratio is followed even in Parliament and all elections where few constituencies are earmarked for those from certain communities.

In a few states like Tamil Nadu, the percentage of reservation is 18% for SCs and 1% for STs, being based on local demographics. In Andhra Pradesh, 25% of educational institutes and government jobs for BCs, 15% for SCs, 6% for STs and 4% for Muslims.

1.3.1.2. Management Quota

Most controversial quota is the Management quota according to the advocaters of Pro-caste reservation people. It is also been seriously criticised by leading educationalists as it is a quota based on economic status irrespective of caste,race and religion as anybody who has money can buy his seat. It reserves about 15 % seats in private colleges for the students who are decided by the college management's own criteria. The criteria involves the colleges own entrance exam or minimum %age of 10+2 legally.

1.3.1.3. Gender-based

Women's reservations Women get 33% reservation in gram panchayat (meaning village assembly, which is a form of local village government) and municipal elections. There is a long-term plan to extend this reservation to parliament and legislative assemblies. In addition, women in India get reservation or preferential treatments in education and jobs. Certain men consider this preferential treatment of women in India as discrimination against them in admissions to schools, colleges, and universities. For instance, several law schools in India have a 30% reservation for females. Progressive political opinion in India is strongly in favor of providing preferential treatment to women in order to create a level playing field for all of its citizens. The Women's reservation Bill was passed by the Rajya Sabha on 9 March 2010 by a majority vote of 186 members in favor and 1 against.It will now go to the Lok Sabha, and if passed there, would be implemented.

1.3.1.4. Religion-based

The Tamil Nadu government has allotted 3.5% of seats each to Muslims and Christians, thereby altering the OBC reservation to 23% from 30% since it excludes persons belonging to Other Backward Castes who are either Muslims or Christians. The government's argument is that this sub-quota is based on the backwardness of the religious communities and not on the religions themselves. Andhra Pradesh's administration has introduced a law enabling 4% reservations for Muslims. This has been contested in court. Kerala Public Service Commission has a quota of 12% for Muslims. Religious minority status educational institutes also have 50% reservation for their particular religions.

1.4. Women and Reservation Politics

Equitable representation of women in the highest decision making body is an urgently required measure to empower the women politically. No nation could stand proud if it discriminates against any of its citizens, and no society could claim to be part of the modern civilized world unless it treated its women on par with men. In keeping with the point to provide gender equality in political arena the present government, the United Progressive Alliance (UPA), has already promised in the Common Minimum Programme, and has been trying to bring consensus among all political parties in favour of the women's reservation Bill. The government has introduced women's reservation bill, in the year 2008, in the Rajya Sabha amidst protests from opposition parties. After this several attempts were made to introduce the bill in the Parliament but the government could not pass the bill, due to various political reasons.

The idea of reserving certain seats to women, it seems, was mooted by former Prime Minister Rajiv Gandhi in the late 1980's. In 1988, the National Perspective Plan for Women suggested that a 30 per cent quota for women be introduced at all levels of elective bodies. Women's group insisted that reservation be restricted to the panchayat level to encourage grass-roots participation in politics. The consensus around this demand resulted in the adoption of the 73rd and 74th amendments to the Indian Constitution in 1993. In 1995, the question of quotas was raised again, but this time the focus was women's representation in Parliament.

In 1996 the United Front government led by Deva Gowda introduced the reservation bill in the Parliament but the bill was rejected in an uproar with, some male politicians arguing that women should stay at home where they really belonged. The media had described the debate as the "battle of the sexes".

Attempt to introduce the reservation bill in the Parliament reserving 33 per cent of seats for women have been scuppered by protests in the chamber of the lower house of the Parliament in the year

1998. Male opponents of the bill, who said it would benefit only middle-class city women, continually disrupted proceedings, forcing several adjournments. The then Prime Minister, Atal Behari Vajpayee described the opposition reaction to the bill as "disgracefull".

The present United Progressive Alliance (UPA) government led by Congress party is was keen to give 33 per cent reservation to women in Parliament. The Prime Minister convened the meeting of UPA constituents and its supporting parties, including the Left parties, on the proposed women's reservation Bill. The meeting did not produce consensus but several parties said they had agreed "in principle" with the idea of reserving one-third of the total number of seats for women in the state legislatures and also in Parliament. The reservation bill has been referred to the Parliament standing committee headed by senior Congress party leader Sudarshana Natchiappan.

1.4.1. Trend at the International Level

The recent UNO report shows that Women hold just over 18 per cent of the seats in parliaments around the world. This represents a 60 per cent increase since 1995 but it is still a long way to go to achieve equality with men in national legislative bodies, the Inter-Parliamentary Union (IPU) has said in its annual report card. "We still feel that progress is slow," said Philippines Senator Pia Cayetano, President of the IPU committee of women parliamentarians. She stressed that of there are 5 legislators there is only one women among them. "The challenges that women face in accessing politics are immense," she told a news conference. "Prejudices and cultural perceptions about the role of society are among the greatest obstacles to women's entry."

During 2008, parliamentary elections and renewals took place in 54 countries and women's representation increased to 18.3 per cent — up from 17.7 per cent last year and 11.3 per cent in 1995, the IPU report said. The U.N. Economic and Social Council had set a target of having a minimum of 30 per cent women lawmakers in all parliaments by 1995. According to the IPU, 15 per cent of parliamentary chambers reached the 30 per cent goal for the first time in 2008. That translates to 39 out of 264 chambers in 32 countries.

At the other end of the spectrum, 25 per cent of parliamentary chambers have less than 10 per cent women members. In the recent election only, for the first time in the political history of Kuwait, four women MPs were elected to the legislature. Right to contest in the election was granted to women in Kuwait in the year 2005 only. Elections were conducted in Kuwait in the year 2006 and 2008, not even single woman MP was elected to the nation's highest decision making body.

"It is unfortunate that we are not seeing progress being made across all parliaments of the world," IPU President Theo-Ben Gurirab said in a statement. "While there were some impressive gains made in 2008, particularly in Africa, where Rwanda's lower house elected a majority of women members, more needs to be done in those countries where women are largely absent from decision-making bodies." Rose Mukantabana, Speaker of Rwanda's Chamber of Deputies which is the only body to have a majority of women members — 56.3 per cent — told reporters that the high female representation is the result of a quota of 30 per cent of seats that was reserved for Women. Of the 2,656 seats won by the women in 2008, the IPU said 1,707 women were directly elected, 878 were indirectly elected and 71 were appointed.

Latin American women registered "some impressive gains," taking a 26.5 per cent share of seats in the 12 chambers that were renewed — largely due to the success of women candidates in Cuba, Belize and Grenada. In the U.S., both houses of Congress elected their highest proportions of women members — 17 per cent in each chamber, the report said. But that still ranks the U.S. below the global average.

Europe, with Sweden, Finland and the Netherlands were the countries that stand first for women in parliament, sustained its "consistent pace of progress" with gains in Belarus, Spain, Macedonia, Monaco and France's upper house, but there was a drop in women's representation in Romania, Malta and Serbia, the report said. The IPU said African countries continued to make strides in 2008 with Angola electing morc than 37 per cent of women members in its first election since 1992.

Angola joins other southern African countries including Mozambique, Namibia, South Africa and Tanzania which have elected more than 25 per cent of women members to Parliament, the report said. "Asia has registered the slowest rate of progress in terms of women's access to parliament over the past 15 years, reaching a regional average of only 17.8 per cent," the IPU said. It cited significant gains in Nepal where women took 32.8 per cent of the seats, in contrast to Iran where women won just 2.8 per cent of seats. In the Arab world, women took just over 9 per cent of the seats, but the lowest percentage of women — less than 4 per cent on average — was in the Pacific island nations, the IPU said.

1.4.2. Trend in India

In India The women representation in lower house of Parliament, the House of People, was not impressive in all the general elections. Over the Fifteenth Lok Sabha elections the representation of women has witnessed a very slow improvement, despite the fact that women comprise almost 50 per cent of India's population. As for Rajya Sabha from 1952 to 2002, 160 women have become members of the Rajya Sabha. However, the representation of women in Rajya Sabha at any given point of time has not gone beyond 30. In 1980, there were 29 women members out of a total of 242 members constituting 11.98 per cent of the House, which was the highest ever strength of women members in the House. At present, there are 25 women members in the Rajya Sabha.

In the first general elections, held in the year 1952, out of 499 total seats there were 22 women members elected in the lower house of the Parliament which was 4.4 per cent of the total. A record of 59 MPs have been elected to the 15th Parliament the highest ever since independence and 17 of them are aged less than 40 years. A Majority of 23 MPs are from Congress. The BJP has 13 women members. Uttar Pradesh has the maximum number of 13 women MPs to representing the most populous state. It is followed by West Bengal with seven MPs. Fifteen per cent of 543 MPs in the present Parliament are in the age group of 25-40 years. While in the 14th Lck Sabha the figure was only 6.3 per cent, according to PRS Legislative Research Report. In all, 556 women had contested the 2009 general elections, of which 59 were elected.

For instance in 1957 general elections male candidates' percentage of winning was 31.7 but at the same time women candidates' percentage was 60 per cent. In the 1998 elections women candidates percentage was 15.7 whereas the male candidates percentage of winning was 11.2 only. In May 2004 elections 45 of 355 women contestants (12.6 per cent) won the elections compared with 498 of 5,050 men contestants (9.8 per cent). There were 30 women fielded by the BJP in the may 2004 elections, 10 (33.3 per cent) won. The female success ratio was 62.5 per cent for the CPI (M) and 26.6 per cent for the Congress 12.

1.5. Political Parties' Stand over Reservation Bill

Consensus still eludes women's reservation Bill in meeting among the UPA constituents and its supporting parties. Several parties said they agreed "in principle" with the idea of reserving seats for women in state legislatures and Parliament. A Different tune was heard from the Samajwadi Party (SP) and Rastriya Janata Dal (RJD), with the former asserting that it would oppose the bill in Parliament. The chief of SP, Mulayam Singh Yadav, made three points. One, he favoured making it Mandatory on all parties providing 10 per cent of ticket to women; two, if inadequacy of representation was the issue why not reservation for Muslim women (three or only two in the present Lok Sabha); and three, if 33.3 per cent reservation was given to women when 22.5 per cent already existed for SC and ST, more than 55 percent of seats in Parliament would become reserved which would not be fair or just for other sections of the population. Later the SP announced its decision to mobilize the public opinion against the reservation Bill. But finally the party has come up with an idea to reserve only 15 to 20 per cent of the seats to women.

The RJD president, Lalu Prasad Yadav, said his party would not oppose "10 to 15 per cent reservation for women" under the old proposed Bill or the new proposal to increase the number of Lok Sabha seats to 900 and the state Assemblies by 3000. Further, he demanded quotas for Backward class and Muslims within the women's Quota. But the BJP was very much against the idea suggested by the RJD. Sushma Swaraj of BJP assured that the BJP would support a women's reservation Bill in what ever form, "Provided there is no quota within a quota".

As far as the Left parties are concern, there was a shift in their stands. They had earlier stated their preference for the "original 1996

Bill" proposing reservation of one third of the current strength of all seats in legislatures for women without any sub quotas within this reservation. But later the CPI has made it clear that while they favoured the original Bill" the Left will not stand in the way of a consensus". The DMK, a principle allay of Congress, wanted 33 per cent reservation for women to be implemented before taking up the demand for a quota for BC, MBC and Muslims within the overall reservation.

Since 1996 intensive efforts were made several times to introduce the reservation Bill in the Parliament but it faced with staunch opposition of the political parties. On the extreme, the government was prevented from introducing the bill in the Parliament in the year 1998 and 2008. Several reasons were cited for not enacting the legislation and most important one is the lack of consensus among political parties and their main argument was the reservation would benefit only middle-class city women and upper caste women. Substantiating the argument, a study reveals that in the Tenth Parliament most of the women MPs were members of the higher castes. For example, there were six women from the Brahmin caste. This represents a sizeable 17.14 per cent of the women MPs, while Brahmins comprise only 5.52 per cent of the population. Further, the number of women who are able to avail of India's caste-based reservation system remains small. While 22 per cent of the Parliamentary seats were reserved for SCs, those women occupy only 4.1 per cent of the reserved seats16. But in other Lok Sabha elections women from across the section were elected to the Parliament and this is not enough or healthy reason to prevent the bill.

In this situation it is significant to note that, 33 per cent seats were already reserved to women in local bodies, by the 73rd and 74th constitutional amendment bill. As the available data shows that the elected women members and chairpersons of Panchayats in different states, especially Karnataka, Maharastra, West Bengal and Kerala, have been contributing positively for the developments of their village panchayats. The then Union Minister for Panchayat Raj, Mani Shankar Aiyar, in his interview to *Frontline* in 2008, says that, at present we have approximately 12 lakh women in the Panchayats alone. As against the reserved quota of 33 per cent, their actual presence ranges around 38 per cent. This means that approximately 5 million women have been liberated from the kitchen and the courtyard and brought in to the public domain. This is an extraordinary act of social and political empowerment, said Mani Shankar Aiyar.

Though, Indian constitution says that reservation for women must be for not less than 33 per cent. Bihar is spoken of as a very feudal, traditional, socially backward backwater. But the credit must go to Bihar for being the very first state to have legislated that reservation for women may be increased up to 50 per cent. In the last elections, 55 per cent of the candidates elected to the Panchayats were women. The example set by Bihar has now been picked up by Chhatisgarh, Madhya Pradesh, Rajasthan and Himachala Pradesh. All these states have raised their reservation quota to 50 per cent. Sikkim has raised it to 40 per cent.

The present effort, by the UPA government, to enact legislation on reservation for women in Parliament and state Legislatures has been facing so many hurdles. For instance, (i) The issue of 10 to 15 per cent reservation for women; ii) Quotas for Backward classes and Muslims; and iii) Whether to accept original 1996 bill introduced by UF government, or in Keeping with the proposed increasing of Parliament seats to 900 and state Legislatures to 3000. Women members of the Parliament are solidly backing the bill, regardless of their party affiliation.

The proposed women's reservation bill is possibly the most important measure to empower the women politically. But the present development has no sign of improvement, with each and every political party has different views and demands over the bill. All the objections, raised by the parties, will definitely elude reservation quota for women unless no series effort to bring consensus among political parties. The general feeling, among the women members of the Parliament as well as in Indian society, is that the issue has been hanging fire for too long.

The government should bring the legislation in the Parliament with a consensus among political parties without diluting the real spirit and other issues such as quotas with in the quota may be taken up for discussion latter. The present situation, women's representation in the Parliament, is not impressive even while compared with Pakistan and China. Unless there is a reservation women will find it difficult to get elected in large numbers.

References

Dahlerup, Drude ed., *Women Quotas and Politics*. London and New York: Routledge, 2006.

Drèze, Jean and Amartya Sen, "Gender Inequality and Women's Agency", in Class, Caste, Gender, ed. Manoranjan Mohanty. New Delhi: Sage, 2004.

Krook, Mona Lena, "Competing Claims: Quotas for Women and Minorities in India and France". Presented at the European Consortium for Political Research, Budapest, September 8-10th 2005.

Mumtaz, Khawar, "Women's Representation, Effectiveness and Leadership in South Asia". UNIFEM, 2005.

Rasheeda, Bhagat, "Getting women into parliament- why the quota system is crucial", The Hindu Business Line, 29 July 2003.

Sumita, Ray, Women's Reservation Bill. Advocacy Internet: Vol. 5; Issue No.4; July-Aug 2003; National Centre for Advocacy Studies.

UNICEF, "Women and Children: The Double Dividend of Gender Equality". 2007.

2

India's Women's Reservation Bill

Women's Reservation Bill or the The Constitution (108th Amendment) Bill, is a pending bill in India which proposes to provide 'thirty three per cent of all seats in the Lower house of Parliament of India the Lok Sabha and state legislative assemblies shall be reserved for women. The Upper House Rajya Sabha passed it on 9 Mar 2010. The seats to be reserved in rotation will be determined by draw of lots in such a way that a seat shall be reserved only once in three consecutive general elections.

Women get 33% reservation in gram panchayat (meaning village assembly, which is a form of local village government) and municipal elections. There is a long-term plan to extend this reservation to parliament and legislative assemblies In addition, women in India get reservation or preferential treatments in education and jobs. Certain men consider this preferential treatment of women in India as discrimination against them in admissions to schools, colleges, and universities. For instance, several law schools in India have a 30% reservation for females. Progressive political opinion in India is strongly in favour of providing preferential treatment to women in order to create a level playing field for all of its citizens. The Women's reservation Bill was passed by the Rajya Sabha on 9 March 2010 by a majority vote of 186 members in favour and 1 against.It will now go to the Lok Sabha, and if passed there, would be implemented

2.1. Possible benefits

— More women participation in politics and society.

— Social norms in India strongly favour men, therefore, reservation for women is expected to create equal opportunity for men and women.

— Due to female foeticide and issues related to women's health, sex ratio in India is alarming at 1.06 males per female. It is expected this will change the society to give equal status to women.

— Women are supposedly more resistant to corruption. therefore, this bill might prove to be a factor restraining the growth of corruption.

2.2. Possible Drawbacks

Passing the Women' Reservation Bill may cause bias in the democratic process because of the following reasons:

— It may hurt the self respect of women who have come up on their own ability, it may result in lesser respect for women in the society. It may also bring down the quality of leaders.

— It is likely to begin/increase the hatred between genders as male may feel deprived of certain privileges, in turn create more social issues.

— Parties will be forced to find women whether or not the women identify with the overall party agenda and the rest of the issues concerning all citizens, as opposed to just women's issues. There are no provisions to prevent discrimination against men because of finding women who are inclined towards women's issues alone, or, in other words, biased against men.

— Powerful male members of parties will be tempted to find female relatives to 'reserve' the seat for themselves during the following cycle.

— It is feared that reservation would only help women of the elitist groups to gain seats, therefore causing further discrimination and under-representation to the poor and backward classes.

2.3. Importance of the Bill

History does not repeat itself is a self-evident maxim which most people tend to accept without demur. But now we are witness to seeing history being repeated every year in Parliament in the matter of hypocrisy of all political parties in the context of the Women's Reservation Bill.

Every political party for the last six years has been assuring its support to the Bill which disarms women activists. And then a farce rather than a tragedy is played out by so-called radical politicians, jumping into the well of the House, tearing copies of the Bill and making impossible for proceedings to continue—the House gets adjourned, the Bill is thrown into the dustbin till it is revived in subsequent years with the same result. It is time this mockery stopped, considering that the Congress, the BJP and Left parties proclaim that they are for the Bill in the present form, and really want it to become a law.

Women are not asking for gracc and charity. Their contribution to the cause of nation-building exceeds that of men. An International Labour Organisation study shows that "while women represent 50 percent of the world adult population and a third of the official labour force, they perform nearly two-third of all working hours, receive a tenth of world income and own less than one percent of world property." Therefore, reservation for women is not a bounty but only an honest recognition of their contribution to social development.

An alternative to the Bill suggests amending the Representation of People Act, 1951, to compel political parties to mandatorily nominate women candidates for at least one-third of the seats on the pain of losing recognition. This is politically flawed and not even constitutionally permissible.It may be violative of the fundamental rights to form an association guaranteed under Article 19(1) (c) of the Constitution. The only permissible restrictions are those in the interest of sovereignty and integrity of India or public order or morality, and such an amendment would not fall within these.

That apart, this alternative will not achieve the objective behind the Amendment Bill, because even if a third of women candidates are put up by political parties, there is no guarantee that the same number will get elected.

It is freely admitted by all parties that because of the inbuilt prejudice against women, male candidates will have an unfair advantage in elections. This aspect is freely admitted even by Left parties. Thus, parties will tend to allow women candidates to fight elections from their weak constituencies. Though I am all for the Bill in its present forms, it is unwise to underestimate the opposition from the male constituency in Parliament. Given the present instability in political coalitions, and the material that is in Parliament, to expect one-third of the male members to accept political hara-kiri is unrealistic. They are no Gandhians. They will not give up their privileges so easily.

There is also some merit in the objection that the reservation of seats for women would mean rotation of seats at every general election with the result that the members will not be able to nurse their constituencies and also that candidates will be uncertain of anticipating their future constituencies. This will be thus breaking their link with the electorate. Notwithstanding these ticklish problems, I would have continued insisting on the present Bill. But there is another alternative which can give one-third seats to women without in any way asking the male members to make the way.

This alternative gets further strength now that the Delimitation Commission has been asked to adopt the 2001 census for delimiting the constituencies, and therefore the same inevitable consequences must follow.

Article 81 provides for the Lok Sabha to have not more than 530 members. Further amendments were made to freeze the number of Lok Sabha members on the basis of the 1971 census till another census after 2000 had been published.

Article 82 provides for the allocation of seats upon the completion of each census. As per the 1971 census, the population of India was about 54 crores. Now after the 2001 census, it has risen to about 102 crores. So the strength of the Lok Sabha can be easily increased by one-third to 750 well within the requisite formula. This will take away the fear of any male member to vacate the present seat. These extra seats could be dovetailed into double-member constituencies, which win ensure the reservation of one seat for women and, even permitting two to be elected, if the other woman candidate gets the maximum of the votes polled.

This is what happened in former President Giri's case during the 1957 general election when both seats were won by Scheduled Caste members—one reserved and the other a general seat—because SC candidate got more votes than Mr. Giri.

The argument that the women's quota wilt be monopolised by urban women is a red herring. There are about 200 OBC candidates in the Lok Sabha, it is a stark reality dial, it is not their public service, but merely the caste configuration that has preferred them. Similar results will follow even after the reservation for women. The only difference will be a big Chink in the male bastion. That is the real reason for opposition by male MPs.

The provision of a sub-quota for the OBCs runs the risk of being held as unconstitutional. A sub-quota for Muslim women would violate secularism, a basic feature of the Constitution, and even an amendment would be illegal. Article 325 provides for one general electoral roll for every constituency and mandates that no person shall be ineligible for incursion on grounds of religion.

In the matter of the fight against injustice and discrimination, women as a class should not be weakened by seeking to bifurcate them on caste lines. Reservation for women would check the muddy politics that the men folk have brought about. It would bring social consciousness to political life. It will also help in brushing the criminal-politician nexus—the real danger to our democracy.

All women's organisations, irrespective of political affiliation, should form a common platform with a single agenda. It must become a mass social movement and send out a message to all political parties, warning them that women will withdraw their backing in the next election if they do not support the Bill now.

The fulltext of the Bill is given below:

2.4. The Constitution (One Hundred and Eighth Amendment) Bill, 2008

Be it enacted by Parliament in the Sixty-first Year of the Republic of India as follows:—

1. (*1*) This Act may be called the Constitution (Ninety-Sixth Amendment) Act, 2010.

   (*2*) It shall come into force on such date, as the Central Government may, by notification in the Official Gazette, appoint.

2. In article 239AA of the Constitution, in clause (2), in sub-clause (*b*), for the words "Scheduled Castes", the words "the Scheduled Castes and the women" shall be substituted.
3. After article 330 of the Constitution, the following article shall be inserted, namely:—

"330A. (*1*) Seats shall be reserved for women in the House of the People

(*2*) As nearly as may be, one-third of the total number of seats reserved under clause (*2*) of article 330 shall be reserved for women belonging to the Scheduled Castes or the Scheduled Tribes, as the case may be:

Provided that where the seat reserved for the Scheduled Castes or the Scheduled Tribes, as the case may be, in relation to a State or Union territory is one, then, in every block comprising of three general elections to the House of the People, the seat in the first general elections shall be reserved for women belonging to the Scheduled Castes or the Scheduled Tribes and no seat shall be so reserved in the other two general elections:

Provided further that where the seats reserved for the Scheduled Castes or the Scheduled Tribes, as the case may be, in relation to a State or Union territory are two, then, in every block comprising of three general elections to the House of the People,—

(*a*) one seat shall be reserved for women belonging to the Scheduled Castes or the Scheduled Tribes in the first two general elections in such a manner that the same constituency is not reserved for women in both the aforesaid elections; and

(*b*) no seat shall be reserved for women belonging to the Scheduled Castes or the Scheduled Tribes in the third general elections.

(*3*) As nearly as may be, one-third (including the number of seats reserved for women belonging to the Scheduled Castes and the Scheduled Tribes) of the total number of seats to be filled by direct election to the House of the People in a State or Union territory shall be reserved for women and such seats may be allotted by rotation to different constituencies in that State or Union territory in such manner, as Parliament may by law determine:

Provided that where the seat, not being a seat reserved for the Scheduled Castes or the Scheduled Tribes, in relation to a State or Union territory is one, then, in every block comprising of three general elections to the House of the People, the seat in the first general elections shall be reserved for women and no seat shall be so reserved for women in the other two general elections:

Provided further that where the seats, not being seats reserved for the Scheduled Castes or the Scheduled Tribes, in relation to a State or Union territory are two, then in every block comprising of three general elections to the House of the People,—

(*a*) one seat shall be reserved for women in the first two general elections in such a manner that the same constituency is not reserved for women in both the aforesaid elections; and

(*b*) no seat shall be reserved for women in the third general elections.".

4. In article 331 of the Constitution, the following proviso shall be inserted at the end, namely:—

"Provided that where such nominations are made, in relation to every block comprising of three general elections to the House, one seat shall be reserved for nomination of a woman of Anglo-Indian community to every House constituted after first two general elections and no seat shall be reserved for the women of that community in the House constituted after the third general elections.".

5. After article 332 of the Constitution, the following article shall be inserted, namely:—

"332A. (*1*) Seats shall be reserved for women in the Legislative Assembly of every State.

(*2*) As nearly as may be, one-third of the total number of seats reserved under clause (*3*) of article 332 shall be reserved for women belonging to the Scheduled Castes or the Scheduled Tribes, as the case may be:

Provided that where the seat reserved for the Scheduled Castes or the Scheduled Tribes, as the case may be, in relation to a State is one, then, in every block comprising of three general elections to the Legislative Assembly of that State, the seat in the first general elections shall be reserved for women belonging to the Scheduled Castes or the Scheduled Tribes, as the case may be:

Provided further that where the seats reserved for the Scheduled Castes or the Scheduled Tribes, as the case may be, in relation to a State are two, then, in every block comprising of three general elections to the Legislative Assembly of that State,—

(*a*) one seat shall be reserved for women belonging to the Scheduled Castes or the Scheduled Tribes in the first two general elections in such a manner that the same constituency is not reserved for women in both the aforesaid elections; and

(*b*) no seat shall be reserved for women belonging to the Scheduled Castes or the Scheduled Tribes in the third general elections.

(*3*) As nearly as may be, one-third (including the number of seats reserved for women belonging to the Scheduled Castes and the Scheduled Tribes) of the total number of seats to be filled by direct election in the Legislative Assembly of every State shall be reserved for women and such seats may be allotted by rotation to different constituencies in that State in such manner, as Parliament may by law determine.".

6. In article 333 of the Constitution, the following proviso shall be inserted at the end, namely:—

"Provided that where such nomination is made, in relation to every block comprising of three general elections to the Assembly, the seat in the Assembly constituted after the first general elections shall be reserved for nomination of a woman of the Anglo-Indian community and no seat shall be reserved for the women of that community in the Assembly constituted after the second and the third general elections.".

7. After article 334 of the Constitution, the following article shall be inserted, namely:—

   "334A. Notwithstanding anything in the foregoing provisions of this Part or Part VIII, the provisions of the Constitution relating to the reservation of seats for women in the House of the People, the Legislative Assembly of a State and the Legislative Assembly of the National Capital Territory of Delhi shall cease to have effect on the expiration of a period of fifteen years from the commencement of the Constitution (Ninety-sixth Amendment) Act, 2010:

   Provided that nothing in this article shall affect any representation in the House of the People, the Legislative Assembly of a State or the Legislative Assembly of the National Capital Territory of Delhi until the dissolution of the then existing House, Legislative Assembly of a State or the Legislative Assembly of the National Capital Territory of Delhi, as the case may be.".

8. The amendments made to the Constitution by the Constitution (Ninety-sixth Amendment) Act, 2010 shall not affect any representation in the House of the People, the Legislative Assembly of a State or the Legislative Assembly of the National Capital Territory of Delhi until the dissolution of the House, the Legislative Assembly of a State or the Legislative Assembly of the National Capital Territory of Delhi, as the case may be, in existence at the commencement of the said Act.

References

Drude Dahlerup (ed.), *Women Quotas and Politics*, Routledge, 2007.

Report of the Joint Committee of Parliament on the Constitution (Eighty-first Amendment) Bill, 1996.

Supporting Gender Mainstreaming, Office of the Special Advisor on Gender Issues and Advancement of Women, United Nations, March, 2001.

Women in Parliament: Beyond Numbers. International Institute for Democracy and Electoral Assistance (IDEA).2005.

Madhu Kishwar, The Logic of Quotas, Women's Movement Splits on the Reservation Bill, *Manushi,* Volume No. 107.

3

Women's Reservation in Legislatures

In India, normatively, women have been given an exalted position in society. During ancient times they were treated at par with men even in political and philosophical spheres. However, down the centuries, the position of women in society deteriorated and politically they were pushed to the background. It was only in the twentieth century, particularly during the freedom movement under the charismatic leadership of Mahatma Gandhi, that involvement of women was accepted as the natural course in India. In fact, Gandhiji's notions and approach towards the role of women in the freedom struggle stood in sharp contrast to the age-old prejudices against them ingrained in the Indian psyche. The social condition of women was quite appalling in those times and it was primarily due to the conscious efforts of the leadership, at the forefront of the freedom struggle, that women fought against the might of the British empire in partnership with men.

Gandhi*ji* believed that women have to play a much meaningful role in politics, making it more accountable, transparent and corruption free. Writing in *Harijan* on 21 April 1946, he emphasised the need to "enroll women as voters, impart or have imparted to them practical education, teach them to think independently, release them from the chains of caste that bind them so as to bring about a change in them...If they will do this, they will purify the present unclean atmosphere." He prophetically said, "as long as the women of India do not take part in public life, there can be no salvation for the country."

Our freedom struggle was viewed by the national leaders in a wider perspective of restructuring the socio-economic and future political set up, to provide in it, among other things, equality of both men and women. It is worth mentioning that way back in 1920 Smt. Sarojini Naidu and Ms. Margaret Cousins led a group of women to demand equal rights of representation for the fair sex in the Indian Provincial Legislatures. Lokmanya Bal Gangadhar Tilak was of the view that political action on the part of women could be independent of their social status and that political action was possibly more important than social reform in empowering women. The attitude of our national leaders was evident from the Resolution on Fundamental Rights and Economic Programe which was adopted in 1931 by the Indian National Congress. The Congress declared that it could agree to a Constitution which provided for equal rights and obligations of all citizens, without any bar on account of sex and provided for adult suffrage. Thus, although the British Government turned down the demand for women's franchise, the Indian National Congress in 1931 adopted a resolution in favour of women's franchise and representation.

In independent India, women have held important political and administrative positions. For instance, Shrimati Indira Gandhi guided the destiny of the country as Prime Minister for more than one and half decades. Women have also served as Governors, Chief Ministers, Ministers in Union and State Governments, Presiding Officers of Legislative Bodies, Judges of the High Courts and Secretaries to the Government of India. Currently, we have a woman as the President of our Republic. Despite the fact that Indian women have held important positions both at the national and international levels, women's participation in the political arena and in the decision making bodies is not in proportion to their population, except in the local bodies. Their effective participation, even in these bodies, leaves much to be desired.

3.1. Constitutional Provisions

Adoption of our Constitution heralded a new era of equality for women of India. It guarantees equal political rights including the right to vote to women. Also, almost all the provisions contained in the UN Convention on the 'Elimination of All Forms of Discrimination against Women' are there in the Indian Constitution. Not only does the Constitution guarantee equal political status to women, there is even a scope for 'positive discrimination' in their favour as is evident in Article 15(3) of the Constitution. There are many other provisions in the Constitution which lay stress on equality between men and women. Article 14 provides for equality before law. Article 39(a), states that the State shall direct its policy towards securing equally to men and women the right to an adequate means of livelihood, and 39(d) enjoins the State to direct its policy towards securing equal pay for equal work for both men and women. Article 42 provides for securing just and humane conditions of work and for maternity relief and Article 51(A) (e) refers to the fundamental duty of citizens to renounce practices derogatory to the dignity of women.

3.2. Women in Parliament/State Legislatures

Political representation was initially based on the premise that it deals primarily with individuals. It was believed that though very few women were actually joining politics at a given time; the overall improvement in terms of education and employment opportunities would necessarily percolate into the political sphere too and their representation would commensurately increase. During the first general elections, 66 women contested the elections to Parliament and 19 were elected to the House of the People. Shri Jawaharlal Nehru was quite appalled at the low representation of women in Parliament. Expressing his anguish and pondering over the issue he wrote thus on the matter in his letter to the Chief Ministers:

> I have been meeting our new Members of Parliament. There are over 700 of them as between the two Houses. I have noticed with great regret how few women have been elected. I suppose this is so in the State Assemblies and Councils also. I think we are very much to be blamed. It is not a matter of showing favour to any one or even of injustice, but rather of doing something, which is not conducive to the future growth of our country. I am quite sure that our real and basic growth will only come when women have a full chance to play their part in public life. Wherever they have had this chance, they have, as a whole, done well, better if I may say so, than the average man. Our laws are man made, our society dominated by man, and so most of us naturally take a very lopsided view of the matter. We cannot be objective, because we have grown up in certain grooves of thought and action. But the future of India will probably depend ultimately more upon the women than the men.

3.2.1. In Lok Sabha

Even six decades after Independence, the representation of women in the Lok Sabha do not present an impressive picture. It has not crossed 10 per cent (Table 2.1). In the First Lok Sabha, there were only 22 women constituting 4.4 per cent of the House. It increased marginally over the years except in the Sixth Lok Sabha when the House had only 19 women members. In the Thirteenth Lok Sabha, there were 49 women members. However, in the Fourteenth Lok Sabha, the strength of women members is 51.

Table 2.1. Number of Women Elected to Lok Sabha

General Elections	No. of Women Elected	Percentage
First	22	4.4
Second	27	5.4
Third	34	6.7
Fourth	31	5.9
Fifth	22	4.2
Sixth	19	3.4
Seventh	28	5.1
Eighth	44	8.1
Ninth	28	5.29
Tenth	39	7.02
Eleventh	40	7.36
Twelfth	44	8.07
Thirteenth	49	9.02
Fourteenth	51	9.51

3.2.2. In Rajya Sabha

Similarly, in the Rajya Sabha, in 1952, the number of women members was merely 15 constituting 6.94 per cent of the membership of the House. Over the years, the percentage of women has increased and now, out of 242 members, 23 are women constituting 9.50 per cent of the House. In the Rajya Sabha, the representation of women has never crossed 12 per cent (Table 2.2).

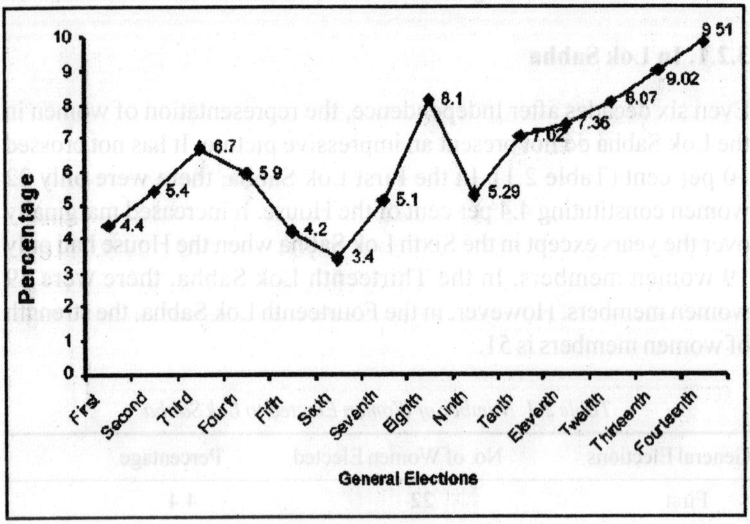

Figure 2.1. Percentage of Elected Women in each Lok Sabha

Table 2.2. Women Members of Rajya Sabha and their Percentage (1952-2008)

Year	Number	Percentage
1952	15	6.94
1954	17	7.79
1956	20	8.62
1958	22	9.52
1960	24	10.25
1962	18	7.62
1964	21	8.97
1966	23	9.82
1968	22	9.64
1970	14	5.85
1972	18	7.40
1974	18	7.53
1976	24	10.16
1978	25	10.24
1980	29	11.98
1982	24	10.16

1984	24	10.24
1986	28	11.98
1988	25	10.59
1990	24	10.34
1992	17	7.29
1994	20	8.36
1996	19	7.81
1998	19	7.75
2000	22	9.01
2002	25	10.20
2004	28	11.43
2006	25	10.41
2008	23	9.50

3.2.3. In State Legislatures

Women representation in State legislatures has also been equally dismal. At present the average percentage of elected women in State Assemblies is 6.94 per cent, the highest being 14.44 per cent in Haryana and the lowest being 1.34 per cent in Karnataka. States like Arunachal Pradesh, Manipur, Mizoram, Nagaland and Union Territory of Puducherry have no representation of women in their Assemblies (Table 2.3).

Table 2.3. Women Members in Legislative Assemblies and their Percentage

Sl. No.	Name of State/UT	Total No. of Seats	Women Members	Percentage
1	Andhra Pradesh	294	28	9.52
2	Arunachal Pradesh	60	0	0.00
3	Assam	126	13	10.32
4	Bihar	243	25	10.29
5	Chhattisgarh	90	5	5.56
6	Delhi	70	6	8.57
7	Goa	40	1	2.50
8	Gujarat	182	16	8.79
9	Haryana	90	13	14.44

10	Himachal Pradesh	68	5	7.35
11	Jammu & Kashmir	87	2	2.30
12	Jharkhand	81	5	6.17
13	Karnataka	224	3	1.34
14	Kerala	140	7	5.00
15	Madhya Pradesh	230	19	8.26
16	Maharashtra	288	12	4.17
17	Manipur	60	0	0.00
18	Meghalaya	60	2	3.33
19	Mizoram	40	0	0.00
20	Nagaland	60	0	0.00
21	Orissa	147	11	7.48
22	Punjab	117	7	5.98
23	Puducherry	30	0	0.00
24	Rajasthan	200	13	6.50
25	Sikkim	32	3	9.38
26	Tamil Nadu	234	22	9.40
27	Tripura	60	2	3.33
28	Uttar Pradesh	403	25	6.20
29	Uttarakhand	70	4	5.71
30	West Bengal	294	37	12.59
	Total	4120	286	6.94

It is unfortunate that in India after 58 years of the working of the Constitution, women are still fighting for their empowerment; women's representation in Parliament is merely 8 per cent. It is not surprising that the Global Gender Gap Report 2007 of UNDP had placed India at a disappointing rank of 114 out of 128 countries studied, based on indicators, among others, of political empowerment.

3.3. Women Contestants in General Elections

Even though women enjoy equal political rights, very few of them are actually participating in the elections. In the Sixth General Elections out of the total contestants of 2439 only 70 candidates were women and in the Fourteenth General Elections, out of the total numbers of contestants of 5435, only 355 were women. Though the number of women participating in the elections may be increasing gradually, they continue to constitute a very small percentage of the total number of contestants.

Another startling fact is that out of the number of women who actually contest the elections, the percentage of women who finally make it to the Lok Sabha is very less. In fact, over the years, the percentage of women who have found their way to the legislature has reduced. In the Sixth General Elections, 27 per cent of the women contestants won the elections and by the Fourteenth General Elections, less than 15 per cent actually made it to the Lok Sabha (Table 2.4).

Table 2.4 No. of Women contestants and Women elected in General Elections

General Elections	Total No. of Women contestants	No. of Women elected	Percentag
Sixth	70	19	27.00
Seventh	143	28	19.58
Eighth	162	42	25.92
Ninth	198	29	14.64
Tenth	314	44	14.01
Eleventh	599	40	6.67
Twelfth	274	43	15.69
Thirteenth	284	49	17.25
Fourteenth	355	50	14.08

There is no denying the fact that a political party is an authentic institutional voice in a democracy. In a multi-party democracy, such as India, the role of political parties in elections, in mobilising public opinion and also in governance process cannot be overemphasised. Therefore, the backing of a political party for the success of a candidate in election is also imperative. This trend was evident when women contestants fielded by political parties won in larger numbers in comparison to independent candidates (Table 2.5).

Given the low representation of women in politics, there has been a consistent demand for more meaningful ways to increase their representation in decision-making bodies. In pursuance of this notion of empowerment of women, the Constitution (Seventy-third

Amendment) Act, 1993 and the Constitution (Seventy-fourth Amendment) Act, 1993 reserved seats for women at the local level bodies, namely, the Panchayats and Municipalities with the hope that these measures will set the trend to provide women their legitimate place in public life.

Table 2.5. Women candidates from National Political Parties

General Elections	Total No. of Women contestants	Women contestants from Political	No. of Women elected Parties	No. of Women elected from Political Parties
Sixth	70	41	19	17
Seventh	143	77	28	27
Eighth	162	63	42	39
Ninth	198	87	29	26
Tenth	314	N.A.	44	N.A.
Eleventh	599	125	40	36
Twelfth	274	107	43	31
Thirteenth	284	104	49	35
Fourteenth	355	110	50	30

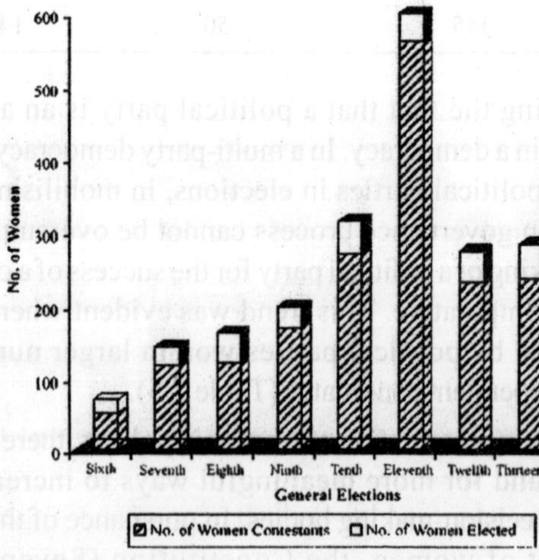

Figure 2.2. Women contestants and Number of Women elected in General Elections

After these amendments, Articles 243 D and 243 T were added to the Constitution to provide that not less than one-third (including the number of seats reserved for women belonging to the Scheduled Castes and the Scheduled Tribes) of the total number of seats to be filled by the direct election in the local bodies (Panchayats and Municipalities) would be reserved for women and such seats may be allotted by rotation to different constituencies in the local bodies.

This, indeed, makes a historic beginning for the effective participation of women in the decision-making process at the grassroots level. In the elections to these local bodies, more than one million women were have been elected every five years.

In 2006, 9,75,116 women were elected to Gram Panchayats; 58,094 women to Panchayats at Intermediate level; and 5779 women to Panchayats at the District level. It is but natural that a larger number of women have participated in these elections and this signifies a very encouraging trend for women's empowerment. Though it has taken time for women to translate their numerical strength into active participation in the rural and semi-urban areas, the results have been truly astounding.

Before reservation, the percentage of women in this area was merely 4.5 per cent, which after reservation has gone upto 40 per cent. As per the *Fifteenth Anniversary Charter on Panchayati Raj*, "Today more than 26 lakh representatives stand elected to the three levels of Panchayats. Of these, over 10 lakh are women. The last fifteen years of Panchayati Raj, have thus succeeded in empowering marginalised groups who have gained political representation and valuable experience. Many of them have successfully taken on the challenge of governance and brought about enduring social change through their close links with the community." Women have prioritised issues of health, education and access to basic services and in some cases have been able to ensure a significant change in living conditions for the entire community. The efforts and work of several women representatives in Panchayats in Maharashtra, Gujarat and West Bengal have been widely acclaimed.

3.4. Reservation for Women in Lok Sabha/Assemblies

Attempts to have seats reserved for women in the Lok Sabha and the

State Legislative Assemblies have had a chequered legislative history. After years of painstaking struggle by the women's groups, the Bills for women's reservation were earlier introduced in Parliament in 1996, 1998 and 1999, respectively, without being passed. The Constitution (Eighty-first Amendment) Bill, 1996, was introduced on 12 September, 1996. Some of the significant features of the Bill were as under:-

(i) One-third of the total number of seats filled by direct elections in the House of the People and in Legislative Assemblies of the States shall be reserved for women.

(ii) One-third of seats shall be reserved for women belonging to the Scheduled Castes and the Scheduled Tribes from amongst the seats reserved for the Scheduled Castes and the Scheduled Tribes under clause (1) of article 330 and clause (1) of article 332 of the Constitution.

(iii) No reservation of seats in Lok Sabha for women from a State having less than three seats in Lok Sabha.

(iv) If the number of seats reserved for the Scheduled Castes or the Scheduled Tribes was less than three in any State, no reservation for women belonging to the Scheduled Castes and the Scheduled Tribes was provided for in the State.

(v) The seats were to be reserved for women by rotation in the manner laid down by law of Parliament.

(vi) No time limit up to which reservation for women was to continue.

(vii) It did not provide for reservation of seats for women belonging to the Other Backward Classes.

(viii) It did not provide reservation of seats for women in the Rajya Sabha and the Legislative Councils of the States.

After intense debates and dissenting opinions, the Bill was referred to a Joint Committee of Parliament consisting of 31 members from both Houses of Parliament. The Committee chaired by Smt. Geeta Mukherjee presented its report on 9 December 1996.

The Committee in its report, *inter alia,* recommended as under—

(i) The words 'not less than one-third' occurring in the Bill should be replaced with 'as nearly as may be, one-third'.

(ii) The Legislative Assembly of the National Capital Territory of Delhi should also be brought under the purview of the Bill.

(iii) The provision for reservation of seats for women should also be made in respect of nominations made under article 331 and 333 of the Constitution.

(iv) The provision of reservation for women should cease to have effect on the expiry of a period of fifteen years from the commencement of the Constitution (Eighty-first Amendment) Act, 1996.

(v) The issue of extending the benefit of reservation to Other Backward Classes may be considered by the Government at the appropriate time.

(vi) The Government should work out the modalities for providing reservation of seats for women in Rajya Sabha and in the Legislative Councils and bring out suitable legislation in this regard at the appropriate time.

The Constitution (Eighty-first Amendment) Bill, 1996, as reported by the Joint Committee of Parliament, lapsed with the dissolution of the Eleventh Lok Sabha.Thereafter, a similar Bill, namely, the Constitution (Eighty-fourth Amendment) Bill, 1998 was introduced on 14 December 1998. The said Bill also lapsed on the dissolution of Twelfth Lok Sabha.Yet another attempt was made by introducing the Constitution (Eighty-fifth Amendment) Bill, 1999 in Lok Sabha on 23 December 1999. But this Bill also could not be pursued due to lack of consensus amongst the political parties.

3.4.1. Current Initiative

The Constitution (One Hundred and Eighth Amendment) Bill, 2008, popularly known as Women's Reservation Bill, was introduced in the Rajya Sabha on 6 May 2008. The Bill aims at eliminating gender inequality and discrimination against women, by political empowerment of women, so as to fulfill people's mandate of Women Empowerment as envisaged in the National Common Minimum Programe of the Government and seeks:

— *reservation for women,* as nearly as may be, one-third seats of the present strength of the House of the People and the Legislative Assembly of every State;

— to provide, as nearly as may be, one-third *reservation for women* including one-third the number of seats reserved for the Scheduled Castes and the Scheduled Tribes in the House of the People and in the Legislative Assembly of every State to be reserved for women of that category;

— to provide for *reservation for women* in respect of nominations of members of Anglo-Indian community in the House of the People and in the Legislative Assemblies of the States;

— to provide *reservation for women* in the Legislative Assembly of the National Capital Territory of Delhi; and

— to provide that *reservation of seats for women* should cease to have effect on the expiration of a period of fifteen years from the enactment of the Bill.

The Women's Reservation Bill introduced in the Rajya Sabha has been referred to the Parliamentary Standing Committee on the Personnel, Law and Justice, headed by E.M. Sudarsana Natchiappan for examination.The 31 Member Committee has been seized of the matter and would submit its report, to both Houses of Parliament after making wider consultation on various issues involved in the Bill.

3.5. Perceptions about the Reservation for Women

The Bill has evoked mixed reactions across the political spectrum, both inside the House as well outside. While some political parties are unanimous that the Bill, which seeks to provide 33 per cent reservation for women in the Lok Sabha and the State legislatures, be passed in its present form at the first available opportunity, others are demanding quota to be fixed for the women belonging to backward sections of the society within this 33 per cent. Otherwise, they contend, benefit of this reservation is likely to be cornered by the women belonging to upper and well-off sections of our society.

One party has stated that it is committed to the demand for the 33 per cent reservation for women. It has, moreover, favoured the Election Commission's proposal for making it mandatory for parties to reserve 33 per cent seats for women.

Most of the parties have pledged their support for the Bill provided there is consensus on it. Some parties while maintaining that they are not opposed to women's reservation, contend that the interests of women from *Dalits,* backward classes, Muslims and other religious minorities should be adequately protected. Others are of the view that if 33 per cent reservation for women is added to the already existing 22.5 per cent for scheduled castes and tribes, then more than 55 per cent of seats in Parliament would be reserved. This would not be fair to other sections of the population. However, they favour making it mandatory for political parties to give 10 per cent of election tickets to women. They also argue that if inadequacy of representation is the issue, Muslim women also deserve this kind of benefit as there are only two women in the present Lok Sabha from this category.

Reserving one-third seats in our legislatures would undoubtedly bestow special powers and privileges on the approximately 180 women who would make it to Parliament and many more to State legislatures on the strength of the quota system. It would also create new aspirations among women at large. However, the larger question is whether it will actually "empower" ordinary women citizens.

Has the presence of 500 plus male legislators in Parliament empowered the men of India? Have these MPs facilitated the growth of men's freedom from abuse and harassment? Freedom from hunger and malnutrition? Do men feel secure and safe in today's India? If most men in this country have not benefited from the preponderant presence of male parliamentarians, why should we naively believe that 180 women in Parliament will change the fate of women in India?

3.6. Alternate Proposals

Few alternate proposals have been suggested to address the concerns of women's reservations without having 33% reservation for women in Lok Sabha and State Legislative Assemblies. These are enumerated as under:

— to make it mandatory for every recognised political party to nominate women candidates for election in at least one-third of the constituencies.

— to increase the strength of the Legislatures to the extent of one-third of the total number of existing seats and provide one-third (*i.e.* to increase seats by 33% and make reservation) seats to women.

— to implement the proposal of the Election Commission of India (known as the Gill formula) to make it mandatory for the recognised political parties to ensure putting of minimum agreed percentage for women in State Assembly and Parliamentary elections so as to allow them to retain the recognition with the Election Commission as political parties.

— to provide for adequate enabling measures for improving the conditions of the women socially, educationally and economically so that women stand up on their own with their intrinsic strength. Occupation of seats in legislatures must be earned by women not through a scheme of reservation but through a positive enabling environment alive with gender equality in terms of access and opportunities, distribution of resources and so on.

— *The Economic Times,* in an editorial, suggested that given the lack of consensus on the issue of quota for women in the Parliament, they should effect a tactical shift in their emphasis towards other areas of institutional life. They should, for one, put in place legislation mandating quotas for women on boards of companies. Norway, with its legally mandated 40 percent quota for women on boards of its companies, could be a good example to follow.

3.7. Gender Quotas

It is an accepted fact that without being proportionately present in the political system, a group's ability to influence policy-making, or indeed the nature of representative system, is rather limited. Greater the number, greater the possibility of wielding power and influence. However, despite the women constituting about half of the world's population as well as the labour force, they do not have any major and effective say in the decision making and priority setting.

The equal participation of women and men in public life is one of the cornerstones of the Convention on the Elimination of All Forms of Discrimination Against Women (CEDAW) adopted by the United Nations (UN) General Assembly in 1979, and in force since 1981. India is a signatory to the Convention. Despite that, discrimination in matters of representation of women in decision-making bodies continues.

In 1995, the UN Fourth World Conference on Women held in Beijing generated renewed pressure for the implementation of the CEDAW provisions: the Beijing Platform for Action identified 'inequality between men and women in the sharing of power and decision-making at all levels' and 'insufficient mechanisms at all levels to promote the advancement of women' as two areas of significant concern where action was critical for the advancement of women.

Given the slow pace at which the number of women in politics is growing, different policy measures are being introduced to bring about gender balance in political institutions. Quotas present one such mechanism to increase, and safeguard, women's presence in Parliaments and are now being introduced in many countries. What are the arguments for and against the use of quotas? What types of quotas have led to substantial increase in women's political representation in practice?

Quotas for women entail that women must constitute a certain number or percentage of the members of a body, whether it is a candidate list, a parliamentary assembly, a committee or a government.

Quotas aim at increasing women's representation in publicly elected or appointed institutions such as governments, parliaments and local councils.

Gender quotas draw legitimacy from women's under-representation due to exclusionary practices of the political parties and the political institutions at large.

Quotas place the burden of candidate selection basically on those who control the selection process, first and foremost the political parties.

Quotas force those who nominate and select to start recruiting women and give them chance which they otherwise would not get.

3.7.1. Types of Quota

The two most common types of electoral gender quotas are candidate quota and reserved quota.

3.7.1.1. Candidate Quota

It specifies the minimum percentage of candidates for election that must be women, and apply to political parties' lists of candidates for election. It could be done in following manners:

— *Legal candidate quotas* are laid down in the Constitution, in electoral laws or in political party laws. Such quotas as are enacted in legislation, force all political parties to nominate/select the required percentage of women.

— *Voluntary party quotas* are adopted voluntarily by political parties, and are most common in centre–left-leaning parties, while liberal and conservative parties generally tend to be reluctant about or strongly opposed to adopting quotas.

3.7.1.2. Reserved Quota

It sets aside a certain number of seats for women among representatives in a legislature, specified either in the Constitution or by legislation. One might argue that reserved seats should not be counted among electoral quotas. However, reserved seats today come in many different types, some excluding, others including, the election of women, rather than appointment, to fill these seats. In Uganda 56 seats, one elected in each district by a special electorate, are reserved for women. In Rwanda, 30 per cent of the seats, elected by a special procedure, are reserved for women according to the Constitution. In Tanzania 20 per cent of the seats are reserved for women and allocated to the political parties in proportion to the number of parliamentary seats won in an election. Reserved seats can also be filled by appointment, as in Kenya and some Arab states. Previous notions of having reserved seats for only one or for very few women, representing a vague and all-embracing category of women, are no longer considered sufficient. Today, quota systems aim at ensuring that women constitute at least a 'critical minority' of 30 or 40 per cent or aim for 'gender balance' as demanded in various international treaties and conventions. Quotas may be seen as a temporary measure, that is to say, until the barriers for women's entry into politics are removed.

Most quotas aim at increasing women's representation because the problem to be addressed is usually the under-representation of women. This is particularly relevant since women constitute more than

50 per cent of the population in most countries, but worldwide they hold less than 16 per cent of the parliamentary seats.

3.7.1.3. Gender-neutral Quotas

Quota systems may, however, be constructed as gender-neutral also. In this case, the requirement may be, for example, that neither gender should occupy more than 60 per cent or less that 40 per cent of the positions on a party list or in a decision-making body. While quotas for women set a maximum for men's representation, gender-neutral quotas construct a maximum limit for both sexes. Gender-neutral quota rules are sometimes used as a strategic choice in order to refute the arguments of opponents of quotas that they are discriminatory against men.

3.7.2. Quotas/Reservations: Pros and Cons

Various arguments have been put forward the world over, for and against, the introduction of reservations as a means to increase the political presence of women. These are given as under:

3.7.2.1. Pros

— Quotas for women do not discriminate, but compensate for actual barriers that prevent women from their fair share of the political seats.

— Quotas imply that there are several women together in a committee or assembly, thus minimising the stress often experienced by the token women.

— Women have the right as citizens to equal representation.

— Women's experience is needed in political life.

— Men cannot represent the interest of women. Only many women can represent the diversity of women.

— Election is about representation, not educational or other qualifications.

— Women are just as qualified as men, but women's qualifications are downgraded and minimised in a male-dominated political system.

— Quotas do not discriminate against individual men. Rather quota rules limit the tendency of political parties to nominate only men. For the voters, the opportunities are expanded, since it now becomes possible to vote for women candidates.

— Introducing quotas may cause conflicts, but only temporarily.

— Several internationally recognised conventions on gender equality have set targets for women's political representation, including the Convention on the Elimination of All Forms of Discrimination Against Women (CEDAW) which 179 countries are now party to, as well as the 1995 Beijing Platform for Action.

— How can it be justified that men occupy more than 80 per cent of the parliamentary seats in the world?

3.7.2.2. Cons

— Quotas are against the principle of equal opportunity for all, since women are given preference.

— Political representation should be a choice between ideas and party platforms, not between social categories.

— Quotas are undemocratic, because voters should be able to decide who is elected.

— Quotas imply that politicians are elected because of their gender, not because of their qualifications, and that better-qualified candidates are pushed aside.

— Many women do not want to get elected just because they are women.

— Introducing quotas creates significant conflicts within the party organisation.

— Quotas for women will be followed by demands for quotas for other groups, which will result in a politics of sheer group-interest representation.

Electoral gender quota represents 'the fast track' to equal representation of women in contrast to 'the incremental track'. It rejects the idea of incremental improvement in women's representation. It is assumed that an increase in resources might not automatically lead to equal representation. Exclusion and discrimination are regarded as the core of the problem and the solution to which could very well be affirmative action. There is growing impatience and the Scandinavian experience cannot be considered as a model today because it took 70 to 80 years to get that far. Today women are not willing to wait that long.

In general, quotas for women represent a shift from one concept of equality to another. The classic liberal notion of equality was a notion of 'equal opportunity' or 'competitive equality'. Removing the formal barriers, for example, giving women voting rights, was considered sufficient. The rest was up to the individual women.

Following strong feminist pressure in the last few decades, a second concept of equality is gaining increasing relevance and support—the notion of 'equality of result'. The argument is that just removing formal barriers does not produce real equal opportunity. Direct discrimination, as well as a complex pattern of hidden barriers, prevents women from getting their share of political influence. Quotas and other forms of active equality measures are thus a means towards equality of result. The argument is based on the experience that equality as a goal cannot be reached by formal equal treatment as a means. If barriers exist, it is argued, compensatory measures must be introduced as a means to reach equality of result.

Research on women's representation shows that women are often met with double standards. Women politicians are accused often of lacking knowledge and education but at the same time criticised for representing a small group of educated elite women; women politicians are often accused of being tokens of their clans, families and parties. The concept of tokenism or 'proxy women' is often used against women elected on the basis of quota regulations. The argument is that quota women are dependent on their husbands and families, political parties or an autocratic leader both before and after the elections.

It is important also to state the obvious: quota provisions do not solve all problems for women in politics and that they may even create new ones. If there are prejudices in society, quotas or reservations do not themselves overcome this difficulty. However, it might make it possible for women to surmount some of the barriers that prevent access to certain opportunities. They could enable a 'jump start' where women have almost no representation at all.

3.8. Quotas for Women in Legislatures: International Scenario

More than 40 countries have introduced electoral quotas by amending the constitution or introducing different types of legislation. In more than 50 other countries, major political parties have voluntarily introduced quotas requiring women to comprise a certain percentage of the candidates they nominate for election. Because of quotas, countries like Argentina, Costa Rica, Mozambique, Rwanda and South Africa are now contending with the Nordic countries, nations which for many decades have topped the ranking in terms of women's parliamentary representation.

Most legal gender quota systems were introduced only during the last decade. Different types of quota are prominent in the world's regions. In Latin America, the leading region in terms of quotas, constitutional or legal changes have opened up the way for gender quotas in politics. In the regions of Africa, the Balkans and South Asia many different types of quota regimes have been introduced recently. In Western Europe quota mainly come in the form of voluntary party quotas, but with France and Belgium as exceptions. In Eastern and Central Europe very few parties have passed quota regulations and no legal gender quota regulations for Parliament are in place. The legacy of quotas as 'forced emancipation' under communism strengthens the opponents of quotas in this region, even if this legacy partly rests on a myth. In the Arab world, quotas as reserved seats for various groups (religious, ethnic and clan) are well known, and very recently a number of countries have included 'women' as a group for whom certain seats should also be reserved.

As a consequence of gender quotas, a dramatic change has taken place recently in the global ranking order of countries based on their level of female political representation. As a result of quota provisions, Rwanda, Costa Rica, Argentina, Mozambique and South Africa are now placed very high in the world league of the Inter-Parliamentary Union. The five Nordic states, Denmark, Finland, Iceland, Norway and Sweden, which for a long time were virtually alone at the top of the ranking table, are now being challenged.

History seems to prove that the implementation of a quota system is made easier in a new political system than in an older one, where most seats might be 'occupied'. In general, it is less complicated to implement quotas for an appointed post than for an elected one. Also, gender quotas are easier to implement in proportional list systems than in plurality–majority systems, where each party only presents one candidate in each constituency. In post-conflict societies, the international community today is putting strong pressure on the actors of reconstruction to take effective measures to include women. Thus we see gender quotas of 25-35 per cent being introduced in strongly patriarchal cultures where very few women were represented earlier, for example, in the post-conflict societies of Afghanistan and Iraq. Quota provisions have also been introduced in the Balkans following strong pressure from the local women's movements in alliance with the international community.

3.8.1. Quota within a Quota

The greatest impediment to the passing of the Bill is the insistence from certain political lobbies on a "quota within a quota" for women of other backward classes (OBC). The concern is that, without these provisions, elected women will come from the ruling classes alone and will selectively represent the interests of this socio-political elite.

OBCs and Muslim women are not currently represented within the Women's Reservation Bill simply because there is no *general reservation* for OBCs and Muslims, and as such a sub-quota within the Women's Reservation Bill may be unconstitutional. Whilst it might be possible to add a sub-clause, the push should first be for a Constitutional Amendment that enables a general OBC quota and/or a non-secular quota for Muslims.

This was the recommendation of the Joint Select Committee formed in 1996, which responded to a common delegation of backward caste MPs with the assertion that sub-reservations for OBC women were not legally permissible until a separate constitutional amendment established a general quota. In addition to a number of minor technical adjustments, the Committee then recommended that the bill be passed into law as soon as possible.

Interestingly, neither Mulayam Singh Yadav of the Samajwadi Party nor any other leader has of yet brought a proposal for reservation for OBCs or other minorities to be debated and discussed in the parliament. Once the Women's Reservation Bill is passed, quotas for general reservation for other social groups can be raised in the parliament as a separate issue, with one third of the seats within these distinct quotas subsequently reserved for women. Even with no general quota, it is difficult to understand why it is assumed that OBCs will be less well represented upon the implementation of women's reservation. To quote the former Judge of Delhi High Court, Justice Rajinder Sachar, "There are about 200 OBC candidates in the Lok Sabha... It is not their public service, but merely the caste configuration that has preferred them. Similar results will follow even after the reservation for women." Subsequently, women's organisations and the National Commission for Women (NCW) have accused detractors in parliament of making demands for OBC sub-quotas simply to undermine the bill and safeguard their own seats, or alternatively to keep their Muslim and OBC vote bank intact at a highly opportune time. They claim that, within the parties most protesting about the need for female representation from backward classes, there are remarkably few female candidates or elected representatives: the Samajwadi Party (SP), for example, has 2 women representatives out of a total of 39 MPs. If these MPs were truly concerned about the lot of OBC women, it should have been possible before now to distribute party tickets to female candidates from OBCs and other minorities. There are also very real dangers in compartmentalising the issue of women's empowerment. The NCW have noted that quotas are one of the few issues to unite women in parliament from across party lines—often because many of these women have personally witnessed the systemic discrimination that impedes women's participation in electoral and political procedures. Reservation is a tool that begins to repair the damage caused by centuries of discrimination that exists ubiquitously across political parties, across social classes and across community divisions.

Of any excluded group, the most deprived member will always be a woman. 22.5 per cent of seats in Parliament are already reserved for SC/ST—of which just over 7 per cent are held by women—and around 200 MPs are from OBCs (well over a third of the Lok Sabha). In contrast, just 8 per cent of seats in the national legislature are held by women. There is undoubtedly a need to further the participation of lower castes and classes, but an alternative prop is needed to the

Women's Reservation Bill. The government cannot continue to be sidelined on this issue because there are men in Parliament who apparently possess more pressing concerns than the liberation of half the population. Ultimately, men's very presence in Parliament will always enable them to shout louder and more often until the Bill is passed.

Some vociferous critics of the current Bill are arguing for a reduction in the proportion of reserved seats for women to as little as 10 or 15 per cent. Discussions between party leaders are rumoured to be taking place that aspire to a compromise of 20 to 25 per cent without any provision for an OBC sub-quota. This would pay no more than lip-service to the principles of egalitarianism—symbolic policy under external pressure that is intended to effect no real or sustainable change within existing structures. Global experiences have demonstrated that restricting women's presence to a point below critical mass can inspire little lasting change in existing dynamics and leave elected women vulnerable to stigmatisation. Furthermore, this cap is actually less likely to open access to the legislatures for women of lower socio-economic status—ironic, given that this is the overt justification for the reduction in the allocation of seats.

The demand for 33 percent reservation is partly based on research that took place in the United States in the 1970s, which concluded that 30 per cent representation by minorities in a decision making body could significantly influence the majority verdict. It is far below the proportion of women in the general population.

It has been raised as a concern that only women from the ruling classes will be elected, and that these women are likely to be "proxy women" acting under direction from husbands, family members or party officials. One response to this has been to recommend a clause that restricts the participation of women who are directly related to a serving politician. However, electoral politics is centred around such networks, and it is surely unrealistic to throw the charge of tokenism at women as if men are wholly autonomous of networks and party connections. Ultimately, male politicians are equally dependent on the political leadership for their (re)nomination.

Women are bound by double standards when it comes to politics. They are at once too uneducated or too elite to participate in politics;

they do not represent women enough or they do not behave like "real" politicians, i.e. men. Undoubtedly, there are women in politics who will fit these criteria; there will also be women who are part of clans, dynasties, party networks and so forth. However, there are also men who obtain their position through precisely such networks, and find they can then use their elected positions as they wish within the party limits. Once a woman is elected, she will have to perform her duties, attend parliament, attend events etc. This cannot be done by any non-elected agent in her place: she will have to think for herself, and, if a Bill is to be passed in a non-discriminatory form, policy makers must believe that she is capable of doing so.

Parties already select candidates who will stand in a given constituency, i.e. it is not a completely free choice by the electorate. Since women have been unable to participate alongside men as equals, there is a need for differentiation which tackles injustice, so as to enable a route to cultural de-differentiation, i.e. a levelling of the current imbalances in the power dynamic that has of yet chosen to ignore the "merits" of half the population. Discrimination is different treatment of equals, whereas affirmative action is an attempt to do justice and redress entrenched privilege that has created inequality. Given such insignificant progress in enabling women's access to national legislatures, it is naively optimistic and extremely detrimental to sit back and assume that prejudice against women will simply disappear over time.

A more substantial criticism concerns the longevity of the terms of the Bill. Reservation of seats is designed as an interim measure to enable women to overcome the historical disadvantages they face in accessing traditional systems of power. The worry should not be that the quota will remain after fifteen years, but that, without supporting measures, fifteen years may not be long enough to rectify centuries of historical damage exerted by disabling women's access to the public domain.

This is not to say that reservations do not work, but that they cannot exist in isolation: they constitute *necessary* but not *sufficient* reform. The Human Development in South Asia Report, 2003 discusses an "embedded system of patriarchy in South Asia", which has meant that "discrimination against women in South Asia is far worse than in most other developing countries." Even where the physical and economic condition of women noticeably improves in the region—as has been the case in Sri Lanka—the social *position* of women rarely changes. To improve women's social standing, political participation is crucial, but unfortunately political participation does not exist outside of the "embedded patriarchy". Examples from South Asian countries have demonstrated that, when quotas are removed, the situation can decline rapidly to reveal few systemic improvements from the point of inception of the quota.

Quotas can form only one part of a multi-faceted strategy for tackling the exclusion of women, and are not an end in and of themselves. Reservation is, of course, a means of providing the opportunity to participate, but from there significant will and commitment will need to be invested to render this participation meaningful. Amongst other measures, women's participation must be translated into all decision making bodies—including committees and advisory boards.

Finally, it is important to understand that political equality inside the governing institutions can only exist in duality with the promotion and protection of women's rights on the ground. For sustainable change, increased political participation must thereby feed into and emerge from wider redistribution of socio-economic resources, with continuous assessment of how resources, opportunities, responsibilities and rights are distributed, accessed and reinforced.

Only with this depth of commitment will there be any possibility of achieving sustainable change within a fifteen year timeframe.

Under the present bill, a system of rotation will be established which will randomly determine one third of the total number of constituencies to be reserved solely for women candidates. The lottery system for earmarking reserved constituencies will provide few incentives for aspirants and incumbents to nurse their constituencies, as neither men nor women will know in advance which constituencies will be open to them until the elections It should be disheartening to openly assume that politicians will refuse to work for the public good if they do not have absolute guaranteed certainty of standing again, since this is in effect the nature of elections and democracy. Politicians are ultimately accountable to the political parties which they represent, and it is not in party interests to have a poor or non-performing member within any particular constituency.

There will be no good women candidates in any constituency: if there are men who are capable of running for election, there will also be women. In practice, it is in party political interests to nominate the best possible female candidates in all reserved constituencies, since they will be competing against women from the other political parties and need to have the best possible chance of winning. The advantage of the quota system is that it forces the nominating bodies, especially the political parties, to engage in an active recruitment process. In doing so, they will need to address the conditions and culture in which party politics plays out, thus taking positive steps to make political participation more attractive for women. This will be especially important in areas where there are not already clearly identified female candidates. It might be unlikely that any woman will get elected more than once to the Lok Sabha or State Assemblies, which will effectively mean that women candidates enjoy no more than a token stint inside the legislative bodies.

With support from political parties, four or five years should be long enough for women to demonstrate their capabilities and win over the public vote. It is not, in practice, a short space of time. However, the current Bill will also allow for reservation of seats to be frozen for two consecutive terms, which will provide women members with more time to establish stable networks within existing systems. In either case, it will be imperative for parties to secure lasting power bases for women members during the period of their tenure, so as to ensure that women candidates remain electable once the seat is unreserved.

For this reason, it is essential that political parties take steps to "integrate" women into political processes and ensure that they capture equal influence among key stakeholders. Various Indian political parties nominated female candidates at the time of the elections to the Lok Sabha in 2004. The Congress has 15 women out of a total of 152 party members in the parliament: about 10 per cent. In terms of percentage, the CPI (M) fares better, with 5 women MPs out of 43 and 12 per cent representation. The BJP has 11 women MPs among its 129 MPs—9 per cent. The DMK has 19 per cent women's representatives in the parliament, which amounts to 3 out of its total of 16. The NCP has the highest percentage (36) of women's representatives: 4 out of 11. The figures are not impressive, but a majority of the political parties claim to firmly support the Women's Reservation Bill and included it as a matter of primary importance in their 2004 election manifestoes.

3.8.2. Political Parties and Quota

At the time of elections, the quota system touches the very foundation of the democratic process, and according to opponents it may clash with the principle of the voters' right to choose the representatives they want. However, nominations are the crucial stage and the power of the nominations rests with the political parties, not with the voters. Since the political parties in most countries are the real gatekeepers to political office, quotas may lead to a dispute between the central and regional/local branches of the political parties. The local branches often fight for their right to choose their own candidates without the interference of the central party organisation. Undoubtedly, it is easier to introduce quotas for women when other forms of quotas are also formally introduced, for example, quotas based on occupational or ethnic criteria. Regional 'quotas' which distribute the parliamentary seats to various parts of the country, not just according to their share of the population, but giving non-proportional shares of the seats to certain regions over others, are in fact used in most countries. However, such arrangements are seldom called quotas.

The 'fast-tracking' of women into legislatures through gender quotas is not necessarily accompanied by sufficient sensitisation among parties and voters to the need for women in political life. For their part, political parties play an ever-increasing role in the management of parliamentary politics, and it is therefore at the party level that the principle of equality must be put into practice. Political parties, which are traditionally male bastions, need to be further encouraged to revise their statutes, admit more women into their internal structures and include them as candidates in elections.

The examples of France and Belgium are illustrative. From a paltry 5.6 per cent in 1995, women now represent 17 per cent of the French Senate (an increase of 11.4 percentage points). Over the same time period, women's parliamentary representation in the Belgian House of Representatives increased from 12.2 to 35.3 per cent. In both countries, the electoral laws were amended to oblige political parties to present an equal number of men and women on their electoral lists.

Some political parties in France showed tremendous resistance to complying fully with the law. In some instances, they even preferred to pay a fine rather than include women on their electoral lists. While change has come gradually, the results of the latest elections to the French Senate, which saw women's representation improve from 11 to 17 per cent, give cause for some optimism.

3.8.3. Need for Stronger Quota Rules

Whether a quota system meets its objective depends largely on the process and method of implementation and enforcement. While reserved seats are by their nature enforceable, candidate quotas are often not enforced. If the method of implementation is not clearly defined and enforceable, a candidate quota requirement of 30, 40 or 50 per cent is not likely to be met. The quota must be embedded in the selection and the nomination processes of political parties from the very beginning.

Political parties may meet the requirement that 30 per cent of their candidates must be women but place them at the bottom of the lists, in largely unwinnable positions. Additionally, if the number of seats to be filled in a constituency is small and many parties stand for election, by and large men will be elected as they usually hold the top positions on a party list. In some countries using a proportional representation (PR) electoral system with open lists, voters may demote women candidates (or promote male candidates), thereby negating women's chances of election. For these reasons it is crucial that quota systems and their rules for enforcement are introduced that work with the electoral system. Several quota laws have been amended, or today are drafted, with placement mandates specifying which positions women are to hold on electoral lists.

While quotas seek to ensure their proportionate presence in Parliament, there is no guarantee that women will be able to use that power effectively. The debate about quotas, particularly in some Asian countries, continues today with the criticism as to how reservations have afforded women the visibility, but not empowered them. There is the dire need for training of women and the need for greater gender sensitivity in the administration. There is the need to look beyond numbers to develop strategies to increase women's skills and ability to participate actively in politics. There are always questions around whether quotas should be instituted on a temporary or permanent basis. Some argue that quotas should be considered as a temporary measure, not only for strategic reasons when seeking to have them introduced, but also because the quota in itself should change perceptions about gender equality, thereby levelling the playing field for men and women to contest elections on an equal basis.

While significant gains have been made in Scandinavian countries, they should not be considered the model, as it took 80 years to shift from no women in Parliament to 35-45 per cent. In Scandinavia, quotas were not introduced until women already had obtained 20-25 per cent in Parliament, thus consolidating women's political power. Quotas ensure a quantitative jump, shifting from a concept of equality of opportunity to equality of result. However, this will only happen if quotas are properly implemented. In Sweden, the Social Democratic Party has an internal quota of a minimum of 40 per cent women, combined with a 'zipper' system. Similarly, the African National Congress party in South Africa has a 30 per cent quota for women. Yet countries like France have different electoral systems and different quota rules, which have a direct effect on the number of women elected in the system. For example, the implementation of quotas was successful at the local level but less successful at the national level in France.

The lack of comparative research makes it difficult to generalise about successful strategies and to present 'best cases' of how quotas can be implemented. It is, therefore, extremely important to generate more comparative research and to learn both positive and negative lessons of individual country experiences with quotas.

Without specifications regarding the ranking of candidates on party lists, as well as sanctions for non-compliance, quota provisions may be merely symbolic. On the other hand, where electoral gender quotas have fulfilled these qualifications, they have proved extremely effective in increasing the political representation of women the world over.

References

Drude Dahlerup (ed.), *Women Quotas and Politics,* Routledge, 2007.

Report of the Joint Committee of Parliament on the Constitution (Eighty-first Amendment) Bill, 1996.

Report on Regional Workshop towards Women's Political Empowerment, Economic and Social Commission for Asian and the Pacific high-level Intergovernmental Meeting to review regional implementation of the Beijing Platform for Action, 26-29, October, 1999.

Statistical Reports of Lok Sabha Elections, The Election Commission of India.

Supporting Gender Mainstreaming, Office of the Special Advisor on Gender Issues and Advancement of Women, United Nations, March, 2001.

Women in Parliament: Beyond Numbers. International Institute for Democracy and Electoral Assistance (IDEA). 2005.

Madhu Kishwar, The Logic of Quotas, Women's Movement Splits on the Reservation Bill, *Manushi,* Volume No. 107.

4

Women's Reservation in Local Bodies

The 73rd Amendment paved the way for a fundamental change in the way public goods are delivered in rural areas in India. Through the structure of the Panchayati Raj, local councils directly elected by the people are responsible for making decisions on an array of public good decisions. Twice a year, the councils must also convene village meetings, where the villagers must approve their plan and their budget. Eventually, the Gram Panchayats are supposed to be given control over an even broader array of social services, including basic education and primary health care.

However, in a country with a heterogeneous population, a danger is that decentralization will make it more difficult to protect the interests of weaker segments of the population, notably women, the Scheduled Castes (SC), and the Scheduled Tribes (ST), and, in particular, to ensure that they get their fair share of public goods. To alleviate this concern, the 73rd Amendment required that a fraction of seats at all levels be reserved to women, SCs and STs. While reservations for SCs and STs are in place in other elected bodies, the 73rd Amendment is the first one in India that mandated women's reservation, and this made it a landmark piece of legislation as well as, to some extent, a test case.

A necessary condition for the efficacy of the reservation policy is that the elected representatives have independent power and autonomy, over and above not only the direct control of the villagers, but also above the control of the bureaucracy, the parties' hierarchies, and the local elites.

4.1. The Panchayat System

The Panchayat is a system of village-level, block-level, and district-level councils, members of which are elected by the people, and are responsible for the administration of local public goods. Each Gram Panchayat (GP) encompasses 10,000 people in several villages. The GPs do not have jurisdiction over urban areas, which are administered by separate municipalities. Voters elect a council, which then elects among its members a Pradhan and an Upa-Pradhan. Candidates are generally nominated by political parties, but have to be residents of the villages they represent. The council makes decisions by majority voting.

The Panchayat system has existed formally in most of the major states of India since the early 1950s. However, in most states, the system was not an effective body of governance until the early 1990s. Elections were not held, and the Panchayats did not assume any active role. In 1992, the 73rd Amendment to the Constitution of India established the framework of a three-tiered Panchayat system with regular elections throughout India. It gave the GP primary responsibility for implementing development programs, as well as in identifying the needs of the villages under its jurisdiction. Between 1993 and 2003, all major States but two had at least two elections. The major responsibilities of the GP are to administer local infrastructure and identify targeted welfare recipients. At this point, the GP has no direct control over the appointments of government-paid teachers or health workers, but in some states there are Panchayat-run informal schools.

The Panchayat is required to organize two meetings per year, called "Gram Samsad". These are meetings of villagers and village heads in which all voters may participate. The GP council submits the proposed budget to the Gram Samsad and reports on their activities in the previous six months.

In West Bengal, the Left Front government gained power in 1977 on a platform of agrarian and political reform. The major political reform was to give life to a three-tiered Panchayat electoral system. The first election took place in 1978 and elections have taken place at five-year intervals ever since. Thus, the system put into place by the 73rd Amendment all over India was already well established in West

Bengal. Following the Amendment, the GP was given additional responsibilities in West Bengal. In particular, they were entrusted to establish and administer informal education centers, an alternative form of education for children who do not attend school.

In Rajasthan, unlike West Bengal, there was no regularly elected Panchayat system in charge of distribution of state funds until 1995. The first election was held in 1995, followed by a second election in 2000. Since 1995, elections and Gram Samsads have been held regularly, and are well attended. The setting is thus very different, with a much shorter history of democratic government.

4.2. Status of Reservation

In 1992, the 73rd Amendment provided that one-third of the seats in all Panchayat councils, as well as one third of the Pradhan positions, must be reserved for women. Seats and Pradhan positions were also reserved for the two disadvantaged minorities in India, Scheduled Castes and Scheduled Tribes, in the form of mandated representation proportional to each minority's population share in each district. Reservations for women have been implemented in all major states except Bihar and Uttar Pradesh.

In West Bengal, the Panchayat Constitution Rule was modified in 1993 so as to reserve one-third of the councilor positions in each GP to women, and a share equal to their population for SCs and STs; in a third of the villages in each GP, only women could be candidates for the position of councilor for the area. The proportion of women elected to Panchayat councils increased to 36% after the 1993 election. To conform to the 73rd Amendment, the Panchayat Constitution Rule of West Bengal was again modified in April of 1998 to introduce reservation of Pradhan positions for women and SC/STs. In Rajasthan, the random rotation system was implemented in 1995 and in 2000 at both levels.

In both states, a specific set of rules ensures the random selection of GPs where the office of Pradhan was to be reserved. All GPs in a district are ranked in consecutive order according to their serial legislative number. GPs that have less than 5% SCs (or STs) are excluded from the list of possible SC (or ST) reservation. A table of random numbers (in the electoral law) is then used to determine the seats that are to be reserved for SCs and STs, according to the numbers that need to be reserved in these particular districts. Using these lists, every third GP starting with the first on the list is reserved for a woman Pradhan in the first election.

4.3. Patriarchy and the Problem of Gender

Since independence, both governmental and non-governmental organizations have initiated a number of projects and programs in India with the intention of empowering and advancing women in society. While there have been attempts to empower women in all areas of society, including the social, economic and religious sectors, some of the most visible attempts have occurred in the political realm. The most recent policy change in government occurred in 1992 when Parliament passed the seventy third amendment of the Constitution, reserving 33% of the seats for women in the panchayats, the local governing system. While this constitutes a positive step for women, it is necessary to assess the extent to which this legislative action has affected women's position in Indian society. In order to do this one must first consider carefully the nature of women's power in society, and then determine to what extent women's power in government influences the other spheres of women's lives.

While advancements in the political sphere are essential for the overall "empowerment" of women, the implementation of seat reservations with the intention of empowering women carries a number of assumptions concerning power. One of these assumptions is based on the overall importance of political power in comparison with power exercised in the social or economic spheres. Increasing the number of women in governmental positions does open doors for women in terms of presence and visibility. Moreover, the critical mass of women in political life itself increases the potential for the transformation of gender consciousness. However, it does not guarantee it. Numbers alone do not indicate that the situation for women has improved. It is very important that those who fill the seats are aware of the problems that women face and are interested in creating change within the community. Often, it is argued that changes in legislation will be ineffective without the support of educational or training programs that promote gender consciousness. Therefore, if the actions taken by women in positions of political power do not benefit women outside of politics, then this legislative change provides a limited form of agency for women.

There are many forms of power that dictate behavior and patterns within every culture. Before further evaluating the role of power in society, there must first be an understanding of what power actually is and what type of power the governmental structure provides.

V. Spike Peterson and Anne Sisson Runyan argue that there are a variety of ways of looking at power. Political power offers what they refer to as "power-over," which is basically the ability of one person to make someone do something they previously had no intention of doing. They argue that the conceptual notions of power themselves are based on masculine qualities and ideals. "This definition of power is masculinist to the extent that it presuppóses androcentric notions of strength, competition, aggression, and coercion, and because it focuses on power understood only in terms of public-sphere activities that are dominated by men." Historically, women have been able to effectively assert this type of power on an individual level, but it can be argued that they are merely becoming part of a patriarchal power structure that omits other important forms of power. This is the reason definitions of power exercised by women that pertain to the private-sphere and the public sphere outside the realm of politics are often overlooked.

Patriarchy by definition is a social system in which the father is the head of the family and men have authority over women and children. The structure of the governmental system, which exists in India and throughout much of the world, is based on a patriarchal system. Relating to politics in India, even if there are members of government and policies within the government that support women or give particular powers to women, the basic system still benefits men over women.

But the goal of many feminists is not to establish a matriarchal governmental structure in its place, but rather to find a way to remove the engendered structure that causes the oppression of one gender over another. Peterson and Runyan address this issue in discussing gender ideologies. It is in this sense that the hierarchies are *structural* and not simply individual or idiosyncratic." Therefore, in order to create long-term change for women's involvement in politics, there must be structural changes. Individual advancement does not promote the progression of all women in society.

When making this policy change in a patriarchal system, it is often the case that those creating the change do not fully understand the complexity of the position of women in society and especially how women came to take on the roles that they did. Before an effective method of eliminating these barriers can be found, the key issues that women face must first be evaluated. The patriarchal ideology that stems from this type of structure can be found in other realms of life besides the public political sphere. However, the origin and the role of the ideology within the structure are essential, given that it dictates the policies and actions visible in government today.

Robert Connell has done extensive research on the role of gender in politics. He argues, "If the modern state is itself 'the general patriarch,'...then demanding that the state redress injustices worked by the 'individual patriarch' in the family is merely appealing from Caesar unto Caesar. Seeking reform through the state is an exercise in futility, perhaps even in deception." He creates a convincing argument that the state cannot assume control of removing 'power-over' type relationships since the state itself is responsible for this type of relationship that is found within the public and private spheres. However his argument goes much further than this point. At the forefront of his argument, there is an understanding that "the state as an institution is part of a wider social structure of gender relations." The "power over" relationship that Peterson and Runyan refer to is widely found in gender relations. Connell's argument emphasizes the importance of legislative change.

Quotas for women's representation in governing institutions are largely a response to liberal feminist demands for equality. Liberal feminists believe that the answer to women's subordination is the acquisition of individual and equal rights. Since individual rights and the state are interconnected, Connell maintains, the liberal feminist argument is based on the assumption that the state can reverse this subordination and lesser status of women. Furthermore, he asserts that liberal feminism lacks a solid understanding of the actual structure of government and the extent to which gender is institutionalized.

Connell suggests that, Liberal feminism has brought to the surface the suppressed truth that the state is gendered, and has used this truth to inspire a formidable and sustained politics of access. But it has not been able to grasp the character of gender as an institutional and motivational system, nor to develop a coherent analysis of the state apparatus or its links to a social context.

While the efforts of liberal feminists have been influential to a degree, their theory's effectiveness is limited by its failure to comprehend the nature of gender relations within the public and private sphere. Connell explains that liberal feminism assumes patriarchy is a surface problem that can be really removed with laws. Under this assumption, it seems logical that a seat reservation quota would be implemented as an effort to reverse men's "overrepresentation." But the patriarchal structure of the state goes much deeper than the overrepresentation of men.

The state's role in women's oppression is often difficult to identify because it is not always direct and is often combined with other oppressive cultural factors. According to Connell, perhaps one of the most influential factors of oppression in the state's structure is the state's ability to appear neutral on issues, specifically those affecting women, while operating under gender biased procedures and systems. Connell contends that the state "plays a part in establishing or regulating 'systems' in which women are oppressed. But the state can appear in itself to be gender-neutral; and this is a vital aid to legitimacy." The state's neutral stance comes from the fight for equality and sameness between the sexes.

Simplistic notions of patriarchy and male domination suggest falsely men intentionally oppress women and consciously attempt to hold power over them. Women's entrance in politics may simply further support this patriarchal structure than reverse women's position in society. Connell insists that generally there "is a broad *similarity* between women's and men's political attitudes, interests, and partisanship.

4.4. Male Dominance and Cultural Differences

In theory the state is the central location of power. Connell makes the argument that the family, while an important source of power, is peripheral and isolated into individual situations, or "cells." Connell is referring to the state of power relations in the modern era. Foucault would agree with Connell's assessment of the present day allocation of power and its implications in relation to the private sphere. Connell believes that the state is the central location of all power relations. Through laws, programs and policy, according to Connell, the state is able to assert this power in an administrative and far more central way than the family structure ever could. However, Connell fails to account for the inability of the state to implement these state laws and policies which they create.

While potentially the state could hold power over violence, property, sexual violence and other male-dominated practices, it is often unable to influence these actions as much as it claims it will. He overestimates the effectiveness of the state to have total control over the everyday life of people. Therefore, it may not be the state's power that dominates the private sphere but rather a different type of power relationship that does not necessarily result from the state's laws, programs or policies. The implementation of the reservations differs greatly from its conception in theory. However, Connell does argue that women's economic and religious involvement in society has placed gender at the base of the state structure.

Seat reservation for women in government at the local level is advancement towards empowerment in the political realm and a step forward in the dismantling of the repression of women in this sphere since this is a visible change for women. However, questions that follow this statement must be: To what extend does the seat reservation translate into changes in the rest of society? What are the factors that cause this method of change to be a limited form of empowerment for women? These factors include social values, patterns of governance, limitations in or gains from political parties, basic modes of establishing political power and the lack of a gender-conscious education.

Some of the greatest obstacles in cross-cultural research are the assumptions embedded in the differing perspectives. The Western perspective especially creates barriers for researchers and impinges our ability to make accurate assessments of women's roles in developing societies. In her article "Under Western Eyes: Feminist

Scholarship and Colonial Discourses," Chandra Talpade Mohanty criticized earlier work by Western feminists who failed to acknowledge their own assumptions about non-Western women. Liberal feminists, specifically during the 1970s, typically characterized "third world women" as one large homogeneous group under the heading of the "Other." Certain Western feminists gave the impression that women in India, Africa, and the Arab world are all culturally bound by something that men of the same culture are not also bound by. However, women cannot be looked at apart from their culture. By doing this, women's roles in society are largely discredited. Women's roles are necessary and often recognized within their cultures as being important.

While women may experience oppression in both the public and private spheres, they are certainly still members of their culture and not an entirely separate entity simply bound by shared oppression. Western feminists often overlook this fact. Mohanty reasserts that "this is what the 'colonizing' gaze of Western feminism does not acknowledge." This notion of the "other" that Mohanty found in modern Western feminist writings has been very influential in anthropological research as well. Kamala Visweswaran finds this notion of the "other" extremely prevalent in most cross-cultural anthropological research. Without the understanding of the use of this concept of the "other," the researcher will not be able to adequately represent the situation as it actually is.

Mohanty goes on to address the issue of "male dominance." She believes that the misinterpretation of the concept of male dominance is one of the greatest barriers when performing anthropological research in third world countries. She argues, "An analysis of 'sexual difference' in the form of a cross-culturally singular, monolithic notion of patriarchy or male dominance leads to the construction of a similarly reductive and homogeneous notion of what we call the 'third world difference' –that stable, ahistorical something that apparently oppresses most if not all the women in these countries." This implies that women in third world nations are held down by a singular force in a way that women in the Western world are not. They are almost implying that women have not been affected by the changes in culture, let alone played a role in forming the culture, based on the fact that they have been oppressed by this "monolithic notion of patriarchy."

4.5. Implementation of Quotas for Women

A little on the history of women's reservations is necessary to disentangle the various discursive strands that have, willy-nilly, to be taken into account to arrive at an understanding of the basis and tenor of diverse positions on the current demand for one-third reservations for women in the state assemblies and in the Union Parliament.

The issue of separate political reservation for women came up during the course of the nationalist movement in the 1920s. The principal reason for opposing the idea of reserved seats was that it deflected from the demand for universal adult franchise and to stand for elections on the same terms as men. Besides, it was felt that there should be no hint of succumbing to the British strategy of "divide and rule" by referring to divisions within the national movement. "The public, official language of politics especially before a colonial government, had to be a language of equality and for fundamental rights of citizenship irrespective of sex, caste, religion or creed." This opinion was supported by the prominent and leading women's organizations of the time and by the Home Rule League, the Indian National Congress and the Muslim League. The women's organizations also endorsed the declaration of the Fundamental Rights to Citizenship in India made by the Karachi session of the Indian National Congress, 1931, which called for equality before the law, irrespective of religion, caste, creed or sex, universal adult franchise and women's right to vote, represent and hold public office. The assumption was the urban women would be in a better position to represent the women of India. But the opposition to reservation remained and merit was to be the only criterion.

It is, however, important to note that the opposition to the idea of reservation was not restricted to the question of women alone. The All-India Women's Conference (AIWC) in their resolution expressed their opposition to the British "Communal Award" of 1932 which sought to provide separate electorates and reserved seats to Anglo-Indians, Christians, Muslims and Sikhs, and for the "depressed classes". The rationale behind such opposition was that divisions along the lines of religion, caste and sect would weaken the struggle against colonial rule and that legislatures must be filled by those who would rise above personal or communal considerations and think of the country's best interests. There were dissenting voices: Begum Sakina Mayuzada felt that desiring the good of one's community need not be at the cost of inflicting harm on others; and K.B. A separate resolution calling for the abolition of untouchability was adopted. What is relevant to our present discussion on the issue of women's reservation is that a certain definition of nationalism came to prevail, which claimed to be above the sectarian pulls of caste and community and which was quite different from that which prevailed till the early twentieth century, when, in fact, discrete religious communities were not viewed as inconsistent with an overarching national identity. Women's organizations like the AIWC shared these perceptions.

It is important to note, however, that the nationalist movement did arrive at a consensus on the issue of affirmative action or reservation for the depressed classes and this was given a constitutional status in 1950, when special provisions for the "scheduled castes" and "scheduled tribes" were written into the Constitution of India. These groups were to be given reservation in the parliament, state legislatures, education and employment in proportion to their population.

4.5.1. Committee on the Status of Women

The question of women's reservations came up once again in the Committee on the Status of Women in India (CSWI) in 1974. The Report noted that in spite of equal rights and universal adult suffrage guaranteed by the Indian constitution, women's presence in the state and central legislatures had been declining steadily over 25 years. Those who are against any form of affirmative action, particularly in public or government service, often take recourse to Article 15(1) or Article 16. The dominant opinion in the CSWI was against reservations, though there were two notes of dissent. The arguments in favour of reservations dealt with:

(a) the difficulties of women to gain entry into male-dominated political parties and hence the necessity of reservations;

(b) that reservations for women would ensure a significant presence enabling women to act as an important pressure group; and

(c) the presence of a critical mass of women would heighten the sense of responsibility among women and this would ensure that women's interests would be adequately represented.

The arguments against reservations were:

(a) reservations for women would be a departure from the constitutional principle of equality;

(b) women's interests cannot be isolated from the economic, social and political interests of groups, strata and classes in the society and linked to this was the notion that women are not a community, they are a category; and

(c) systems of special representation for women may spiral into similar such demands from other groups and interests and thus threaten national integration.

The two notes of dissent in the CSWI are very significant because they mark a shift in the perception of the "daughters of independence" generation and also because they raise questions about the way political representation has functioned. Sarkar and Mazumdar note with disarming and refreshing candour that as members of the pre-independence generation, they had never been supporters of special representation and that they had in academic discussions criticized the system of reservations for scheduled castes and scheduled tribes as "... a legacy of the colonial period which institutionalised the backwardness of certain sections of our population". The main reasons for dissenting with the majority opinion within the CSWI also arise out of and are consistent with the findings of the Committee; that is, despite progressive legal changes, the actual situation of the mass of Indian women has not changed significantly and the continuing under-representation of women prevents them from participating in the decision-making process of the country. The authors also draw attention to the narrow social base of women legislators, representing mainly the upper strata of society.

4.6. Women in Local Self-Governing Institutions

The recommendations of the CSWI remained in cold storage till the early 1990s, when the Indian Parliament passed the Seventy-Third Amendment to the Indian Constitution with near unanimity in December 1992 and the Amendment came into effect from 24 April 1993. The purpose of this amendment was to revitalize local self-governing village councils. The Seventy-Third Amendment has been considered historic and one of the most significant attempts at transforming the Indian polity in the direction of greater democratization and decentralization of powers.

The amendment has mandated a wider representation for historically marginalized and excluded groups like the scheduled castes, the scheduled tribes and women thus deepening the roots of democracy. Following the amendment, people from the scheduled castes and tribes are now represented in proportion to their population in the area of the panchayat — in its membership and in proportion to their population in each state in the positions of the chairpersons of these panchayats; one-third seats are reserved for women in general in each panchayat, that is, at the village cluster level, at the block level, and at the district level. Finally, there is one-third reservation for women among the positions of the chairpersons of these bodies.

The reservation is to be rotated among the various constituencies and panchayats to ensure the widest spread. Regular elections are to be held every five years and financial resources are to be devolved by the setting up of state finance commissions and central finance commissions. The states have been mandated to make the panchayats institutions of self-government and to give them responsibility for planning and implementation of schemes for economic development and social justice for which appropriate functions and responsibilities have to be devolved. The logic behind the system of reservations is that institutionalized inequalities require institutionalized counter-measures from above to ensure some semblance of genuine democracy.

The most significant and new feature has been bringing about a certain uniformity regarding representation of the weaker sections. While reservation of seats for scheduled castes and tribes has been written into the constitution from the very outset, the reservation for women is new and the most important contribution of the amendment. According to many analysts, it has brought a critical mass of women to these institutions and holds forth tremendous potential.

What has been the experience of women's participation for the first time in these institutions, both in terms of transforming these institutions and for the women themselves? This will have to be assessed in terms of India's traditional social structure, which is characterized by a socially legitimized hierarchy, based on the caste system, an integral element of which has been gender discrimination. Women's marginalization is almost a given in the Indian social situation. Given this, has the formal change brought about a significant change in this situation? Evaluations done on women's participation in the PRIs have highlighted the following dimensions.

1) Women have responded overwhelmingly and participated with full enthusiasm in the elections and in the proceedings of the PRIs, thus exploding the myth that women were uninterested in politics and public life.
2) While there is a great degree of variation across the different states in the country, nonetheless one generalization can be made — approximately about 40 per cent of the women who have got into these bodies come from marginalized sections and communities, though the positions of chairpersons tended to be occupied by women from the more well-to-do sections of rural society, like well-off middle peasant families.
3) The women representatives generally got the support of the families during the elections and also in the performance of their new political roles.
4) The self-esteem of the women has gone up tremendously, and that is an observation that holds true across the board. The stepping of women into the public realm has long-term implications for gender relations in society and the family.
5) While the presence of women in these institutions over the last eight to nine years has not transformed the power structure in the rural areas in any significant manner, and vested interests have tried to use the provision for women's reservation to consolidate their position, the overall experience has been positive. Thus women are engaging in power struggles that used to be dominated by men, sometimes as actors and at other times as pawns.

But regarding the question of women's empowerment: (a) Are women beginning to break their silence, to challenge patriarchal ideology? (b)

Are they beginning to transform institutions and structures of gender subordination and inequality? (c) Are the new women in panchayats beginning to gain access and control over material and knowledge resources and altering their self-image? (d) Are they gaining new skills and gaining self-confidence? (e) Are they succeeding in avoiding cooption and dilution of the empowerment process by pervasive patriarchal forces with new ways of exercising power and becoming a political force?

Buch's study of the women in the PRIs in the three most backward states concludes that less than half a decade is too short a period to have a major shift in the dominant patriarchal structures reinforced by an equally patriarchal and paternalistic state apparatus.

4.7. PRIs and Women's Reservation Bill

The Eighty-Fourth Constitution Amendment Bill meant to provide one-third reservation of seats to women in state and central legislative bodies and the current discussions and controversies around it mirror the contradictions of Indian society and the contestations in access to power and resources between those who have been traditionally excluded and the socially and politically dominant sections of Indian society. The Women's Reservation Bill once again throws up questions of certain kinds of identity, specifically caste and religious identity, the intermeshing of gender identity with caste and religion and their articulation in the public realm, in the field of politics.

The core questions to our mind relate to the hierarchy of Indian society and the manner in which this hierarchy operates in the field of politics and political representation. It also raises questions about the nature of representation.

The near unanimous support for the Bill among national level women's organizations is premised on a certain understanding of the patriarchal forms of oppression and exclusion that characterize Indian society and the undeniable reality of declining participation of women in political life, specifically in the legislatures. And historically the suppression and exclusion of women has been extremely important in maintaining a Brahmanical and caste-dominated social order, and affirmative action for women will undoubtedly contribute towards the democratization of society.

The protagonists of the Bill highlight the traditionally sanctioned exclusion of women from the public sphere as crucial. However, emphasizing the dimension of gender oppression at the expense of other oppressions glosses over the complex and intricate ways in which gender oppression is embedded in these categories. Historically, women's suppression has no doubt been very important in maintaining upper-caste exclusivity and hegemony. Even so, certain recent developments suggest the need for addressing gender oppression in more subtle and nuanced ways, if access to power and resources to all categories of women is to be ensured.

The continued dominance of the upper castes in education, administration and structures of government is a reality that cannot be glossed over. This has been paralleled by an increasing presence and visibility of women from the upper-caste middle classes. On the other hand, the women (and men) from the subaltern communities and classes have largely been victims of "development".

The opponents of the bill in its present form point out that it is likely to exclude women from the "other backward classes" (OBCs) and the minorities. Almost all the political parties except the Communist Party of India (CPI) and the Communist Party of India (Marxist) — CPI(M) — are deeply divided on this issue. The Hindu nationalist party in government, the Bharatiya Janata Party (BJP) leadership, is in favour of the Bill in its present form, although one of its women members of parliament had expressed reservations to the Bill on the ground that OBC women were likely to get excluded. Needless to say, there is also a strong resistance on the part of a considerable number of political leaders to "encroachments" into what has been a traditionally male preserve.

The media has trivialized the debate by often characterizing it as a battle between "feminists" and "casteists". The crux of the issue is whether indeed the generalized oppression and exclusion of women characteristic of society is a sufficient basis for transcending the divisions of caste, religion and ethnicity and whether indeed the women's movement is representative enough to effect such a unity. The tendency on the part of women's organizations has been to point to stronger patriarchal norms prevalent among the OBCs and the Muslims and the attitudes of the men of these communities as being particularly "backward" and "male chauvinist", thus focusing on the family as the principal site of patriarchal control and oppression and ignoring its wider social context.

Recent analyses of the Women's Reservation Bill raise important though disturbing issues regarding the relative ease with which the question of women's reservation has been accepted by the ruling elites in the 1990s, as compared to the resistance to this in the 1970s.

However, it is the changing composition of the parliament with a significant number of members from the backward castes, which challenges the hegemony of the upper castes and has made the question of women's reservation more acceptable. Thus gender has been pitted against caste. And it is not a coincidence that this is accompanied by the rise to political dominance of right-wing Hindu chauvinist forces. Besides, there is another dimension: the fact that the women's movement is no longer perceived as a threat to the social order is also a result of the cooption of gender issues both by the state and the NGOs.

There are other opinions from women activists and scholars who seriously question the efficacy of reservations as an instrument for the achievement of the goal of equality. These scholars focus on the fact that even the experience with women's reservations in the institutions of local self-government has not been entirely positive and that women need to traverse a long road before they reach the portals of parliament. They point out to the loopholes in the manner in which Panchayat Raj institutions have functioned; the crying need for training of women and the need for greater gender sensitivity among the administration. It is important to note that usually this reservation about quotas for women is also accompanied by a reservation about the whole question of quotas on the basis of caste. There is a fear that the question of women's reservations will raise the question of caste, religion and other divisive categories.

What is happening to Indian society is a criss-crossing of movements of various oppressed sections. Often these movements pull in different and even opposite directions, thus defeating the process of democratization in the short run. It is a challenging task both for the leaders of these movements and social analysts to unravel the myriad oppressions that characterize Indian society and to draw out the major strand which will strengthen and contribute to the overall process of democratization of society.

4.8. Women's Participation in Local Governments

India, with a population of around one billion persons is the second most populous country in the world after China. Located in South Asia, the country is spread over an area of 3.2 million square km, which makes it the seventh largest country in terms of area. The country was under British Rule for about one hundred and fifty years before 1947, when it became independent. In the year 1950, it declared itself a republic.

India is a federal system of government with 25 states and 7 union territories. It has a population of about 1 billion out of which 26 percent live in urban areas. The per capita GDP of India is about US$ 370. Agriculture accounts for 31.1 percent of the economy, while industry and services account for 23 percent and 45.9 percent respectively, of the economy. The sex ratio of the population is 48.1 percent and is rather skewed in favour of males. These overall figures show considerable disparities between men and women, which arise from traditional views of men being superior to women. However, India is a diverse country and these figures vary from state to state.

There still exists a significant gap in the education levels of men and women. The literacy level is a lowly 39.3% for women. Regional disparties are also quite significant, with Kerala having achieved cent percent literacy and Rajasthan having a dismal 20.4 percent literate women population.

Urban population increased 3.5 times from 62.4 million in 1951 to 217.6 million in 1991 with an average annual growth rate at 3.2 per cent. In 1951 the urban population accounted for a mere 17.3 percent of the total Indian Population. In the next four decades this figure has gone up to 25.7 percent.

India has 23 cities with populations over 1 million. However, only about 33 percent of the urban population lives in these cities, including about 19 percent who live the top 5 urban centers.

The political and administrative structure of the country is largely inherited from the British. The British introduced local democracy in India by constituting municipal councils and the municipal corporations in the last quarter of the nineteenth century. They also provided a federal structure to the country with the Government of India Act, 1935.

The country today has a quasi-federal structure. Apart from the Government of India in New Delhi, there are twenty-five States with their own state governments. The Seventh Schedule to the Constitution of India divides the subjects of State activity between the Union and state governments. The executive powers of the central government are vested in the Council of Ministers with the Prime Minister at its head. Similarly, the executive powers in the State governments are vested in its Council of Ministers with the Chief Minister at its head. However, following the Westminster pattern, the Head of the State is not the Prime Minister but an indirectly elected President, who broadly performs the role as the Head of State. India has a bicameral parliament, with the Lower House directly elected by the people on the lines of the House of Commons in the U.K. or the House of Representatives in the U.S.A.

Although local government in India is a subject of the State governments, the seventy-third and the seventy-fourth amendments to the Constitution of India now make it obligatory for the State governments to organize local bodies, to hold regular elections to them and to give them appropriate finances.

The urban local bodies are of three grades; municipal corporations for cities with a population of more than (0.3 million), municipal councils for towns smaller than this population limit and nagar panchayats for villages in transition to becoming towns. These bodies are elected on a universal suffrage basis, with all citizens above the age of eighteen years of age having a right to vote.

The rural local bodies are organized in three tiers, the village panchayat at the village level, the block panchayat samiti for about 100 villages and a district council for a district comprising about 1000 villages. The rural local bodies do not have many resources of their own. They actually spend the state government funds as implementing agencies.

The civil service in India is a closed system, with a very limited scope for lateral entry at senior level. Most permanent officials join the service as a lifetime career through an entrance examination/ interview conducted by the Public Service Commission. The age of entry is usually 21 to 30 years and the age of retirement either 58 or 60 years of age.

The subject matter of the Government of India is divided between the Union Government and the State Governments. The respective governments recruit most of their employees independently. However, the Government of India obtains the services of these officers at higher and middle management levels through deputation for a period of about five years. This enables a regular exchange of officers between the field and the central levels. Senior Indian Administrative Service Officers who have had their initial grounding in different States of India thus man the top secretariat posts in most ministries of the Government of India.

The elections to both the urban and rural local bodies in India are ward based. The local area is divided into wards of more or less equal population. Each ward sends one representative to the concerned local body. After the Seventy-third and Seventy-fourth Amendments to the Constitution of India, one-third of the wards are reserved for women candidates and only women candidates can contest elections from these wards. Apart from the reservation for women candidates, some other wards are reserved for candidates from socially underprivileged sections.

India became independent in the year 1947. In all the elections held since independence, women had the voting rights. The percentage of seats won against the seats contested is showing a declining trend only because the number of women contesting elections has increased sharply. However, it may be seen that voting for women in all tiers of Government has always been a feature of the Indian polity since 1947.

4.8.1. Political Participation

Women play a dual role in politics – as voters and political representatives. On the voting front, though adult franchise was granted in 1937, it was the progressive spirit that pervaded the making of the constitution that made it a reality.

Generally, in India, registration and participation of women as contestants is less than that of men. In recent past, records show that there has been an increase in the percentage of women who vote. Such participation is also contingent on the mobilisation efforts made by political parties, NGOs, Action Groups and the general awareness among the community of the importance of women exercising their franchise. Usually, however, countries that do hold regular elections show an improved recognition of women as a political constituency and parties and candidates tend to adopt pro-women stances and appeal specifically to women's votes, especially at the time of elections. This becomes very evident when we look at consecutive elections in the Indian context, wherein there is a growing consciousness of the need to woo the woman voter and the need to pay attention to the needs and issues of women, in the election manifestos of political parties.

Since Independence, due to exercise of their franchise, Indian women have been exposed to the political processes and are showing increasing awareness about not only lack of rights but also their utility. Women get easily mobilised in the political processes by the political parties who approach women very often for party issues and for short-term goals by winning elections, but not for long-term goals of bringing about social changes and gender equality in political power-sharing.

In all the elections held since independence, women had the voting rights. The percentage of seats won against the seats contested is showing a declining trend only because the number of women contesting elections has increased sharply. However, it may be seen that voting by women in all tiers of Government has always been a feature of the Indian Polity since 1947.

The number of women contestants in Parliamentary elections has not increased significantly over the years. Political parties are still reluctant to field women candidates at national level.

In the early days of the Indian republic, the number of women representatives was a mere 22, which was a lowly 4.4% of the total seats in the Lok Sabha.

As analysed by the Prasad Leela Devi– Even as early as the 19th century Indian women had begun to appear on the national scene in public and political activity. Women were not only being accepted in public activity but were organising themselves to fight for their rights in different walks of life.

Though women constitute nearly half of the population of the country, it was only after Independence that efforts were made to promote women's participation in public life. As a consequence, women had not advanced much politically and economically. From the records available of the past 50 years, since the independence, it is seen that the strength of women in the political field as reflected in State legislatures remained at an average of 3 % to 5% of those elected. At the level of Parlaiment, the position of women members has varied between 5 to 7%.

It is seen that women in large numbers have come out against atrocities on women, in defense of their traditional control over crucial resources, water, forests, and land, mass literacy drives and other issues. They are also coming out in large numbers over ecological degradation, price rise or protests against police repression, etc.

Amongst the several reasons for such a situation is the growing money power and muscle power required to contest even the smallest of elections in India, the intimidation, violence and slander that a woman candidate has to face combined with the traditional male domination that seeks to keep her indoors. And if they are fielded at all, kinship and affinity factors play a major role. It is very common to observe that the relatives of politicians are promoted and supported to emerge as politicians.

Increasingly, women have stood for elections and got elected as members of State Legislative Assemblies and the Parliament. However, at the national level there is only one woman Cabinet Minister and 8 Ministers of State in a Cabinet of 70. There is only one woman Governor and one woman Chief Minister.

Some studies of Parliamentary participation indicate that women members participate more actively in 'women's issues' – health, welfare, atrocities against women, crimes like dowry and violations of human rights. In issues such as defense, finance, politics, etc. their participation is relatively limited.

Analysis of trends of women's participation to contest elections to the State Legislatures indicate that there is a gender discrimination which is responsible for poor representation of women in India.

Women's role in decision making is one of the most important questions for consideration in the movement for their empowerment.

The 73rd and 74th Amendments to the Indian Constitution have served as a major break through towards ensuring women's equal access and increased participation in political power structures. There is also a one-third reservation for women for posts of chairpersons of these local bodies. This amendment has initiated a powerful strategy of affirmative action for providing the structural framework for women's participation in political decision-making and provided an opportunity to bring women to be forefront and centre of city development and develop new grass-root level leadership. There are about 1 million elected women representatives in Panchayats and Municipal Bodies in India.

After 1993, women's participation in local governments increased quite radically, with the enactment of the legislation providing 33 percent reservation of seats for women in local bodies. The legislation and its implementation has added another level in political participation.

In Governments too, there has been limited representatives of women. A few eminent women have no doubt, occupied important administrative positions, such as Secretaries of Departments in the National Government as well as in State Governments. It is only 5.71% of the total number of persons in administrative services are women. It is noteworthy that within the premier civil services of India, the representation of women is not that encouraging.

Since relatively few women enter the civil services, several efforts have been made to improve the situation. The Department of Personnel and Administrative Reforms of the Government of India has also provided, wherever possible, women officers on the selection boards for posts and services.

4.8.2. Participation in Governance

The 74th Amendment to the Indian Constitution, 1992 has served as a major breakthrough towards ensuring women's equal access and increased participation in local government. The Constitution Act, 1992 aims at Constitutional guarantees to safeguard the interests of urban local self government to enable them to function as effective democratic and self governing institutions at the grass root level. This Amendment provides for reservation of 33 1/3 percent of elected seats for women at local government level in urban and rural areas. There is also a one-third reservation for women of posts of chairpersons of these local bodies. These provisions have provided great opportunities and challenges to women in India, particularly in the local government field. This is of great significance, since this grass-root level participation has considerably broadened the base of women's participation in politics at city level.

Involvement of women in the political arena and in decision-making roles is an important tool for empowerment as well as monitoring standards of political performance at local level. However, in the present political process of entry into decision making political institutions, there is growing influence of money and muscle power, backroom dealings, communalisation and criminalisation. In many respects women and men elected representatives face similar problems on election to office. The role of political representatives at local level is demanding and all new 'recruits' need time to gain experience and to understand the rules, regulations and procedures governing the administrative bureaucracy with which they now have to work – often quite closely in the urban service delivery system.

Some of the major constraints that prevent women from effective participation at local level are as follows:

1. Lack of orientation / training in urban development issues and municipal administration.
2. No proper knowledge / orientation about municipal acts and rules and regulations.
3. No prior experience about dealing with multidimensional urban development issues / civic issues and its complexities.
4. Lack of knowledge about technical in-puts related to urban service delivery system.
5. Lack of support from senior male / female colleagues in the party / municipal body.
6. Less co-operation from municipal officials understanding about various facets of the budget, such as allocation of budget at ward level
7. Lack of party support and poor organisational structure.
8. Lack of money and resources to sustain the electoral campaigns.

9. Discrimination in decision making at party level.
10. Specific notions towards politics and political atmosphere.
11. Fear and insecurity.
12. Lack of confidence in public speaking.
13. Criminalisation of politics and use of money power.
14. Family responsibilities.

Political system in India works through political parties who contend for power by invoking popular support. Therefore it is necessary that if women want to share power they have to make a place for themselves within the political parties through which the Indian democratic system operates. The experience of the last 52 years show an inability to create 'this space' and recent studies show that there has been no significant change in either the nature of women's functioning or in the political parties' approach to women and women's issues. Women are not seen as a vote bank to be approached, and once the men are mobilised, women will merely endorse their choice of party and candidate. Male candidates rarely have access to the female electorate and there are not enough women involved in political campaigns to be able to reach out to a large section of women even in big cities. As a result, the exposure of women to political debates and issues has always remained indirect. According to women from all parties the political environment was not conducive to women's participation in politics.

Women in India today are agitating at the doors of Parliament, demanding reservation for 33 per cent of the seats. The issue at stake here is more complex than it may seem. It is not only a question of a few more or a few less women in the corridors of Parliament and legislatures but also a response to the fact that a large section of society has historically been denied its legitimate share in the exercise of political power, power that ultimately determines its destiny. Reservation of seats for women in Panchayats/Municipal bodies have shown that it has tremendous implications, not merely in terms of the number of women entering the public arena and holding public office, but also in terms of the social, economic and political impact that these reservations have had for the total system.

It is for these reasons that women are increasingly demanding political roles for themselves. They recognise that constitutional guarantees do not ensure effective participation and that these cannot ensure political equality. Hence the need to gain entry into political institutions and in the functioning of the state, and to share control over the power the state exercises. This alone would lead to a situation where women are able to reverse the existing situation, which has consistently been against their interests, and bring about the necessary changes in policy and the social structure so as to ensure a more equitable and humane order.

The role of women's participation in elected bodies should not be undervalued. Elections are after all a forum for self government and democracy, they are significant in drawing the attention of the nation to the problems and needs of disadvantaged sections; the manifestos, campaigns, promises made by individual candidates, track record and future course of action of political parties are indicative of national concerns as well as mandates for action. Hence, opportunities for participation at this level are significant for the adoption of politics and measures for women's development.

Strong and dynamic women who would not dream of appropriating privilege are today talking of reservation because they have come to recognize that they will not give "easy entry" in the corridors of power without reservation. The demand for reservation should not therefore be seen as either a gift or a privilege that women are seeking. For most women it is the last straw and a desperate measure to ensure their coming into the political mainstream. Their participation becomes vital in the context of the adoption of development strategies that are negative and harmful to women. Today most of the political parties in India have initiated some initiatives to activate political participation of women and develop their capacities. However, most of the political parties have not yet developed any special programmes to meet the special requirements of women in urban or rural areas, despite the fact that most of the women activists felt that if planned efforts were made, they could be easily mobilised. Different debates concerning struggles of women as well as various actions by women's groups and NGOs on local as well as national problems have forced the mainstream political parties to accept women's concerns in their political programmes.

Statistics on women's participation in the electoral process are not very encouraging. It is important not only to pressurise the political parties but also to make the leaders understand the significance of organising systematic training of women possessing leadership qualities, of carefully selecting women candidates and ensuring financial, technical and human resources for affirmative action.

The need to strengthen womens' participation and leadership is constantly emphasised by various institutions viz, All India Institute of Local Self Government, NIUA, HSMI, Rambhau Mhalaji Prabhodini, etc and several NGOs and Women's groups like SEWA, Working Womens' Forum, YUVA, Disha, Prayas, Astha, Winavani, SNDT University, Aalochana, Agni, FASDSP, Stree Mukti Sanghathana, etc.

Many NGOs/CBOs, Womens' groups have provided some training, however systematic training of women possessing leadership qualities is not enough and more concentrated efforts are required to facilitate the process of women's ascent to key positions in political field. The movement must provide a support system for women who enter political processes to win elections. As stated by Nath Kamale 'The women's movement has been a powerful agent of empowerment and has provided an alternative perspective for fundamental structural changes. The movement has created organisational strength of women, has focussed on women's issues and mobilised them around these issues. The women in the movement, however, have shied away from active participation in politics.

The women's groups and women activists thus aim to bring about a change in the women's perceptions, but not necessarily in the structures which subordinate women. If we want to bring about change in the lives of women and transform mainstream politics, there is no other way than to get involved in politics and transform it.

The women's movement and groups have to recognise the importance of women as a constituency and ensure their participation and representation in policy formulation. The movement should also provide a support system for women who enter political processes to win elections. The women's groups working at the grassroots level are small and scattered and have diverse ways of empowering women. There are no infrastructural facilities of networking available that could bring them together and strengthen them while allowing autonomy in their functioning. It is important to create unity in diversity between women's groups, organisations and individuals involved with women's empowerment.

Reservation for women in local government is not just a question of getting a certain number 'in'; it also develops their capacities to play their rightful roles in the development process and makes an important difference as the local governments deals mostly with the quality of life for citizens. Municipal responsibilities relate both to women's practical needs and their strategic needs. Most local governments have initiated orientation / training programmes to encourage women to participate in local governance by organising city-specific induction or theme-based training programmes, wherein intensive training is given in various subject areas, such as, municipal acts and its implementation, laws of meetings, municipal budgeting, budgeting at ward level, municipal taxation, mobilisation of resources, urban service delivery systems, poverty alleviation schemes, community management, environment management, shelter programmes, new reforms in municipal administration, functioning of ward committees, motivation techniques, communication skills, women and development, handling the media etc.

The Ministry of Urban Development, Government of India and Urban Development Department of State Governments organise a number of training programmes, workshops, seminars for women elected representatives at local level through various training institutions. Many municipal bodies have initiated a series of in-house training in m unicipal administration and urban development, in collaboration with premier training institutions in India. Special training / orientation programmes are organised by Ministry of Urban Development and Poverty Alleviation, Government of India under the UNICEF assistance and government's funds in the area of poverty alleviation schemes and its implementation in urban areas.

4.8.3. Gender Sensitizing of local Government

Local governments are using sex-desegregated data for policy and programme formulation. It is an obligatory duty of municipal governments in India to collect, compile and maintain vital statistics in their city limits. Sex-disaggregated data is in use in many cities of the

States in India for policy programme formulation and implementation of some special programmes and projects at local city level.

The Government of India regularly collects, analyses and disseminates quantitative and qualitative data on the number of women and men employed at various levels in government on an annual basis and many mechanisms have been set up within governmental structures for monitoring progress in this field.

The Department of Women and Child Development, Government of India is collecting and using gender-disaggregated data to evaluate development from a gender perspective.

Bringing women to positions of political power in local government is just the first step in social transformation. Gender sensitization of those in power, be they men or women, is of critical importance. Influencing the choices of those at decision – making levels and bringing gender issues to the political agenda are important factors. Over the years, this perspective has gained acceptance within organisations, action groups and political parties.

Government departments, other institutions, non-governmental organisations, and women's organisations have undertaken several programmes to sensitise local governments about the issues and needs of women in their cities.

It is recognised that law enforcement is a critical factor for bringing about enduring changes in gender perceptions. Several initiatives have been taken by the Government of India and the voluntary sector to sensitise law enforcement personnel and policy makers. A National Centre for Gender Training and Research has set up in the National Academy of Administration in Mussourie with the objective of sensitising young administrators and policy makers on gender issues.

The Election Commission of India maintains updated information on women representatives in each Parliament, including categorised information on the number of scheduled castes women representatives. With the recent revolution in information technology, the entire information is available not only in print but also on the Internet in the Parliament and Election Commission websites. This increases out-reach and access of this information to the general public. The Ministry of Rural Development, Government of India maintains updated information on the representation of women in local self-government or Panchayati Raj. The Department of Women and Child Development, Government of India also has come out with publications like 'Women in India – A Statistical Profile' in 1997, which compiled information on all aspects related to women in India.

Besides these, several independent organisations are carrying out their own research and surveys that provide updated information on the same. These are also widely used and are quoted in different public documents. Sensitising the leadership of people's movements in the country to gender issues need to be prioritised.

4.8.4. Legal and Political Initiatives

The number of women in politics at the local level had been very small, and their influence negligible. As stated by Kumari and Kidwai, "Prior to 1990, the women in local politics were generally either politicians who had lost membership of higher institutions, and those who were given such an opportunity to serve the purpose of publicity. In many cases, the motive was partially also to satisfy the aspirations of these few women, since they could be kept under virtual control and denied higher aspirations.

The 74th Amendment of the Indian Constitution in 1992 ushered in a new era in the democratic process of the country as it not only provided constitutional status to the municipal bodies but also provided an enabling environment for women to a direct part in the local self government and brought women to the forefront and centre of local development. Sharing power and responsibilities with immense control over resources for development and social change will be an empowering instrument for women.

Article 243 T (I) of Constitution Amendment states as follows:

"Reservation of Seats:

1) 243 T (1) Seats shall be reserved for the Scheduled Castes and the Scheduled Tribes in every Municipality and the number of seats so reserved shall bear, as nearly as may be, the same proportion to the total number of seats to be filled by direct election in that Municipality as the population of the Scheduled Castes in the Municipal area or of the Scheduled Tribes in the Municipal area

bears to the total population of that area and such seats may be allotted by rotation to different constitutions in a Municipality.

2) Not less than one-third of the total number of seats reserved under clause (1) shall be reserved for women belonging to the Scheduled Castes or, as the case may be, the Scheduled Tribes.

3) Not less than one-third of the total number of seats to be filled by direct election in every Municipality shall be reserved for women and such seats may be allotted by rotation to different constituencies in a Municipality.

4) The office of Chairpersons in the Municipalities shall be reserved for the Scheduled Castes, the Scheduled Tribes and common in such manner as the Legislature of a State may by law, provide.

5) The reservation of seats under clauses (1) and (2) and the reservation of office of Chairpersons (other than the reservation for women) under clause (4) shall cease to have effect on the expiration of the period specified in article 334.

6) Nothing in this Part shall prevent the Legislature of a State from making any provision for reservation of seats in any Municipality or office of Chairpersons in the Municipalities in favour of backward class of citizens."

4.8.5. Training and Support Mechanisms

Attention is being given to the training and capacity developing skills and capacities of all elected representatives in local government, including women. They are trained to acquire skills, knowledge and orientation needed to carry out the onerous responsibilities given to them. A time bound, systematic and comprehensive training programme has been drawn up which will be funded by the Central Government. The Indira Gandhi National Open University has been associated with the preparation of a syllabus on women and development. The Government of India is also committed to capacity building efforts by organising and funding training programmes for women elected to municipal bodies in India. Ministry of Urban Development (MUD) supports several such kind of training programmes through Regional Centre for Urban and Environmental Studies (RCUES) which are functioning in all the regions of India.

Apart from this, some of the theme-based training programmes are organised by State Training Institutions in several States for women elected members in municipal bodies. Human Settlements Management Institute (HSMI) of HUDCO organises some specialised training for women elected representatives in India.

Women elected to local governments have not formed any formal associations, groups and forums. However, all women mayors meet during meetings organised by All India Council of Mayors (AICM), which is an association of mayors representing all cities in India. These meetings give women mayors an opportunity to interact with each other and with other male Mayors and exchange ideas, information about effective urban service delivery, good governance and also provide issue based support. Similarly, various seminars, workshops, training programmes organised by Government of India, State Governments and National and Regional institutions provide wide opportunities for women elected members to meet and interact with elected women members from different municipal bodies in India.

In many cities women elected members have close links with local NGOs, CBOs or Residents' Associations or action groups and through suc h networking women members support each other and initiate networking among themselves about governance at local level or any issues related to women and development. It is observed that women officers from the Indian Administrative Service (IAS), Police (IPS), and Foreign Services (IFS) have their associations in all the States of India. These associations organise periodic meetings and 'get together' which provide an opportunity for the women officials to interact with each other. The City Managers' Association of Gujarat State also provides opportunities for women officials in local government in Gujarat State.

All India Institute of Local Self Government, through its various Centers in India imparts training in the field of municipal administration. Besides short-term specialized programmes, it also organises full time diploma courses on various aspects of municipal administration for junior and middle level municipal personnel. These courses are attended by large number of women employed at junior and middle and senior levels in municipal bodies in India.

4.8.6. Women in Decision-making Positions

One of the variables that go into the Gender Empowerment Measure, as depicted in the Human Development Report, is the proportion of men and women at senior levels of government. In this context the study initiated in 1996 by the Department of Personnel and Training (DoPT), as part of a project 'Capacity Building for Civil Services', was a significant step. In order to crystallize the problems faced by women in Civil Services as well as to isolate areas which needed to be addressed through policy guidelines, a survey was carried out across a cross section of the services, among men and women officers, to ascertain the issues on which guidelines would have to focus.

Various government studies have been undertaken in the past on problems and issues related to the various individual services that constitute the Indian Administration. But this survey broke new ground in terms of coverage of services and levels of both women and men, as well as the range of related issues. A national level Project Steering Committee was set up for carrying out the Capacity Building project, and a Focal Point was identified in the DoPT for examining the sphere of "Women's Issues in the Civil Service".

The Lal Bahadur Shastri National Academy of Administration (LBSNAA) was appointed as consultant for developing a curriculum for Gender Sensitization Programmes and ten Regional Seminars were conducted at nine State Administrative Training Institutes.

The Focal Point identified in the DoPT will begin work towards framing guidelines on women's issues by reviewing existing rules / regulations of various services. The task that has emerged for the Focal Point is as follows :

— Review of existing rules and regulations for possible gender bias and discrimination against women and suggest corrective action.

— Co-ordinate output flowing from various activities of the project related to the issues requiring policy formulation.

In the Civil Services, the overall percentage of women in 1997 was 7.5%, the highest being 12.3% in the Indian Foreign Service. Women are increasing their presence in other sectors such as the Revenue Services, the Railway Management Cadres, Telecommunication etc.

Women's Organisation or other civil society organisation have taken some initiatives in some states of India to encourage women to stand in local government elections, however, these groups or organisations are small and scattered and have diverse ways of empowering women. There are no infrastructural facilities of networking that could bring them together and strengthen them while allowing autonomy in their functioning. It is important to create unity in diversity between women's groups and civil society organisations involved with women's empowerment.

Political participation would make a significant different if it came from those who are at the helm of affairs of political parties, and if women are there wielding power, the situation can improve to a great extent and political participation would give every woman a sense of dignity as a individual.

Nath analysed that the women's movement and groups have to recognise the importance of women as a constituency and ensure their participation and representation in policy formulation. This can be achieved through reorienting existing structures for entry into decision-making including the political party system and introduce quotas or reservation as a temporary means of women's representation. The movement should also provide a support system for women who enter political processes to win elections.

The women's groups working at the grassroots level are small and scattered and have diverse ways of empowering women. There are no infrastructural facilities of networking available that could bring them together and strengthen them while allowing autonomy in their functioning. They need to adopt a common strategy, informed by a common vision, to be able to bring about changes in the policies and structures that perpetuate their subordinate status.

Non-partisan women's groups should provide necessary moral and advisory support to women candidates to increase their chances of being elected to political offices. They should work towards enhancing the capacity of women candidates to win the elections by providing them with a forum whereby they could exchange ideas and experiences and learn from experts on electoral laws and politics and evolve issues and strategies to win elections.

4.8.7. Encouraging Women's to Participate in Politics

The 33 percent for women in municipal bodies has brought into focus the fact that there is a need to bring more and more women into the party. But the problem is that many women are often not equipped to become members of the political parties, as the party expects a certain level of consciousness for membership – not everybody can become a member. Also, women have difficulty in attending party meetings, study circles or demonstrations because of their timings and the pressure of housework.

As analysed by Kumari and Kidwai at one level, the party's ideology itself may be discriminatory, on the other hand its ambiguity in a traditional society may leave adequate space for discrimination. Party workers at times exhibit a sense of lack of gender equality because they carry with them their traditional value systems which are often feudal and patriarchal, into the party. But at the same time women assert that the party does not try to change the attitude of both men and women who come to the party or make them more gender sensitive.

The nature of electoral politics in India also marginalises women and women's issues from the political agenda. Many women feel that electoral politics, at times limits the kind of support women politicians would like to extend to members of their own sex, since they realise that they cannot win elections on women's issues alone. Also, elections are largely conducted by men and with men's support. Electoral expediency requires women participants to compromise to survive in the man's world of politics.

The type of leadership required is of transformational type. Women's entry into processes of governance should create change in the very institutions of governance. In order to effect such change, leaders have to emerge which can occur only through participatory processes. The participation allows empowerment, which then generates leadership. It is only through their leadership, and their implied changes in the hierarchy of party and power that they may provide that they can justifiably participate in governance as representing something 'different'. Prior to 1992, political parties have not been initiating any special initiatives or programmes to encourage women to stand in local government elections. The number of women in politics at the local level has been very small, and their influence negligible. After 1993, women's participation in local governments increased quite radically with the enactment of the legislation providing one-third reservation of seats for women in local bodies. According to women from all parties the one third reservation for women in local governments has brought into focus the fact that there is a need to bring more and more women into the local government field and develop their capacities.

The particular 74th Amendment of the Indian Constitution ushered in a new era in the democratic process in India as it not only provided constitutional status to the municipal bodies but also provided an enabling environment for women to take direct part in the process of local self government and brought women to the forefront of city development. A very active role for women in local governance is envisaged as compared to governance at the state and national levels in India. These provisions have provided great opportunities and challenges to women in India. The challenge now is to transfer this large presence of women at local government level supported by the real delegation of power and responsibilities.

References

Barry, Trudie, Sneha Palnitkar. 1996. *Women and Local Politics in Mumbai and London : The quota Innovation*' Third IIAS International Conference (International Institute of Administrative Sciences) – Beijing, China 8 – 11, October, 1996.

Beall, Jo, 1996, *Urban Governance: Why Gender Matters, Gender* in Development Monograph Series, Number 1, UNDP, New York.

Folasade Ayorinde. 2005*Local Government Budget & Gender, A Guide Analysis of Kuje Area Council Budget, Abuja, Case Study of the Education & Health sectors*, Nigeria Gender Budget Network.

International Union of Local Authorities. 1998. *Women in Local Government. Stockholm: IULA.*

5

Gender Quota Laws: Global Perspective

Women form more than half the population, but constitute only a small minority of all political representatives. According to the most recent figures, they occupy 17% of all seats in national parliaments around the world. However, attention to global averages masks important variations. States like Rwanda, Sweden, and Costa Rica have nearly equal numbers of male and female parliamentarians, while countries like Kyrgyzstan, Qatar, and Saudi Arabia have no women in their parliaments at all. Further, it does not acknowledge the important increases made over the last several years in a number of countries around the world. In Latin America, the two most notable cases are Argentina, where the percentage of female deputies grew from 5% in 1991 to 35% in 2006, and Costa Rica, where the proportion increased from 5% in 1993 to 39% in 2006. In this and other regions of the world, a crucial impetus for change has been the adoption of quota policies to facilitate the selection of female candidates to political office. However, not all quotas are equally successful in increasing women's political representation: some countries experience dramatic increases following the adoption of new quota regulations, while others see more modest changes or even setbacks in the proportion of women elected to national assemblies.

5.1. Gender Quota Policies

Gender quota policies fall into three broad categories: reserved seats, party quotas, and legislative quotas. They vary in terms of their basic characteristics, the countries in which they appear, and the timing of their adoption. Nonetheless, they share striking similarities in terms of the timing of their introduction. In the fifty years between 1930 and 1980, only ten states established quotas, followed by twelve additional countries in the 1980s. In the 1990s, however, quotas appeared in more than fifty states, which have been joined by nearly forty more countries since the year 2000. As a result, more than one hundred countries now have some sort of quota policy, with more than seventyfive percent of these measures being passed during the last fifteen years. Quotas thus appear to reflect a growing international norm regarding the need to promote women's political representation.

Reserved seats are policies that literally set aside places for women in political assemblies. In this way, they guarantee women's presence by revising the mechanisms of election to mandate a minimum number of female representatives. This proportion is often very low, as some reserved seats policies mandate as little as one or two percent of all seats. However, there are important exceptions, like the thirty percent policy that was adopted in Tanzania. These measures first appeared in the 1930s, but have been adopted a s recently as 2005, and have become an increasingly prominent solution in countries with very low levels of female parliamentary representation. They are concentrated geographically in Africa, Asia, and the Middle East. In some states, there are no quotas at the national level, but quotas are used very effectively at the local level, as in India and Namibia.

Party quotas are measures adopted voluntarily by political parties to require a certain proportion of women among their parties' candidates. Given their origins with political parties, these quotas differ from reserved seats in that they concern slates of candidates, rather than the final proportion of women elected. Further, they generally mandate a much higher proportion of women, usually between twenty-five and fifty percent of all candidates. They were first adopted in the early 1970s by various left-wing parties in Western Europe. Today they are the most common type of gender quota, appearing in parties across the political spectrum and in all regions of the world. They continue to be the most prevalent measure employed in Western Europe. However, they also frequently coexist with legislative quotas in Africa and Latin America, where party quotas predate or accompany the adoption of more encompassing quota laws.

Legislative quotas, finally, are measures passed by national parliaments that require all parties to nominate a certain proportion of female candidates. Similar to party quotas, they address selection processes, rather than the number of women actually elected. Unlike party quotas, however, they are mandatory provisions that apply to all political groupings, rather than simply those who choose to adopt quotas. Legislative quotas typically call for women to constitute between twenty-five and fifty percent of all candidates. They are the newest type of gender quota, appearing first in the early 1990s, but have become increasingly common as more and more countries adopt quota policies. With some notable exceptions, these measures tend to be found in developing countries, particularly in Latin America, and/or in post-conflict societies, primarily in Africa, the Middle East, and Southeastern Europe. In many countries, they coexist with – or supersede – provisions for party quotas.

5.2. Gender Quota Adoption

The rapid diffusion of gender quota policies raises the question: how and why these measures have been adopted in diverse countries around the world? Cases around the world suggest four possible explanations.

The first is that *women mobilize for quotas to increase women's representation*. This usually occurs when women's groups realize that quotas are an effective – and maybe the only – means for increasing women's political representation. These women may include women's organizations inside political parties, women's movements in civil society, women's groups in other countries, and even individual women close to powerful men. In all of these instances, women's groups pursue quotas for both normative and pragmatic reasons. They believe that there should be more women in politics in order to promote justice, interests, and resources. In the absence any 'natural' trend towards change, however, they recognize that this is likely to be achieved only through specific, targeted actions to promote female candidates.

The second explanation is that *political elites adopt quotas for strategic reasons*, generally related to competition with other parties. Various case studies suggest, for example, that party elites often adopt quotas when one of their rivals adopts them. This concern may be heightened if the party seeks to overcome a long period in opposition or a dramatic decrease in popularity. In other contexts, elites view quotas as a way to demonstrate some sort of commitment to women without really intending to alter existing patterns of inequality, or alternatively, as a means to promote other political ends, like maintaining control over political rivals within or outside the party. If these motives are correct, the adoption of quotas may be less about empowering women in politics and more about how quotas fit in – perhaps serendipitously – with various other struggles among political elites.

The third is that *quotas are adopted when they mesh with existing or emerging notions of equality and representation.* Evidence indicates that gender quotas are compatible in distinct ways with a number of normative frameworks. Some scholars view quota adoption as consistent with ideas about equality and fair access. They point out that left-wing parties are generally more open to measures such as quotas because these match with their more general goals of social equality.

Others interpret quotas as a method to recognize difference and the need for proportional representation. Quotas for women are thus a logical extension of guarantees given to other groups based on linguistic, religious, racial, and other cleavages. A final observation is that quotas tend to emerge during periods of democratic innovation. In these countries, quotas may be seen as a way to establish the legitimacy of the new political system during democratic transition or the creation of new democratic institutions. Taken together, these arguments analyze quotas in relation to their 'fit' with features of the political context: they do not reflect principled concerns to empower women or pragmatic strategies to win or maintain power.

The fourth explanation is that *quotas are supported by international norms and spread through transnational sharing.* Over the last ten years, a variety of international organizations –including the United Nations, the Socialist International, the Council of Europe, the European Union, the Commonwealth, the African Union, the Southern African Development Community, and the Organization of American States – have issued declarations recommending that all member-states aim for thirty percent women in all political bodies. These norms shape national quota debates in at least four ways.

International imposition occurs in cases where international actors are directly involved in quota adoption, either by deciding to apply quotas themselves or by compelling national leaders to do so themselves. Transnational emulation takes place in cases where local women's movements and transnational non-governmental organizations share information on quota strategies across national borders. International tipping appears in cases where international events provide new sources of leverage in national debates, shifting the balance in favor or local and transnational actors pressing for quota adoption. International blockage, finally, happens in cases where international actors seek to prevent the adoption of gender quotas, despite mobilization by local women's groups and transnational NGOs in favor of these policies.

5.3. Gender Quota Implementation

Quota measures are diverse, and thus differences in their impact are to be expected. However, pinpointing why some quotas are more effective than others is a complicated task: in addition to features of specific quota policies, which affect their likelihood of being implemented, quotas are introduced when variations already exist in the percentage of women in national parliaments. Cross-national variations are thus the combined result of quotas – where they are present – and other political, social, and economic factors that were often at work before quotas were established.

As a result, quotas do not simply lead to gains proportional to the quota policy, but also interact, both positively and negatively, with various features of the broader political context. Three broad explanations have been offered to untangle these effects. The first links variations in quota implementation to *details of quota measures themselves*. Some scholars connect quota impact to the type of measure involved.

Although most studies agree that reserved seats generally produce small changes in women's representation, some claim that party quotas are more effective than other types of quotas because they are voluntary measures, adopted from concerns about electoral advantage. Others insist that legislative quotas are more effective because they bind all political parties, rather than merely those who choose to adopt quotas, and are enforced by state bureaucracies and the courts, rather than simply party leaders.

More recent work delves deeper into variations within and across types, seeking to understand why specific quota measures are more or less effective in achieving changes in women's representation. These scholars argue that the impact of gender quotas stems from the wording of the quota, whether the language used in the policy strengthens the quota requirement or reduces ambiguity or vagueness regarding the process of implementation; the requirements of the quota, whether the policy specifies where female candidates should be placed and to which elections the policy applies; the sanctions of the quota, whether the policy establishes organs for reviewing and enforcing quota requirements and procedures for punishing or rectifying non-compliance; and the perceived legitimacy of the quota, whether the policy is viewed as legal or constitutional from the point of view of national and international law.

A second explanation relates the impact of quotas to *the 'fit' between quota measures and existing institutional frameworks*. Most studies in this vein focus on characteristics of the electoral system, examining how electoral rules facilitate or hinder the potentially positive effect of quotas on women's representation. They observe that quotas have the greatest impact in proportional representation electoral systems with closed lists and high district magnitudes, although they also identify idiosyncratic features of particular electoral systems that negatively affect quota implementation, including the possibility for parties to run more than one list in each district, the existence of distinct electoral systems for different types of elections, and the chance for parties to nominate more candidates than the number of seats available.

Other scholars consider features of the political party system, as well as the characteristics of parties themselves, to discern partisan dynamics that aid or subvert quota implementation. They argue that quotas are more likely to have an impact in party systems where several parties co-exist and larger parties respond to policy innovations initiated by smaller parties, as well as in parties with left-wing ideologies where the party leadership is able to enforce party or national regulations. Still others observe higher rates of implementation across all parties in countries where the political culture emphasizes sexual difference and group representation and lower rates of compliance in countries where the political culture stresses sexual equality and individual representation. A third explanation outlines the *actors who support and oppose quotas and their respective roles in guaranteeing or undermining quota implementation*. Much of this literature focuses on political party elites as the group most directly responsible for variations in the impact of quotas, since the effective application of quotas largely hinges around elites' willingness to recruit female candidates. Most accounts expose the ways that elites seek to mitigate quota impact through passive refusal to enforce quotas to more active measures to subvert their intended effect, to the point of even committing largescale electoral fraud and widespread intimidation of female candidates.

Many also mention other actors who play a direct or indirect role in enforcing quota provisions, including women's organizations both inside and outside the political parties who pressure elites to comply with quota provisions, distribute information on quota regulations both to elites and the general public, and train female candidates to negotiate better positions on their respective party lists; national and international courts who provide an arena to challenge non-compliance and require parties to redo lists that do not comply with the law; and ordinary citizens who engage in public scrutiny of parties' selection practices through reports and reprimands that lead elites to honor and even exceed quota commitments.

5.4. Gender Quota Policies in Latin America

Evidence from around the world suggests that these three sets of factors work together to shape the effects of gender quota policies. Crucially, multiple combinations appear to be successful in improving the numbers of women elected to political office: strict quota policies combined with proportional representation electoral systems and strong elite support often produce gains in women's representation, but similar results have been observed in other countries with vague quota measures, majoritarian electoral systems, and weak elite but strong civil society support. The main recipe for success is simultaneous attention to all three of these dimensions, possibilities which become evident when we compare cases where quotas have succeeded and where quotas have failed to increase women's representation. Because reserved seats are unlikely to be proposed, experiences with party quotas and legislative quotas offer the most insights for designing more effective quota policies in Latin America.

Party quotas take a variety of different forms across countries. Their impact on the overall numbers of women elected depends largely on (1) the number and size of the parties that adopt gender quotas and (2) the percentage of women provided for by the quota policy. In addition, many of the most successful policies 'frame' quotas in ways that resonate in clever ways with local contexts.

The most effective party quotas are those that operate in *Sweden*, where women's representation in parliament is currently 47.3%. Since the 1920s, women have mobilized inside and outside the political parties to pressure elites to select more female candidates. Their efforts resulted in a gradual strengthening of party measures to promote women: from the inclusion of at least one woman per list in the 1950s and 1960s, to recommendations and targets of "at least 40% women" in the 1970s and 1980s, to stricter 50% party quotas in the 1990s and 2000s. Importantly, the final push for equal representation came after women's representation decreased in 1991 for the first time since 1928.

Women from all the parties threatened to leave to form their own women's party if the established parties did not take steps to recruit more female candidates. In response, most parties agreed to alternate between men and women on their party lists. Interestingly, many insisted that this was not a 'quota' but rather the principle of *varannan damernas* ('every other one for the ladies'), which referred to a tradition in Swedish countryside dances where men asked women to dance for one song and then women asked men to dance for the next song. (In many towns, this was also known as the practice of 'democratic dancing'). Similar policies are known as the 'zipper principle' in Western and Eastern Europe and the 'zebra principle' in Southern Africa. Quotas have been particularly effective in Sweden because they have been adopted by all the political parties, they aim for 50% female representation, and –given the context of their adoption – parties believe that they would lose female voters if they do not fully implement these policies. The effects of these policies are heightened by the fact that Sweden has a proportional representation electoral system that employs closed lists, which enables parties to ensure that approximately 50% women will be elected.

Party quotas have been less successful in increasing women's representation in other countries. In some cases, this is because the parties that adopt quotas are very few and very small, for example the many women's parties across Eastern Europe. This indicates that party quotas are unlikely to increase women's representation to a significant degree unless they are also adopted by one or more of the major political parties. Sincere party commitments are also important: some parties adopt quotas but then do not fully implement them, as in France in the 1970s and 1980s. In still other cases, parties adopt quotas but then are forced to abandon them due to legal challenges.

For example, in the *United Kingdom*, the Labour Party instituted a policy in 1993 that pledged to consider only female candidates in 50% of all the districts that the party expected to win in the 1997 elections. However, this policy was soon challenged by two male party members who were overlooked as possible candidates, because their districts were among those that had been designated for all-women shortlists. The quota was eventually overturned by the courts in 1996 on the grounds that it violated the terms of the Sex Discrimination Act, which prohibited discrimination on the basis of sex in applications for employment.

The party did not challenge the ruling, but did not de-select those female candidates that had already been chosen through the quota. As a result, women's representation doubled from 9% to 18% in 1997, due exclusively to the Labour Party policy. Following a modest decrease in the number of women elected to parliament in 2002, the Sex Discrimination Act was subsequently reformed to allow positive action in candidate selection, but women's representation has since stagnated at 20%. Concerns about the legitimacy of the quota, combined with the difficulties in making dramatic increases in a majoritarian electoral system, have made further dramatic increases hard to achieve.

Legislative quotas, which are the most common type of quota policy in Latin America, are similarly diverse. Their impact on the overall numbers of women elected stems mainly from

(1) the percentage of women provided for by the quota law,

(2) degree to which the policy constrains the behavior of political parties, and

(3) the extent to which women's groups remain vigilant over the implementation of the quota policy.

In Latin America, the two countries with the most successful legislative quotas are Argentina and Costa Rica, for very similar reasons. In *Argentina*, both houses of parliament passed a law in 1991 that specified that parties were to nominate at least 30% women in list positions where they were likely to be elected. The idea for the quota emerged through meetings of women from all the major political parties. They had learned about experiments with quotas at the UN Third World Conference on Women, as well as through contacts with women in the Spanish Socialist Party, where quotas had been adopted in 1988, and women's groups in Costa Rica, where a bill proposing quotas was under consideration also in 1988. Confusion over what constituted an 'electable' position, however, led to a series of constitutional and legal debates, as well as a number of presidential decrees, over the course of the 1990s that clarified the precise requirements of the quota law, including the placement of women and the procedures for rectifying non-compliance. As these stricter interpretations took effect, the proportion of women in the lower house of parliament increased from 6% in 1991 to 14% in 1993, 22% in 1995, 28% in 1997, 27% in 1999, 30% in 2001, and 35% in 2005. When these provisions applied to the Senate for the first time, women's representation jumped directly from 3% in 1999 to 35% in 2001, increasing to 43% in 2005.

In *Costa Rica*, a quota law was discussed as early as 1988 as part of the proposed Bill on Real Equality between Women and Men, but the final version passed in 1990 simply recommended that parties adopt their own measures to ensure women's representation. Supporters continued to lobby for revisions to the electoral code, however, and parliament eventually adopted a 40% quota law in 1996. Because the law required all parties to reform their internal rules governing candidate selection, but made no formal requirements regarding women's placement on party lists, advocates appealed to the highest electoral court to pass a judgment on the 'spirit' of the law. While the court rejected placement mandates in 1997, it espoused them in 1999, arguing that in order to conform to the law, parties must include 40% women in 'electable positions,' defined by the court as the number of seats won in the previous election. As a consequence, the proportion of women in parliament increased only from 14% in 1994 to 19% in 1998, but jumped to 35% in 2002 and 39% in 2006. In both Argentina and Costa Rica, therefore, the quotas were increasingly more successful over time because while they initially mandated a high proportion of women, women's groups continued to watch over the implementation of the quota law, calling on political leaders and national courts to make adjustments and clarifications each time the policy was not followed to its fullest extent.

Legislative quotas have been less effective in other countries, leading to stagnation and even decreases in the numbers of women elected. In *France*, both houses of parliament amended the constitution in 1999 and the electoral law in 2000 to mandate that parties nominate 50% female candidates for all elections. The new law set out distinct requirements for different sorts of elections, however, according to the type of electoral system used. For local elections held under proportional representation, the law obliged parties to achieve parity per group of six candidates, with three men and three women in any order, with rejection of the list being the penalty for non-compliance.

For elections to the lower house of parliament governed by two-round majoritarian voting, the law required parties to present equal numbers of male and female candidates across all electoral districts, with no specification as to which districts female candidates should be placed, with a financial penalty for non-compliance. While all parties complied at the local level, regulations at the national level created distinct incentives for smaller versus larger parties: smaller parties generally respected parity, because they were under pressure to maximize the amount of state subsidy that they could claim, while larger parties did not, because they could absorb losses in state funding by recouping money later through winning more seats. As a consequence, the proportion of women in local councils jumped from 26% to 48% in 2001, while women's representation in the lower house of parliament barely rose from 11% to 12% in 2002.

In *Brazil*, quotas were first debated inside the political parties as early as 1986, but proposals for national quotas appeared only in 1995, when both houses of parliament approved a 20% quota for local elections, along with a reform allowing parties to nominate 20% more candidates than seats available. Following the UN's Fourth World Conference on Women, women's groups stepped up their lobbying and no less than eight proposals for various types of quota laws were presented between 1995 and 1997. In 1996, both houses of parliament established a 20% quota for state and federal elections that was raised to 25% in 1998 and 30% in 2000. At the same time, however, members of parliament passed another regulation allowing parties to present 50% more candidates than seats available. Combined, these provisions introduced a crucial escape clause regarding the process of implementation: since parties were simply required to 'reserve' 30% of slots for women, the possibility to nominate 150% meant that they could in practice propose a candidate list consisting entirely of men. As a result, the number of women in the lower house of parliament actually decreased following adoption of the quota law, dropping from 6% in 1994 to 5% in 1998, although this figure eventually increased to 8% in 2002 and 9% in 2006. In France and Brazil, therefore, quota laws have largely failed to increase women's political representation. In both cases, the policies themselves permitted parties various means for circumventing the quota requirements which, combined with the lack of mobilization by women's groups, have produced disappointing results.

In addition, quotas remain very controversial in many countries, despite a growing international norm in favor of gender quotas. This has limited their effects in some cases; in others, quota policies have been subject to legal challenges and subsequently overturned, as in Colombia and Venezuela. While in some cases such developments have taken quotas off of the political agenda, it is worth noting that such setbacks have been successfully overcome in a number of countries outside Latin America. As mentioned above, party quotas were made legal again in the *United Kingdom*, following reform of the Sex Discrimination Act in 2002. The new Act now allows – but does not require – parties to apply gender quotas when selecting their candidates to parliament. The Labour Party quickly resumed its former quota policy in the run-up to elections in 2005, and recent changes inside the Conservative Party indicate that it too may take special steps over the next few years to select more female candidates

In *France* and *Italy*, quotas were declared unconstitutional in 1982 (France) and 1995 (Italy). In both cases, women's groups transformed this legal setback into a strategy for change, focused on reforming the constitutional articles on equality that had been used to overturn the earlier quotas. While difficult, these changes were achieved in France in 1999 and in Italy in 2003 after extensive mobilization. Reforms to the French electoral law soon followed in 2000. However, despite various proposals, similar changes have not occurred yet in Italy, because although various quota reforms have been approved by the Chamber of Deputies, they have never yet reached the floor of the Senate. These cases suggest that legal obstacles surrounding quotas can be resolved in ways that allow new quota policies to be passed, although such changes generally require sustained mobilization by women's groups to ensure that new policies are approved.

This overview of gender quota policies around the world reveals that a wide range of actors are engaged in quota campaigns, and that the issue of women's representation has now reached the political agenda in countries around the world. Viewed together, patterns of adoption and implementation suggest that political action plays a crucial role in shaping women's access to political office. Most obviously, the spread of quotas challenges the idea that increases in the number of women in politics occur 'naturally.' However, while quota adoption appears to be a major reason for these recent shifts in representation in recent years, it is important to recognize that not all quotas have their intended effects.

Many produce increases, but others result in stagnation and even decreases, in the numbers of women elected to political office. These variations suggest that quotas are not a panacea, but constitute a crucial step forward for women's political empowerment worldwide. Designing more effective gender quotas requires attention to three features: the design of quota policies, the 'fit' between quotas and broader political structures, and the relative balance between actors who support and oppose quota policies. These three features may fit together in a number of different ways.

Nonetheless, it is possible to pinpoint some general characteristics of successful quota policies. Party quotas generally have a greater impact on the numbers of women elected to political office when (1) many parties, especially several larger parties, adopt these policies; (2) the quotas adopted call for a relatively high proportion of women to be nominated as party candidates; and (3) the quotas are framed in ways that link them to well-understood and widely accepted cultural practices and traditions. Legislative quotas tend to result in increases in women's representation when (1) these laws require a relatively high proportion of female candidates to be nominated by the political parties; (2) these laws strictly bind the behavior of political parties or, alternatively, create positive incentives for parties to nominate more women; and (3) women's groups continue to monitor compliance with these policies, through legal and political means if necessary, to ensure that parties implement quotas to their fullest degree.

5.5. Gender Quota System in Rwanda

Rwanda has been the most successful country at implementing a gender quota system.

Women in Rwanda are now at the top of world rankings of women in politics, and many othercountries in Africa and beyond are aiming to follow Rwanda's lead in gender equality.Rwandan women not only are members of both houses of Parliament but also hold positions as secretary of state, ministers, and Supreme Court justices.

Rwanda's success took root in the post-genocide era. In 1996, tribal wars and genocide devastated the male Tutsi population. This travesty left Rwanda with a population of 70 percent women. Therefore, women had to assume traditional male roles in society. Post-conflict processes ensured that women were able to take part in the drafting of a new constitution and new legislative structures. In doing so, they had the chance to push for more equality in politics through initiatives such as quota laws. Rwanda illustrates how women in African countries are able to begin breaking existing legislative and cultural structures. Through forming new women's organizations and movements, women empowered other women to fight for equality in politics.

The women's movement that began in post-genocide Rwanda was successful at forming a gender quota system in Rwanda. Today, Rwanda has both a constitutional quota and election law quotas to ensure women's place in Parliament. Rwanda operates on a reserved seat system in which 30 percent of seats in Parliament must be filled by women. However, after the 2008 elections, 56 percent of Rwanda's Parliament is female, far exceeding its constitutional gender quota. Rwanda today has the first majority female parliament in the world. The female parliamentarians have shown effective political power as they have enacted laws related to women's issues. For example, in 1999 the "Inheritance Law" amendment was incorporated into the civil code. This law was a significant step forward for women and allowed women to inherit property, enter into contracts, seek compensated employment, and open bank accounts, all without their husband or father's sanction. Rwanda's success continues to serve as an example for the myriad of other countries seeking to represent women more equally in politics.

5.6. Gender Quota System in Jordan

Jordan remains a patriarchal society in which the attitude of the public must be changed if women are to advance politically. It is tradition in Jordan that politics is a man's job and political parties in Jordan have very few women members today. Women also lack funds to run for political offices because most women are not economically independent from their husbandsand families, which put them at a decided disadvantage from men. There is often illegal activity, such as "vote buying", that requires additional money from the political party's funding. In Jordan, it is only in the past 15 years that women have begun to participate in politics, albeit at minimal levels. In an effort to accomplish this, many nongovernmental organizations (NGOs) mobilize women and have awareness raising programs.

In 2003 Parliament passed an amendment to the 2001 election law requiring that six seats in the House of Representatives be reserved for women. The seats in the Senate are directly appointed by the King. Since the introduction of a quota law in Jordan, Falak Jumaani was the first woman in Jordan to win in an electoral race with her male competitors in the 2007 election. Falak Jumaani is against the quota system because she believes that women can work hard and win without the system by getting to know and achieving a level of trust with their constituents. In doing so, women can compete with male opponents and win. This view is also shared by Toujan Fousal. Toujan was the first women elected to Parliament in Jordan in 1993, before the gender quota laws had been implemented. She also believes that the quota system is both unfair and unnecessary. However, Dr. Eman Al-Hussein believes that the quota system is still necessary because currently women can only win in cases, such as Falak Jumaani's, where there are small districts and the female candidates know the community.

Today, seven out of the 110 members (6.4 percent) of Jordan's Senate are women, and seven out of 55 (12.7 percent) of Jordan's House of Representatives are women. Six of the 14 current women in Parliament achieved their positions through the reserved seats in the quota law. In the 2007 elections, women were more active in both promoting female candidates and in running for office. Women also were finally present on tribal committees that select candidates. Women have even achieved the feat of creating a "Women and Family" committee in the House of Representatives.

Dr. Eman advises that the quota system be extended for one more term and then hopes it will no longer be necessary. She considers the quota system an instrumental force in helping women achieve positions in Parliament, but also thinks that seven women is not a great enough representation of women to lobby Parliament on women's issues. There has been a shifting change in mentality where women and communities have begun to encourage women to run for office. Nevertheless, because of cultural barriers, when the small percentage of women who votein Jordan cast their ballots, they continue to vote for men over women. Dr. Eman believes that women still face many obstacles and believes the quota system is effective in solving them.

5.7. Gender Quota System in Bolivia

Bolivian women have made many strides since gaining the right to vote in 1956 and today make up close to 17 percent of the Bolivian Parliament. Through the influence of NGO's and women's movements, Bolivia enacted a gender quota system in 2001. The 2001 Election Law required that 30 percent of the candidates on the ballot for town councils must be women, that candidate lists for the lower house must have one woman for every three men, and that candidate lists for the upper house must have one woman for every four men. Although this legislation was a promising beginning for women's equality in Bolivian politics, significant challenges remain.

Marisol Aban, a representative for the political party Revolutionary Nationalist Movement, is a WDN activist who was elected to Parliament in 2005. Out of pure luck, Marisol was placed at the top of the candidate list for the Revolutionary Nationalist Movement as the first candidate. This allowed her to gain a seat in Parliament as a congresswoman and actually have effective power. However, she said that most of her colleagues who are women were placed at the bottom of the list and only achieved positions of little power, or won seats as substitutes, who only serve in Parliament when the permanent representatives are absent. Marisol said that the 2001 Election Law was also flawed because it lacked sanctions or penalties if the political parties did not place women on their candidate lists or allow women to be elected to high positions on the ballot. Without sanctions, corruption flourishes. As Marisol said, "Hecha la ley, hecha la trampa," which roughly translates to "for every law there is a loophole." She explained how she does not want that to characterize women's rights in Bolivia, which is why she is working hard to get rid of any loopholes that exist. Marisol explained how in the Revolutionary Left Movement, a Bolivian political party, a man ran for office under a woman's name, and won. She said that this type of corruption is commonplace under the current political system.

In January 2009, the 2001 Election Law was modified, changing the quota to 50 percent instead of 30 percent. Marisol applauded this recent development. Out of every three spaces on candidates list, one space will have to be filled by a woman. Although this new quota aims toincrease women's representation in Parliament, there are currently no sanctions for noncompliance with the new quota. Marisol said that Congress is currently debating how to enforce the new quota. She hopes that noncompliance sanctions will soon pass in Parliament, but believes that the debates will continue on even if sanctions are in place. Marisol's outlook on the future for women's representation in politics in Bolivia is optimistic. She believes that the quota system has been instrumental in providing women with easier access to entering politics. She believes that in the future, it will become an obligation for political parties to include women and the need for quota laws will dissipate. She also thinks that soon, men will see the need for women in parliament and the political atmosphere will begin to shift and begin favoring women more as attitudes change. For now, she advises women to train themselves for political office and demand more participation.

5.8. Gender Quota System in Kenya

In Kenya, women have been struggling for years in order to gain greater representation in Parliament. In 1997, a constitutional amendment was passed that gave Kenya a quota system. The legislation provided that the president appoint 12 people to Parliament, six of whom should be women. As there are 222 members of Parliament, this quota law is numerically fairly insignificant and many citizens of Kenya are unaware it even exists. There is no mandate in the legal electoral framework that requires Kenyan political parties to ensure a minimum quota for women in Parliament. The Democratic Party in Kenya is one party that does implement a quota system, reserving one third of all seats on the candidate list for women. However, there are numerous political parties in Kenya, making the Democratic Party's quota law relatively insignificant as well. Today, Kenya's Parliament consists of close to 10 percent of female representatives.

Honorable Professor Ruth Oniang'o, a WDN member and political activist in Kenya, said that the political atmosphere in Kenya presents women with too many obstacles. For example, passing legislation concerning women's issues is difficult in Kenya. A male dominated parliament is more likely to strike down legislation such as the "Inheritance Law" because it usurps power from men.

According to Professor Oniang'o, other obstacles that impede women in politics in Kenya include economic dependence on men and physical and mental degradation from society.Because women have not been able to pass legislation that would make them financially independent from their husbands and fathers, women have difficulties acquiring the money to run for office. In most cases, only with their husband or father's approval can women obtain the funds necessary to run a political campaign. If women do overcome the financial obstacle, they still face societal disapproval when they run for office because

Kenya continues to have a patriarchal society. The European Union Election Observation Commission reported 33 cases of violent assaults on women during the 2007 elections including "intimidation, physical assaults, threats, and murder." Professor Oniang'o said that there is often planned violence against opponents during campaigns and elections, especially when the opponents are women, and Professor Oniang'o herself was almost killed in the post-election violence of 2007 and 2008. According to Professor Oniang'o, male opponents also often attack the moral character of female candidates, which not only affects the women, but also affects the women's families. Professor Oniang'o said that when she ran for office "the playing field was hostile to say the least". Despite all of the obstacles, Professor Oniang'o is hopeful that the quota system will help increase the representation of women in Parliament. In 2005, UN Security Council Resolution 1325 set a goal for Kenya to target a 30 percent quota for women in the legislature. Two failed initiatives to introduce new quota laws into the constitution in 2005 and 2007 followed. The 2007 initiative would have set a quota that allocated 50 seats to women in the Parliament. Ultimately, 265 women ran for office, but only 23 were both selected and elected. Professor Oniang'o advocates awareness raising programs and organizations such as the WDN who help train and connect women in politics around the world. She has faith that the number of women will eventually rise in politics, but only when "elections are free, fair, and violence and abuse free."

5.9. Gender Quota System in Bangladesh

Although Bangladesh was one of the first countries in the world to implement a gender quota system in their National Parliament, the government has struggled with fulfilling the quota law. The first quota law in 1972 required that 15 of the 315 seats in Parliament be reserved for women. In 1978 the government increased the number of reserved seats for women to 30 seats.

Until 2001 when the quota law requiring that women occupy 30 seats in Parliament expired, the highest number of women in Parliament was 11 women in 1996. Because the quota law hadexpired, in 2004 the National Parliament passed the 14Constitutional Amendment, which reinstated the quota system and required that 45 of the 345 seats in Parliament be reserved for women. However, that number of reserved seats has yet to be reached. There are currently only 19 women in the National Parliament, and 26 reserved seats are yet to be filled. Rekha Shaha, the Director of Steps for Development in Bangladesh and a WDN activist, believes that "when a woman takes initiatives to enter the political field, she has to fight social stigma and endure bitter experiences." Bangladesh is a country in which there exists a discriminatory social system. Rekha said that women are portrayed as incompetent and unable to prove themselves in the political arena. Women lack presence in political parties, and therefore have little decision making power. They face the obstacles of dowries, lack of education, early marriage, and domestic violence. Above the traditional obstacles, she said that there is a rising impediment of religious fundamentalism in Bangladesh, which only perpetuates the cultural traditions that portray women as inferior.

When women do run for office, they face a corrupt political environment. Men who have economic means, unlike women, are able to pay people to vote for them. According to Rekha, men also tend to organize against women, making it very difficult for women to compete with them.

Rekha supports the gender quota system in Bangladesh because she believes that it is necessary in order to surpass those obstacles of a very traditional and patriarchal society. She thinks that affirmative action for women helps women move forward from the backward position they are held in society, and then later, they can succeed in a competitive environment. In Rekha's mind, although the quota system is positive and needed, it is not enough. She believes that awareness raising programs and skills development training are necessary supplements to the quota system and help women to advance in running for office.

One of Rekha's colleagues, Sufia Islam, ran for office in order to give more decision making power to women. She wanted to rectify the existing social situation in which women are "distressed and tortured". She gained a myriad of public support because of her ability to relate to the community. However, she ended up losing the election by only three votes. Because she came so close to winning, Sufia did not want to give up. She decided to participate in a leadership training program, which encouraged her to run again and increased her advocacy skills.

Sofia then ran again and was successfully elected as a councilor in a reserved seat inRajshashi City. She believes that the leadership training she received greatly helped her win the reserved seat made available to women through the quota system.

Rekha said that "unless the political situation in Bangladesh can be changed, the traditional attitude towards women cannot be changed." She has faith that the gender quota system, in conjunction with supplemental training and awareness raising programs, will help mold the new political atmosphere that is necessary for establishing a gender equal society. Since the introduction of the quota system, women in Bangladesh have faced a bumpy road. Although there is slow progress, reaching even higher in 2008, the Election Commission in Bangladesh approved legislation to ensure that women are represented as 33 percent of political parties by 2020. The road to equality for women in Bangladesh's political system will not doubt continue to be steep, but WDN activists like Rekha have hope that if the social and political atmospheres can be changed, women will find an equal place in politics.

5.10. Gender Quota System in Albania

Women's groups in Albania have been fighting for years for a quota mandate in the electoral system. According to Jeta Katro, a WDN activist in Albania, the struggle began after the Fourth World Conference on Women in Beijing in 1995 when Albanian women began discussions with political parties and the leadership in Parliament about the possible introduction of party quota laws. In 2000, women created a petition and received the support of 190,000 people for the introduction of a quota bill into the electoral system. In 2001, Parliament was made up of only 5.7 percent of women. Jeta said that although Parliament did not enact a quota law for the 2001 elections, women began "creating the political climate for change." Women also began creating and participating in training programs so that they could fight for themselves without the presence of the quota law.

Then, in 2004 women in the Millennium Women Network drafted the Gender Equality Law. After years of lobbying Parliament and the political parties in Albania, and with the help of many NGO's, trade unions, businesses, and the media, the Gender Equality Law was revised and finally introduced into the electoral code in 2008. The law states that 30 percent of the candidates on political parties' lists must be women and is being enforced through monetary sanctions. If political parties submit candidate lists that do not include 30 percent female candidates, the Central Electoral Committee will not accept their list and the party cannot run inthe election. This first quota law is a work in progress. Jeta believes that there are many problems with the current law that impede women's ability to achieve effective political power once they have positions in Parliament. The current law only specifies that one of the first three candidates on each list must be female. This allows the parties to put all but one woman at the bottom of the lists so that they can only achieve positions in Parliament that have little power. The women who are elected also tend to forget about women's issues once they have positions in Parliament because they become "party soldiers". Jeta has been leading the women's movement for equality in politics for more than 17 years. She believes that the new quota law will provide easier access for women to enter politics, but that in the long term, the quota system will not be necessary. Furthermore, Jeta believes that the political climate women created contributed greatly to their success in passing quota legislation in Parliament.

Currently Parliament is made up of 7.2 percent of women, a 1.5 percent increase from 2001. Jeta hopes that women's output in Parliament will one day match that of men's, and that there will be more women's issues present in the 2009 platforms of candidates because of the larger presence of women in Parliament.

5.11. Gender Quota System in Georgia

The situation of women in Georgia is much like that of the women in Albania just a few years ago. Georgia currently has no quota system and women represent 7.2 percent of Parliament. The number of women in Parliament has actually decreased in recent years, and the women's movement in Georgia has been working hard to convince Parliament to enact a quota law. For example, the Women's Coalition of Georgia recently gave a petition to Parliament with 32,000 signatures in support of amendments to Georgia's elections legislation that would introduce a quota law and guarantee women positions in Parliament. Their goal is to enact a temporary quota law that will increase women's representation in Parliament to 50 percent. Maia Kuprava, a WDN activist in Georgia, says that they are waiting for the spring session of Parliament to see if the introduction of a quota law will appear on the agenda. Although the Women's Coalition suggests 50 percent representation of women, the percentage could be decreased to 40 percent if the number is too high or unacceptable for Parliament.

Regardless of the percentage, she said that if a new quota law is introduced and passed, it willensure that one candidate out of every three candidates on a political party's list will be a woman.

Maia believes that the main obstacle of women entering politics today is men. According to her, "men dominate political parties and therefore control the rules." Women have tried to work with parties to pass quota laws, but have been unsuccessful. Maia said that the men in Georgia see the quota system as a joke and believe there are no serious obstacles facing women. She said the men use psychological pressure to hold women back and discourage them from getting involved in politics.

Despite the obstacles, Maia is hopeful that a quota law will be passed in the upcoming session of Parliament. She believes that the enactment of a quota system in Georgia will change the country's attitude towards women and promote women's education. She also believes that if women could acquire more funding, they could create more candidate schools, awareness raising programs, and political training programs, all of which would help women compete against their male candidates and even the playing field. Until then, Maia and other women activists like her will continue to fight and hope that they will succeed.

References

Araújo, Clara. 2003. "Quotas for Women in the Brazilian Legislative System." Paper presented at the International IDEA Workshop "The Implementation of Quotas: Latin American Experiences," Lima, Peru, February 23-24.

Baldez, Lisa. 2004. "Elected Bodies: The Gender Quota Law for Legislative Candidates in Mexico." *Legislative Studies Quarterly* 24, no. 2: 231-258.

Inter-Parliamentary Union. 1995. *Women in Parliaments: 1945-1995.* Geneva: Inter- Parliamentary Union.

Jones, Mark P. 1998. "Gender Quotas, Electoral Laws, and the Election of Women: Lessons from the Argentine Provinces." *Comparative Political Studies* 31, no. 1: 3-21. 13

Krook, Mona Lena. 2006a. "Gender Quotas, Norms, and Politics." *Politics & Gender* 2, no. 1: 110-118.

Phillips, Anne. 1995. *The Politics of Presence: The Political Representation of Gender, Ethnicity, and Race*. New York: Oxford University Press.

6

Comparative Analysis of Women's Reservation

The number of countries that have introduced some type of quota system is much larger than expected. Although highly controversial, electoral gender quotas are now being introduced at an amazing speed all over the world. The outcome of introducing quotas should be studied in quantitative and qualitative terms. Electoral statistics can tell the number of women elected. But, unfortunately, the official electoral statistics of many countries do not contain sufficient data on those nominated by sex, which must be provided through other channels such as through the political parties. The consequences of quotas should also be studied in qualitative terms, looking into the intended and unintended ramifications.

With some outstanding exceptions, research on quotas has, until now, primarily been limited to one country, or to the employment of quotas in different electoral systems. It is, however, relevant to widen the perspective, and to discuss how to conduct research that compares quota discourse and implementation processes and results under different electoral systems, different political cultures and different gender regimes. Existing one-country studies seem to come up with quite different conclusion about the ability of quota systems to empower women. Yet, those differences might derive from the chosen approach rather than from actual differences between countries. The introduction of quotas is increasingly influenced by recommendations from international organizations and by cross-country inspiration. However, the new international idea of quotas, or 'quota fever', as it is now called in Southeast Asia, confronts very different contexts. Today, electoral gender quotas are being introduced in countries where women have been almost entirely excluded from politics, as well as in countries with a long history of mobilization of women into the labour market and into political life—such as in the Scandinavian countries, where electoral quotas were not introduced until the 1980s, when women's parliamentary representation already exceeded 25 percent.

The introduction of effective quota systems represents a change in public equality policy, from 'equal opportunities' to 'equality of results'. Quota systems thus represent a break with the widespread gradualism in equality policies. Seen in this perspective, the history of the Scandinavian countries can no longer be considered a model for obtaining equal political representation around the globe.

6.1. Quota systems in Scandinavian Countries

For many years feminist organizations throughout the world have viewed the Scandinavian countries, Denmark, Finland, Norway and Sweden, as a model for women's equality. One key factor has been the very high representation that women have enjoyed in parliaments and local councils in these countries, especially since the 1970s.

Table 1: Percentage of Women in Scandinavian Parliaments in 2003

Country	Women in Parliament	Election Year
Sweden	45%	2002
Denmark	38%	2001
Finland	37%	1999
Norway	36%	2001
Iceland	35%	1999

This extraordinarily high level of representation, seen in a global perspective, has led to the question: how did you come that far? What can we learn from the Scandinavian experience? As Nordic researchers we have tried to answer these questions by pointing to structural changes in these countries, such as secularization, the strength of social-democratic parties and the development of an extended welfare state, women's entrance into the labour market in large numbers in the 1960s, the educational boom of the 1960s, and the electoral system. Strategic factors are also seen as important, especially the various strategies employed by women's organizations in the Nordic states in order to raise women's political representation.

The Scandinavian experience cannot be considered a model today, because it took 80 years to get that far. Today, the women of the world are not willing to wait that long. The introduction of electoral quotas is a symbol of their impatience, as well as an often efficient tool for increasing female representation. A very good example is South Africa, where the introduction of quotas by the African National Congress (ANC) resulted in female representation in this new democracy jumping to an international high of about 30 percent.

6.2. Different Quota Systems

Even if constitutional amendments and new electoral laws may seem more commanding, it is not at all evident that they are more efficient when it comes to implementation than party quotas. It all depends on the actual rules and the possible sanctions for non-compliance, and on the general opportunity structure of the country for quotas. A distinction must be made between quotas for:

(a) the pool of potential candidates;

(b) the actual nominees; and

(c) the elected.

There are examples of quota requirements on all three levels, but most quota systems relate to (b). Here, the crucial question relates to where, for instance, the required 40 percent of women are placed on the lists or in the districts with real chances of election. The partly unsuccessful 'women's short lists' in England provide an example of the employment of quotas on the first level, which broadens the pool from which the selection committee or the primary may chose. 'Reserved seats for women' is a different quota system, in which certain seats are set aside, as in Uganda, for instance, where certain regional seats are reserved for women.

The electoral quota for women may be constitutional (as in Nepal, the Philippines and Uganda), legislative (as in many parts of

Latin America and, for example, in Belgium, Bosnia–Herzegovina, Serbia and Sudan) or it may take the form of a political party quota. In some countries, numerous political parties apply some type of quotas, such as in Argentina, Bolivia, Ecuador, Germany, Italy, Norway and Sweden. But in many other countries only one or two parties have opted to use quotas. If the leading party in a country uses quotas, however, like the ANC in South Africa, this may have a substantial effect on the overall representation of women. Yet, most political parties around the world do not employ any kind of quota system at all.

Gender quotas may apply to the number of female candidates proposed by a party for election, or they may take the form of reserved seats in the legislature. In some countries, quotas apply to minorities based on regional, ethnic, linguistic or religious cleavages. Almost all political systems apply some kind of geographical quota to ensure a minimum representation for densely populated areas, islands and the like. That type of quota is usually not considered as controversial as gender quotas.

Quotas work differently under different electoral systems. Quotas are most easily introduced in proportional representation (PR) systems and other multi-list systems. Also several majority systems have introduced quoows. But even in a PR system, because of the few candidates elected, small parties and parties in small constituencies have difficulties implementing quotas without controversial central interference in the usual prerogatives of the local party organization to select their own candidates.

6.3. Gender-Neutral Quota Provisions

Most quotas aim to increase women's representation, since the problem to be addressed usually is the under-representation of women; this is particularly relevant since women usually constitute 50 percent of the population. An electoral gender quota regulation may, for example, require that at least 40 percent of the candidates on the electoral lists are women. A minimum requirement for women implies a maximum set for the representation of men. Since women are the underrepresented group in political institutions, most regulations seek to secure for women a greater minimum number of seats than before.

Some quota systems, though, are constructed as gender-neutral, which means that they aim to correct the under-representation of both women and men or at any rate establish a maximum for both sexes. In this case, the requirement may be that neither gender should occupy more than 60 percent and no less that 40 percent of the seats. A 50:50 quota is in its nature gender-neutral, and it also sets a maximum in terms of the representation of women, which a minimum requirement for women does not do.

The concept of a 'double quota' is used to refer to a quota system that not only requires a certain percentage of women on the electoral list, but also prevents women candidates from merely being placed at the bottom of the list with very little chance of being elected. Argentina and Belgium are examples of countries with legal double quota requirements.

6.4. Quota Controversies

Quotas are very controversial, yet several countries around the world, including such diverse ones as Argentina, Bosnia, France, South Africa, Sweden and Uganda, have recently introduced gender quotas in public elections. An electoral gender quota system sets up a quantitative prescription for the minimum representation of either sex, such as 40 percent. Sweden's 'every second a women' and 'parité' (France, Belgium) are other names for quota systems.

In political life, quotas have often engendered vehement debate. Research on quotas so far has tended to concentrate on these debates and on the actual decision-making process. These discursive controversies are also an essential part of the present research project, but, in addition, an emphasis is being placed on the too often neglected aspect of the troublesome implementation of quotas and on the consequences of introducing quotas. From studies of single countries, we know that a decision to introduce a requirement of a minimum of, for instance, 30 percent of each gender on the electoral lists does not automatically lead to women getting 30 percent of the seats. Thus, by comparing the use of quotas in many similar and different political systems, it is possible to illuminate whether and under what conditions quotas can be considered an equal policy measure that contributes to the stated goal: equal political citizenship of women. Introducing quotas is always highly controversial, yet the debates are often confused and only understandable if the hidden assumptions about women and women's position are scrutinized. This makes it possible to see why quotas for some are seen as discrimination and a violation of the principle of fairness, while others consider them to be compensation for the structural barriers that prevent fair competition. The idea of quotas is frequently in conflict with other notions like the prevailing discourse of fairness and competence, and the idea of individualism. However, quotas are seen as an efficient measure to attain 'real' equality, that is, equality of results. An unclear debate and lack of legitimacy of the claim often lead to problems at the stage of implementation. In an earlier survey of quotas among the political parties in the Nordic countries and women's organizations in the same parties, the Norwegian Labour Party declared that it took three elections to implement a quota system. Why? Because the party does not throw out a male incumbent member of parliament (MP) in order to include a women.

The results of previous single-country studies are quite diverse. They range from the partial failure of the attempt to introduce women's short lists in a majority electoral system like that of England, which nevertheless showed some positive results,through often 'minimalistic' compliance with the rules by the political parties, which has resulted in small and uneven gains in female representation in Latin America,to the somewhat negative consequences of reserved seats for women in Uganda as they become stigmatized.

Today, we see a worldwide increase in the political representation of women, but the regional differences are immense (the world average is 15 percent in 2003 according to the IPU). The international research community has taken a strong interest in the results of Nordic research, because, since the 1970s, female representation there has been extraordinary high by international standards. This has sometimes been attributed to the introduction of quotas:However, this view is not accurate, since quotas in the Nordic countries were introduced after women's representation had taken off in the 1970s, and not all Nordic political parties use quotas—those that do are mostly the parties in the centre and on the left. Furthermore, the few Danish parties with quotas abolished the system after just a few years. The Swedish principle of 'every second a women' is not even considered a quota system by the general public, even if it is in fact a radical one, demanding and, in many cases, leading to 50 percent of each sex.

We need more international comparative studies of quota systems and of women in politics in general.The many empirical single-country studies and examinations of women in politics carried out over the past two decadeshave paved the way for new, cross-national comparison research projects.

Research on gender and politics has tried to answer the two most frequently asked, yet rather complicated, questions: first, how did this increase in women's representation come about?And, second, what difference does having many women in politics make?The interaction between the elected women and women's organizations has been seen as important to the performance of female politicians and vice versa.One conclusion is especially relevant for the introduction of quotas. In almost all political systems, no matter what the electoral regime, it is the political parties, not the voters, which are the real gatekeepers in regard to elected offices. Consequently, party nomination practices should be kept in focus.A new trend is also the growing interest in theoretical questions within gender studies, including the study of gender and politics. The concept of citizenship has been central to many feminist research projects in recent years, focusing on welfare state development and on the historical connection between political, social and civic citizenship.The concept of citizenship guides our attention to comparisons between the political exclusion and inclusion of women and that of other groupings or categories. The new philosophical discussion of women as a contested category is also highly relevant for studies of gender and politics, and will be examined later.

6.5. Gender Quotas and Discourse Analysis

Gender quotas have been on the political agenda of many countries throughout the world from the late 1970s onwards. The insight that democracy is incompatible with the exclusion or under-representation of women from the decision-making bodies and processes has been gaining increasing recognition, and gender quotas have come to be seen as one possible instrument to remedy women's persistant political under-representation in elected and nominated democratic bodies. However, gender quotas as a political instrument, especially when introduced via the state, remain controversial for practical and normative reasons. Practical issues concern for example the feasability of quota policies and their efficiency under various electoral systems, at various stages of the electoral process, their intended and unintended effects, etc. From a normative point of view, quotas raise questions about the nature of representative democracy, namely about the normative relationship between the representants and the represented; about the relationship between gender equality and social justice; about the existence of "women's interests; etc.

As comparative studies show, gender quotas, when carefully designed, efficiently enhance women's presence in representative bodies. As the number of women elected increases, the chances for a qualitative improvement of representativeness—in terms of "women's interests" grow. Thus, gender quotas can be seen as a possible means to alter the power balance between the genders, both in material and symbolic terms. The precise nature of these changes will have to be assessed over time in those countries that have been applying gender quota policies.

In this section, we would like to take a step backwards and draw attention to the processes the preceed the adoption and implementation of gender quota policies: the discursive struggles around the meaning of gender quotas and their place within representative democracy. Far from being "mere rhetorics", discursive struggles over the meaning of words and over the categorisation of the social world are central to politics: "problems" and "interests" do not exist independently of the ways they are represented or framed through language, and this process of framing involves judgements and normatives choices. Having political power means, amongst other things, being able to impose a certain view of a given situation, setting authoritative definitions or even whole "worldviews", delimiting what counts as "political", what is considered "normal", "feasible", "reasonable" or "acceptable"—and what is no.

In this perspective, discourses are not "just" about talk, but about power and politics, and power struggles begin much earlier than in the decision-making or even the agenda-setting stage. Politics in a wider sense is concerns "all aspects of institutional organization, public action, social practices and habits, and cultural meanings insofar as they are potentially subject to collective evaluation and decisionmaking". This perspective on politics as discourse, inspired by discourse analysis and social constructionism, has the advantage of drawing attention to the fact that debates on gender quotas are of interest to political analysis even when they fail to generate concrete effects in terms of numbers (as it is in part the case with the French parity law), when they are just debated, but not adopted (as in the Swiss case), and even when they are not yet on the political agenda at all. Even then, quota debates reveal something about politics understood as "the locus where society defines itself" and as a "permanent attempt to invent the future by dissociating the old and the new". Gender relations have surely been one of the most contested sites of struggle since the 1970s, and quota debates give us an insight into the ways in which gender issues are politicised or silenced.

6.5.1. The French Parity Law

The French debate on gender quotas can be summarised in three phases. In the first phase, gender quotas were discussed inside the French Socialist Party in the early 1970s and applied for internal party functions. In the second phase, gender quotas were effectively introduced at the state level (25% list quota) after the election of President F. Mitterrand, but had to abolished shortly after following a decision of the Constitutional Counci. A "new" debate labelled gender "parity" debate emerged in the third phase, from the late 1980s on, when gender inequality in politics became a politicised issue known to the wider public in France and also at the international level. In the 1995 presidential campaign, the issue of parity was an important electoral theme. The legislative project for a parity law was launched by Prime Minister Lionel Jospin in 1997.

A constitutional amendment was accepted by the French Congress in 1999, the so-called parity law passed parliament in June 2000. The law has been in application since the municipal elections in March 2001. The parity law introduced a 50% list quota for all proportional elections (Senate, regional elections, European elections) and mixed-system elections (local elections in localities with more than 3500 inhabitants), and a 50% nationwide quota for candidates in uninominal elections (National Assembly). No gender quota applies at the very important level of the départements, nor in small municipalities.

At the municipal level, the parity law has proven to be efficient, due to constraining sanctions (invalidation of lists that do not respect the 50% gender quota): the proportion of women elected into municipal legislative bodies (+ 3500 inhabitants) increased significantly from 25% to 47%. At the cantonal elections 2001 and the senatorial elections 2001, the law had little effect: the proportion of women elected increased from 6,3% to 9,8% for the cantonal assemblies and from 6% to 11% for the Senate. Finally, at the national elections 2002, the law had little effect despite the fact that financial sanctions were applied to those parties that did not respect the nation-wide 50% quota for their candidates: women's proportion grew slightly from 10,9% to 12,3%.

6.5.2. The Swiss Quota Initiatives

A series of popular and parliamentary initiatives aimed at introducing some form of gender quotas for legislative elections were launched in Switzerland during the 1990s. At the local and cantonal level, all of them remained fruitless (rejection either by the parliament of by the people). At the federal level, several attempts failed as well, but one popular initiative reached the state of a popular vote in spring 2000. The initiative was launched in 1993, officially validated in 1995, debated and rejected by the federal parliament in 1998-1999 and finally rejected by the Swiss people in March 2000.

The initiative claimed wide-reaching and constraining result quotas for all federal authorities (unlimited in time). At the legislative level, it suggested namely a 50% quota for the National Counciland a 50% quota for the Council of states. At the executive level, a 40% quota (3 members out of 7) for the Federal Council was claimed. At the judicial level, the initiative aimed at a 40% quota for the Federal Tribunal. Moreover, the initiative proposed regulations for a "balanced representation" of women in the federal administration, public enterprises under control of the federal state and at the universities.

The parliament rejected the popular initiative, but debated over a counter-project (parliamentary initiative) which suggested the introduction of a 30% list quota for the three following elections to the Lower House. This counter-project was finally rejected by the parliament.

At the federal level, women currently represent 23,5% at the Lower House of parliament (National Council)) and 19,5% at the Upper House (Council of states). In the Executive, two of the seven members of the Swiss Government are women. At the cantonal level, women held globally 23% of the seats in the cantonal parliaments and 15% of the seats in the cantonal governments in 1997. At the local level, women represented 28% of the members of the communal parliaments and 22% of the communal governments in localities with more than 10'000 inhabitants.

6.6. Gender Quota and Political Representation

In recent years, questions of representativeness in terms of socio-cultural diversity have become increasingly salient. Until the 1970s, the notorious under-representation of women, ethnic and social minorities (gays, disabled people, etc.) was hardly thematised and was not considered a "problem", neither in the political arena nor in the classical literature on representation which does not give much attention to the socio-cultural representatitiveness of the elected. Under the pressure of multiculturalists and feminists, "diversity" has become an issue, and the "biased" composition of elected bodies—in terms of sex, ethnicity, sexual orientation, age etc.—is not simply accepted as normal or unproblematic any more.

Classical authors like for instance Pitkin rejected the idea of a "mirror representation" with the argument that what matters for representativeness is the result of the activity of representation, not the characteristics of the representants. Contemporary theorists take up this critique and provide more sophisticated arguments in favour of some form of socio-cultural representativeness. The Anglo-saxon literature often uses the term "group representation" when elaborating on this question. This term usually refers to all kinds of minority groups, women being considered a minority in terms of power. Women's under-representation has also been theorised from a different point of view, and deconnected from debates on ethnic or other minorities, in the recent French literature on gender parity.

The representativeness of the political system with regard to gender has been debated in terms of differentialism and egalitarianism, essentialism and materialism, universalism. The terminology used usually avoids the term "group representation", alien to the abstract republican logic of representation, but the idea underlying the parity debate is in some respects similar to that of group representation. Indeed, the theoretical problem explicitly theorised in the Anglo-saxon literature, and more implicit in the French literature, is the link between social positioning, experiences and action, in other words: the conviction that the representativeness of our democratic institutions would be enhanced if the social characteristics of its members would be taken into account explicitly.

The Swiss model of political representation is based on territorial and linguistic pluralism.The link between territorial and linguistic allegencies and representation is explicitly recognised and institutionalised for territorial and linguistic minorities, namely in the form of linguistic quotas at all levels of the political system (including the federal government), cantonal quotas (for the Upper House of parliament, the federal government, commissions, civil servants, etc.), and party quotas (for the federal government, commissions, high-ranking civil servants, etc.).

The Swiss political system is designed to avoid conflicts that may arise out of discrimination of the groups that "count", i.e. that are powerful and politicised enough to break up the Swiss consensus : small cantons, linguistic minorities, interest groups. It is also designed to diffuse power and to prevent attempts towards centralisation. The main institutional instruments for "conflict dilution" and consensus building are: direct democracy, decision-making procedures in terms of Konkordanz, federalism and subsidiarity, and quota regulations. Gender is a contested criterion of representativeness. Since 1993, it has become a criterion that is explicitly invoked for the composition of the federal government. An implicit gender quota (two seats out of seven) seems to be establishing.

In France, the idea of group representation is absent from the republican universalist model of representation institutionalised inherited from the Revolution. This model of representation was constructed historically as a powerful rejection of the monarchy and of a sophisticated regime of privileges and the French political system therefore conceives of the citizen as an "abstract member of the nation, considered as such, independently from any social or economic determinism". The French citizen's social, cultural and economic bonds are deemed "irrelevant", in the sense that they do not count in the normative matrix of citizenship. In the words of the way ex-Minister of Justice Robert Badinter, one of the most salient opponents of the parity law: "We are all citizens, nothing but citizens. These are the foundations of the Republic.

The Republic has ne ver been a mosaic of communities nor a juxtaposition of different components. It does not recognise, and has never recognised, anything else than individuals, human beings and citizens, without any form of discrimination". The French political system, contrary to the Swiss, is designed to centralise and concentrate power. It allows for acertain distance between centre and periphery, between the state and society, between political elites and economic and social elites. As we will see, the conceptual link between social positioning, experiences and interests, and action, remained implicit in the parity debate. In the Swiss debate it was more explicitly debated, as it always is when it comes to electoral issues.

6.6.1. The Parity Debate in France

The parliamentary debates on gender parity in France in the years 1998-2000 were passionate, controversial and mobilised the attention of the wider public, the media and the French "intellectuals". The parliamentary debates took place in two phases: the first debate led to a constitutional amendment, the second phase to the adoption of a parity law. A wide range of arguments for and against gender parity was debated in the course of these parliamentary debates. They can be clustered around two main discourses, or "story-lines".

The story-line of the advocates of a parity regulation was set at the very beginning of the parliamentary debates in December 1998: Justice Minister Elisabeth Guigou opened the debate in the National Assembly by a speech which summarised the main arguments in favour of the parity principle. In this story-line, the parity principle is framed as an "accomplishment" of the universalist revolutionary ideal of equality.

In Guigou's words, the goal of the parity article is "not to destroy the achievements of the French Revolution", on the contrary "we seek to accomplish them!". In this perspective, the gender parity principle is seen—somewhat anachronistically- as the realisation of a 200- year old ideal and as the logical follow-up of the abolishment of slavery in 1848. For Guigou and many others proparitarians, the adoption of a parity principle is justified by the fact that women are "one half of mankind", and not a minority, a category or a "group". They make a distinction between a "good" universalism that will realise gender parity, and a "bad" universalism which recognises only "individuals" (universalisme d'exclusion) and which, they believe, comes down to a patriarcal and exclusive republicanism. In Guigou's words: "By defending universalism, one erases history and reality. Women have been excluded from citizenship because they were women [..] Neutrality has supported male domination...".

The adoption ofa gender parity principle would, then, be a "modernisation of democratic life", a "decision of considerable symbolic importance" after which "the sovereign Nation will no longer be an abstract entity and as such the foundation of the legal order, but an embodied representation of men and women living in their century". Thanks to the parity principle, sovereignty will "be embodied by both genders". As a deputee puts it, France has to choose between "an unfinished democracy and a restored democracy". Beyond the modernisation of French politics, the gender parity principle is seen by some deputees as a motor for modernisation more generally. Women's absence from politics, they claim, has put a brake on the evolution of the French society.

The competing "story-line" of the opponents of the gender parity principle, on the contrary, frames gender parity as a fundamental, and unacceptable, "violation of the republican rule stating that all citizens are equal (..). without any distinction other than their virtues and talents". They defend an abstract conception of representation according to which the elected represent the nation as such, not any particular group. They believe that the parity principle would "give women the imperative mandate to represent women's interests, while men would only be able to speak in men's name" which, in their eyes, is a " disfiguration of the parliamentary function", and a violation of the principle that the Republic is indivisible.

For them, unlike for the advocates of the parity principle, women are a group, and the parity principle is likely to be the first step on the famous "slippery slope", as expressed by a deputee: "After gender quotas, other quotas would have to be adopted, for civil servants, employees of the private sector and the liberal professions; for the poor, the Muslims, the people living in the banlieues". In other words, France will take the road of a dangerous "americanisation", i.e. "communitarisation". In this discourse, gender parity is seen as a step back towards an undue "favouritism based on physical difference" that "brings us back to very ancient times and that is not at all informed by the republican tradition".

6.7. The Quota Debate in Switzerland

Unlike the French parity debate, the Swiss gender quota debate of 1998-2000 was a rather unpassionate, short and shallow one. The media paid little attention to the issue and the parliamentary debate was much shorter than the French debate. A much more passionate discussion on women's place in politics had taken place in 1993, when the quota initiative was launched.

As in the French case, the various arguments debated about in Switzerland can be summarised in two broad competing discourses. The first "story-line" was to say that gender quotas would be nothing but an extension of the already existing wide-ranging quota regulations. The advocates of gender quotas rightly pointed to the fact that quotas are a central element of the Swiss political system, at all levels and for all important functions: "Switzerland is a quota country" and gender quotas would simply be a "refinement of the proportional system". They refer namely to the linguistic quotas which are designed to protect Switzerland's linguistic pluralism and which are very salient namely for the composition of the federal government, of parliamentary and extra-parliamentary commissions, for high-ranking civil servants and for the composition of electoral lists in bi- or multilingual cantons. A sort of cantonal "quota" is in force at the federal level where each canton has two seats in the Council of states, independently of its size. Finally, party quotas are important for some important political bodies, namely for the federal (stable coalition) government for which an informal quota regulation has been applied since 1959. Party quotas also apply to high-ranking civil servants and to the judges at the Federal Tribunal. Gender quotas do not exist officially in the Swiss political system. However, since 1993, a sort of informal women quota seems to be respected for the federal government (two seats out of seven).

For the advocates of gender quotas, the existing pluralist logic of representation should simply have been extended to women who, according to them, can be considered a minority because of their lack of power in society. So, the advocates of the quota initiatives pleaded for an explicit gendering of the existing pluralist model of representation.

The opponents of gender quotas firmly rejected this "story-line". In fact, they did simply not really take into account this "extension" argument and never engaged with this argument. Only the federal government, in a report that was elaborated in the pre-parliamentary phase and submitted to the parliament as a consultative document, mentioned this argument explicitly. According to the Federal Council the existing formal quotas are ma inly designed to protect the cantons. These quotas have "have historical origins rooted in federalism" and "they guarantee the equilibrium of the federal state". Consequently, the Federal Council considers that "their justification is not comparable to the one of the quota initiative". The existing informal (linguistic, political, regional) quotas are simply ruled out with the argument that they have "no juridical validity" since they are not mentioned in the Constitution. Given the history of Switzerland as a federal state constantly threatened by a break-up of the fragile federal consensus, women and other non-territorialised minorities like non-territorialised linguistic minorities, or the Jenisch) have traditionally not been considered important as a political force. Although the issue of women's under-representation has become more widely debated during from the 1990s onwards, the principle of territoriality remains strong enough in Switzerland to make the opponents accuse gender quotas to be "arbitrary", "perverse", "rigid and absurd", a "heresy", a way of creating a "gap between men and women" and even a "step backward to pre-democratic times". Some opponents referred to the well-know argument of the "slippery slope" with an under-tone of indignation, and expressed the fear of an endless fragmentation of the political system. As one deputee puts it:

"After gender quotas, we will have to introduce quotas for elderly people, young people, singles, disabled people or any other group of citizens that experience a particular situation in their everyday life", and this will "lead to a confrontation of particular interests". Another deputee finds the gender quotas as "arbitrary" as the idea of quotas for age groups.

To sum up, the Swiss debate on gender quotas opposed a minority of women and men who believed that time had come to modify the territorial logic of representation in Switzerland by including the non-territorial gender criterion. The majority, however, opposed this idea by sticking to the principal of territoriality and rejecting gender quotas as being totally "out of place".

6.8. Conceptions of Gender Differences

The precise nature of the concept of gender has given raise to many theoretical developments within feminism. Early debates focused on the establishment of a clear sex/gender distinction that defines sex as a matter of biology and gender as a matter of socio-cultural construction. The aim of this conceptual distinction was to overcome the traditional determinist view of women's "nature" from which women's social role as mothers and carers was supposed to derive. In recent feminist accounts, the concepts of sex as a biological "given" that would exist prior to cultural determinations is increasingly questioned. Sex is more and more being theorised as a social construction as well, and the causal connection between sex and gender thereby tends to erode, as does the binary conception of humanity as being divided into men and women on the basis of biological categories. The emphasis is shifting more and more to the power relations underlying social and political definitions of gender difference and gender inequalities, and the links established between them.

Conflicting conceptions of gender differences and inequalities were central in the French and Swiss debates on gender quotas. We will analyse these conceptions using a distinction between gender as a "natural" category, a social category and a political category. The terms "natural" and social category draw on the classical sex/gender distinction. We use the term gender exclusively, also when referring to discourses about "natural" differences, to emphasise the fact that "natural" differences are naturalised through discourse. We add another distinction between gender as a natural and social category on one hand, and as a political category institutionalised by the state on the other hand. Following Badie/Birnbaum, we can define the state as a political actor which is characterised by some degree of autonomy and differentiation with regard to society. Thus, the state tends to function according to its own "logic" which needs not be the same as the logic of the social world, for instance in terms of inclusion/exclusion of certain groups, of norms, etc. By extension, we assume that there may be a gap between the discursive categories that map the social world and the categories which institutionalise certain power relationships. Although the mechanisms of political representation are supposed to link the social world and the sphere of the state, this link can be more or less stringent. Switzerland is a typical "weak" state where state and society are very interdependent and little differentiated.

Political representation is based on a pluralist conception of citizenship in which linguistic andcantonal identities—important categories of the social world and within the state—are extremely salient. France, on the contrary, is a typical strong and centralised state based on a republican universalist model of citizenship. Political representation is conceptualised as an abstract principle: normatively speaking, representation in France is about "abstract" citizens without "particular" identities representing an abstract idea of the "Nation". The quota debates in Switzerland and France were obviously about the institutionalisation of gender as a political category for representation. But as we will see below, the conceptual links between gender as a political, social and biological category differed in these two countries.

In the French parity debate, gender as a conceptual category was constructed in various complex ways. Firstly, it was presented as a biological category, both by the advocates and the opponents of the parit y principle. The opponents accused the constitutional gender parity article to "make possible a form of favouritism based on physical difference". The advocates, on the other hand, claimed the legitimacy of the parity article on the basis that "sexual difference is the founding difference, all other differences are contingent or transitory". As "there are 50% men and 50% women on earth, such a categorisation [of the citizens in terms of sexual difference] can be made".

But purely biological formulation of sexual difference were the exception in the parliamentary debates. More common was an abstract formulation that did not say clearly whether the supposed difference between women and men is to be understood in biological and/or sociological terms. Many proponents of the parity principle based their arguments on the "essential (sexual) mixity of humankind". In the words of a deputee: "Women constitute half of humankind, they are indissociable form the notion of human being. They are not a category, by definition they are part of all categories". Another deputee expressed the same idea a bit differently, without making it clearer whether he was referring to biological and/or sociological differences: "The collectivity of the nation is composed of men and women who are not identical human beings, but who work together and complementarily to assure the perennity of the human species". The secretary of state in charge of women's affairs who intervened at the National Assembly to defend the parity article pointed out that "women are as talented and intelligent as men, but their under-representation does not allow for the expression of different ideas or values".

It is noteworthy that this argument of the "inherent mixity of humankind", which has at least an essentialist under-tone, was also used by the opponents of the parity article. A few deputees conferred an ontological status to this "mixity" argument. For one of them "the institutionalisation of sexual differences [by the parity article] means rejecting a common dimension of republicanism, a common dimension of humanity".

A purely and clearly sociological understanding of gender or gender difference was, astonishingly, absent from the parity debate. Many deputees referred again and again to statistical figures of women's under-representation and discrimination in politics and other areas of society, and to historical moments of exclusion. But when it came to justifying or rejecting the parity article, these figures were never invoked. They were used only to legitimise the global idea that gender parity in politics was an important political issue. The concrete justifications around the parity article itself, however, remained at a quite abstract level where the boundaries between sociological and biological categories were blurred. This may have to do with the fact that in France, the (real and perceived) distance between the state and society is relatively big, compared with Switzerland. The French state is has more autonomy with regard to society than weak and states such as Switzerland, where political action tends to be very reactive: the Swiss state has neither the power nor the means to impose political change against the will of the people, nor to prevent a social change from penetrating the state at least to some degree. The French state, on the contrary, is more autonomous in his action which can be initiated rapidly and efficiently.

The inherent mixity of humankind was the main argument in favour of the parity article, i.e. of an explicit institutionalisation of gender as a political criterion for representation, whereas the fear of an "americanisation" of French politics was an important argument against. In France, the legitimacy of the state to intervene in electoral politics via amodification of the constitution and of the electoral laws was never fundamentally put into question, and political action "from above" was implicitly accepted. The idea that the state is authorised to intervene actively in order to orient societal change and to push towards an evolution of the mentalities, was not at all contested, rather the opposite: several deputees insisted on the active role of the state and on the importance of political will ("The legislator sometimes needs to stimulate democracy"). In their eyes, the parity principle was to be understood as "an instrument, a motor, not only in the field of politics, but also in social and professional fields".

In the Swiss parliamentary debates, gender was clearly and consistently defined in socioeconomic terms: being a woman was defined as having a "lower probability of being elected", having "fewer resources", less "prestige", "less power, influence, money", less "access to networks", having more difficulties (than men) acquiring "professional qualifications" and "combining parenting and a career", doing "more house-work" and being "less present in the media", being excluded politically, culturally and economically. Only very rarely is gender considered in biological terms, for instance by a deputee who was obviously irritated about the fact that "physical characteristics are now becoming relevant" for political representation.

Gender was rejected as a political category by a majority of deputees, gender as a nonterritorial criterion being framed as wholly "arbitrary" and illegitimate to ground political categorisations. In the words of one deputee, "defining different categories of citizens (..) is a manipulation of democracy which lays the ground other exclusions or segregations". The introduction of gender quotas was also considered to be a step into the direction of a wholly illegitimate "state interventionism". This argument is to be put in the context of the Swiss tradition of decentralisation and subsidiarity which engendered a widely shared sense of suspicion against decision-making "from above". The opposition against gender quotas can therefore be understood not only as a resistance against the empowering of women, but also as a resistance against the central state.The advocates of the gender quota initiatives argued that gender should become a political category precisely because of the social causes of women's under-representation. In other words, both the opponents and the proponents of gender quotas agreed on the fact that gender is to be understood as a social positioning, not as a biological fact. However, there were disagreements on the exact evaluation of the fact that one gender is socially disadvantaged.

.For some deputees, the political under-representation of women simply wasn't a "problem" since "a maximum of individuals from all social backgrounds can express their claims"within the political system. For others, women's under-representation is a problem, but one that is not due to the political system or to social barriers, but to the women themselves who, supposedly, do not want to be candidates, or who resign too easily.

It is noteworthy that the political system was not considered as having some kind of autonomous effect that would disadvantage women candidates (in terms of networks, recruitment strategies, political careers). Even the advocates of gender quotas who suggested to make gender become an explicit political category for representation considered gender only as a social reality. Implicitly, most deputees did not want to make a difference between the social world and the political system. This is consistent with the overall logic of the Swiss political system which is characterised by a low degree of autonomy and differentiation with regard to society. However, the strong opposition against gender quotas in Switzerland shows that quota regulations problematise the sensitive question of the political-institutional use of a given categorisation. As the French case shows, social change can very well be initiated from above. Introducing a political category top-down is certainly harder in a decentralised state than in a centralised one, but the underlying issue remains nevertheless the same: it has to do with power and with the willingness of the political actors to consider gender inequalities worth of action and engagement.

6.9. Gender and Power Relations

Since Simone de Beauvoir's Second Sex, feminists have theorised gender relations in terms of social power. The explanations of gender inequalities in society range from structural (economic, symbolic, etc.) determinism(s) to cultural stereotyping and socio-political categorisations of the social world. There is a overarching consensus among feminist scholars that gender is predominantly about power, and not about "differences", diversity or nature. However, in the political debates, this insight—supported by a large and expanding literature—is not easily accepted. As the quota debates in France and Switzerland illustrate, the issue of the distribution of political power was eluded by most opponents of gender quotas, and was openly addressed only by a few advocates.

Gender quotas can certainly be opposed for a variety of "good" reasons, be they practical reasons of feasability or implementation or normative ones. For the purpose of this analysis, we will leave these debates aside and focus on another point: the power of the social norm. Feminist scholars have shown that men—as a category—are implicitly considered to be "the norm" in political discourse as well as in political theory. Women as a category tend to be given the implicit status of a "deviant" group whose claims are considered "suspicious". Some elements of the French and Swiss gender quota debates illustrate the ways in which the norm is discursively established and maintained, most of the time implicitly.

The issue of the power relations underlying the parity debate have not been very explicitly thematised in the French parliamentary debates. A few advocates of the parity principle nevertheless pointed directly to some of these issues. One deputee thematised the question of the distribution of power within parliament. For her, the parity project was a "challenge for the male politicians" since "one seat more for a woman means one seat less for a man". Such a choice, as she says, "is never easy". Another deputee denounced a tendency towards the "confiscation of power" by the political elites. Another deputee reminded that "parity is a struggle" and that "in France, changes in institutions or political rights have always been through struggles". " Other deputees insisted on the fact that women's under-representation is due not only to "mentalities" or social disparities, but also to obstacles within the political sphere, for instance: patterns of candidate recruitment of political careers, the generalorganisation of political life that imposes a too big workload on women or the parties' lack of political will to recruit women. Another woman deputee reminded the assembly that woman had had to take up a "fierce political struggle" to get accepted as deputees.

A Communist deputee problematised issues of social power in a broader perspective. For him, the "division of labour imposed by modern liberalism subjects women to wide-ranging exclusion, exploitation and feelings of guilt". For him, the struggle in favour of gender parity is part of a wider effort for a different world, namely for a different division of labour, the defence of the service public, the struggle against wage discrimination etc.These few interventions aiming to thematise issues of social power and gender relations were not discussed by the other deputees. Most advocates of the parity principle explained their position with reference to issues such as the modernisation of political life—an omnipresent theme throughout the debate on the constitutional article—and the need to increase the legitimacy of politics in the eyes of the citizens.

Some opponents of the parity principle, however, engaged with power issues indirectly, mainly by trying to disqualify the parity project. One deputee made a lapsus which was a revealing example of the power issues at stake. According to this deputee, " the project [for a constitutional parity article] will not guarantee women's promotion, it will even be counterproductive and insulting to women. It is aimed only at generating an immediate media effect, but will not generate any positive result for men... for women, I wanted to say".

Other deputees invoked the supposed undesirable effects of the parity principle as well: some deputees simply spoke of "negative" or even “disastrous consequences”, others identified more threatening dangers. Quoting the French philosopher Alain Renaut, one deputee did not even hesitate to compare the gender parity principle and the Nuremberg laws (!):”Any parity principle and any quota policy bring us back to a perspective which is closer to the Nuremberg laws than to the idea of democracy”. Others compared the French parity article with American affirmative action programmes which, according to one deputee, have been “an instrument of exclusion and racism” in that they “generated an anti-women and anti-Black racism has it had never existed before in the USA... Affirmative action is an extraordinarily harmful, toxic and counterproductive. It is against the interests of women and other minoritiesit is meant to defend”. Still other saw in the gender parity principle nothing less than a “regression of women’s cause”, a “discreditation of women”, a “regression of the Republic” and a “violation of the Constitution”.

A very negative image of gender quotas prevailed also among other opponents of the parity principle. Some of them were convinced that “women do not need quotas, they will succeed by natural means”. In the eyes of this deputee, women who would have been elected thanks to quotas would have no value at all, since they “would have been taken from a special contingent of intellectually under-developed persons” (!). If quotas were introduced, “women would not any more be required to prove their ability, their qualities, their talent”, which is obviously not desirable, since women’s presence in political life “ has to be a natural, happy, joyful and kind-hearted one, and not a presence experienced as constraining and resulting from authoritarian mechanisms”.

In the Swiss parliamentary debates, the issue of the distribution of social power among the genders was not very salient, although is was explicitly thematised by some advocates of the gender quota initiatives. As one deputee put it, gender quotas “are a matter of justice meant to distribute resources and power positions equally among women and men”. For others deputees, gender quotas are about “normality and power monopolies”, about “power and loss of power”. For them, the strong resistance against gender quotas reveal “men’s very big and old fear to loose power. (..) They consider their privileges as something totally normal and unquestionable, even as divine”(gottgegeben). Obviously, “no-one gives up power without resisting". Some advocates of gender quotas explicitly thematised the social "construction" of gender inequalities—"women's discrimination in society and politics is wanted and created by society"—and insist on the fact that gender relations can be altered. They emphasise the role of political will as a motor for social and political change. One deputee defended gender quotas by pointing to the fact that until recently, men had the privilege of a "100% quota" and that even today, most political functions have a clear "male profile". The opponents of gender quotas did not engage with this type of critique directly. But indirectly, they minimised or denied that gender relations are indeed power relations and that these power relations influence women's representation. They went to great lengths to disqualify gender quotas as a political instrument. Many deputees insisted on the fact that competencies, not gender, should be the criterion for the election of a candidate. According to them, women elected thanks to gender quotas would be "devalued as quota women" or as "pure quota material" (sic)"; women would be "victimised", mobilised as pure "alibi candidates", and if they were still elected, their election would be "artificial".

Implicitly, the tenants of these arguments suggest that the men elected are so on the basis of their competencies alone and that getting elected has nothing to do with social prestige, particular identities, networks, and social norms. There is some irony to this argument in a country where linguistic quotas, cantonal quotas and interest group affiliations are very explicitly and openly debated at each election of the federal government, at each nomination of a highranking civil servant, at the composition of each important parliamentary or extraparliamentary commission. And there is also a reactionary undertone, in the sense of Hirschman, to the argument that a measure intended to favour women would end up discriminating against them. As Hirschman shows, turning a potential improvement for a social group into a supposed disadvantage is a common feature of reactionary discourse. Some deputees rejected quotas because a 50% women quota would "make it impossible for women to be over-represented". It is noteworthy to know that this problem would currently arise with regard to two cantons (out of 23) that are represented by two women in the Council of states... But not only women would be the "victims" of gender quotas, men would too:. For some deputees, "quotas discriminate men", they even constitute a "consequent exclusion of men".

Finally, in the eyes of the opponents, gender quotas are an illegitimately restriction of the voter's freedom and a threat to the "transparency" of the electoral process". As for the previous argument, it is interesting to see that such restrictions are deemed unacceptable only for gender quotas. The overall lack of transparency of the highly complex Swiss electoral system does not seem to trouble the opponents of gender quotas. Indeed, in Switzerland, each canton has its own electoral law (proportional in some cantons, majoritarian in some small cantons) for the election of the National Council, and list combinations are allowed in most cantons with a proportional system. The result is a system in which the exact relationship between voices and seats is extremely intransparent to the voter. To sum up, we can see that both in the French and the Swiss debate, issues of power and gender relations were openly addressed by some deputees, usually by the advocated of gender quotas who tried to gain legitimacy for their cause by pointing to the issue of power. The counter-strategy of the opponents—some, not all—was to try to disqualify the claim for quotas by treating them as out of place, exaggerated, dangerous or counter-productive.

Gender quotas are not "only" about women, but—amongst other things—about the relationship between the citizens and the state, conceptions of representative democracy, identities, and about the power to define the social world. Discursive struggles over gender quotas are instructive in that they reveal competing conceptions of politics, democracy and the public sphere. The aim of this analysis was to highlight three issues that were at stake in the French and Swiss quota debates in the late 1990s.

The first issues concerns the relationship between discourses on gender quotas and institutionalised conceptions of representation and citizenship. In France, the advocates of the parity principle campaigned in favour of a conceptual gendering of republicanism, whereas the opponents aimed at maintaining the status quo, i.e. an abstract universalism. In Switzerland, the existing pluralist model of citizenship centered on territorial and linguistic identities and interests was contested by the advocates of gender quotas who tried to "stretch" this pluralism by introducing a non-territorial formal criterion of representation. In both cases, some opponents tried to frame these attempts towards a gendering of the existing model as arbitrary and illegitimate. In Switzerland, the territorial logic was strong enough to prevent a gendered redefinition of the pluralist model.

Putting gender quotas discourses into a broader perspective informed by comparative political and historical sociology moves the focus from philosophical arguments to discursive strategies, from conceptual coherence to efficiency The empirical and comparative perspective reveals the discursive strategies mobilised by the political actors in their situationspecific struggles for power and influence. This focus is complementary to philosophical analyses and case studies.

The second point illustrated by this analysis is that gender is a contested concept not only in political theory, but also among political actors. In France, both the advocates and the opponents of gender parity mostly referred to gender differences and inequalities in a rather abstract way that did not clearly separate gender as a sociological reality from gender as a biological reality. The legitimacy of state action as such was not fundamentally contested, not even by the opponents of the parity principle. What was contested was the idea of a dual (gendered) conception of universalism as suggested by the advocates of the parity principle. In Switzerland, gender was consistently framed as a sociological reality; biological understandings of this concept were almost absent from these debates. Unlike in France, the legitimacy of state action from above was highly contested, notwithstanding the fact that gender quotas were claimed by a popular initiative. What was also rejected by the opponents of gender quotas was the idea that Swiss pluralism could be gendered. These varying understandings of gender reflect the differences between two very dissimilar political systems. The abstract way framing of gender issues in the French party debate reflects both the republican tradition and the acceptance of a strong and directive state. The sociological understanding of gender and the hostility towards state action in Switzerland reflect the strong interpenetration of the state and society, as well as the federalist tradition.

The Swiss-French comparison highlights the context-boundedness of struggles over categories, and points to the need for more sophisticated analysesif we aim to understandthe full dynamics of these struggles. The few hints pointed to in this chapter should perhaps simply make us aware of that gender quota debates are not only about the pros and cons of quotas, but also about the meaning of gender.

The third point we tried to bring to the fore in this analysis is the issue of gender relations as power relations. The feminist literature provides a vast body of theoretical and empirical analyses that show support the view that gender relations are indeed power relations. In the gender quotas debates in the French and Swiss parliament, issues of power and gender were explicitly articulated only by a few deputees, mostly advocates of gender quotas. Most of the time, the issue remained implicit, but nevertheless omnipresent. As a few quotations have illustrated, some opponents accused gender quotas of being nothing less than a perverse, arbitrary, heretic, authoritarian, "racist" and discriminatory instrument meant to destroy democracy or, alternatively, a counter-productive measure that will increase women's exclusion. Such arguments are revealing of a social norm in favour of the more powerful gender: measures which are a considered wholly unproblematic when applied to a majority of men (for example candidate selection on the basis of criteria other than "competency") or to groups other than women (linguistic quotas for instance) are suddenly doomed highly problematic when used in favour of women; features of the political system which have been accepted until now (intransparency, complexity) become unacceptable when it comes to gender quotas.

This discourse-analytical perspective on the social norm reminds us that political discourses are about power, not only (but also) about conceptual coherence. The normative coherence of an argument as such does not yet say much about the impact this argument is going to have in a given context and situation, nor about the meaning that will be given to a concept in a given context. The term "quota" for instance has a wholly different connotation in France—where it is linked to the "ghost of americanisation"—and in Switzerland where it is linked to linguistic minorities. If we aim to understand quota debates, we therefore need to be attentive to the dynamics of power and to discursive strategies used to disqualify competing arguments, "categorising out" issues, denying or minimising issues, denigrate political opponents, etc.

References

Bacchi, C. L. *Women, Policy and Politics. The Construction of Policy Problems*. London: Sage. 1999.

Badie, B. and Birnbaum P. *La logique de l'Etat*. Paris. Hachette. 1982

Bataille, P. and Gaspard, F. *Comment les femmes changent la politique et pourquoi les hommes résistent*. Paris : La Découverte. 1999.

Karam, A. *Women in Parliament. Beyond Numbers*. Stockholm. International institute for democracy and electoral assistance IDEA. 1998.

Knapp, A. and Wrigh, V. *The Government and Politics of France*. London/ New York: Routledge, 4th ed . 2001.

Opello, Katherine A. R. 2006. *Gender Quotas, Parity Reform, and Political Parties in France*. Lanham: Lexington.

Phillips, A. "Democracy and representation: Or, why should it matter who our representatives are?", in Phillips, A. (ed), *Feminism and Politics*, Oxford: Oxford University Press, pp. 224-240. 1998

Pitkin, H. *The Concept of Representation*. Berkeley: University of California Press. 1967.

Squires, J. *Gender in political theory*. Cambridge: Polity Press.1999.

7

Marginalisation of Women in Politics

India has adopted and enacted the Constitution in 1950 guaranteeing to its citizens' Justice, Liberty, Equality of Status and of Opportunity and Fraternity assuring dignity of the individual and unity and integrity of the Nation. In addition, the State is under obligation, as per the Directive Principles of State Policy to provide enabling conditions and secure minimum standards to its citizens, in furtherance of the fundamental rights. And, in accordance with its principles, the Government has undertaken many initiatives – legislative and executive policies, schemes and programs towards this.

India is also a signatory to several International Treaties and Conventions. One of the important Conventions impacting women is The International Convention for the Elimination of All Forms of Discrimination against Women (CEDAW), which has been ratified by a majority of UN member states. India has ratified the treaty in the year 1993.

The United Nations initiatives, which include the three UN Decade for Women, Conferences held at Mexico (1975), Nairobi (1985) and Beijing (1995); and the CEDAW, have had a substantive impact on the status of women in India. 'Towards Equality', the first national report outlining the status of women followed Mexico conference. Following the Nairobi conference, Government of India announced 'The Perspective Plan for Women' and it outlined policy directions and new administrative structures for the development of women. At Beijing, the government of India announced 33 per cent reservation for women in local governing bodies. Another significant change worth mentioning is the shift in focus of the United Nations Initiatives and the International Women's movement in the last three decades. It has moved from a needs assessment through country wide status reports in the 1970s, to economic development for women in the 1980s, and finally to empowerment – socioeconomic and political, of women in the 1990s.

The question of reservation for women had surfaced even before Independence because women from the elite classes of that period – who wanted to play some role in public life, realised the hurdles in their way. This view was again reflected during the review of the Committee on the Status of Women in India, (CSWI) in 1974. The Committee observed that "the rights guaranteed by the Constitution have helped to build an illusion of equality and power which is frequently used as an argument to resist protective and accelerating measures to enable women to achieve their just and equal position in society". Social scientists also who undertook studies on the Committee's request came back with a uniform finding that while women's participation as voters had been increasing at a faster rate than men's, their representation as candidates – successful or unsuccessful –registered in fact an opposite trend.

The marginalising trend has continued till date. In Lok Sabha elections between 1952 and 1996, the percentage of women contestants remained virtually stagnant at 3.2 per cent. The exception was in 1957, (the second general election), where their percentage was 4.4, the stagnation was very marked. In the success ratio on the other hand there was a definitive decline from 43.1 per cent in 1952 and 50 per cent in 1962 to the lowest ever 7.9 per cent in 1996. In state assemblies there were variations in representation, ranging from 1.8 in 1952 to the maximum of 6.3 in 1957, and stagnation around 4.5 per cent in the rest of the elections. In the state averages covering the period 1952 to 1997 the variation is negligible, again showing a stagnation around 4 per cent. Surprisingly thc CSWI, whilc rccommcnding unanimously reservation for women in statutory women panchayats at the village level rejected the demand for reservation in legislative bodies. The majority decided to stand by the position taken by their seniors and ignored the junior cadres of women political activists, who complained bitterly to the CSWI about the discriminatory treatment meted out to them by political parties in offering nominations. Only three members of the Committee (all women) dissented on this, because they felt the Committee was being unwise in ignoring the need for institutionalised measures to eliminate or at least weaken institutionalised inequalities which universal adult franchise had failed to dislodge.

The draft recommendations of the Government of India's National Perspective Plan (NPP) for Women 1988, acknowledged the problem of under-representation and recommended 30 per cent reservation for women in local governance, pahchayat, zilla and in local municipal bodies.. There was however a provision that in the initial years this quota may be filled in by nomination/co-option. National women's organisations called for a national debate to discuss the NPP. When the Government disregarded the call, they organised themselves and critiqued it. They rejected outright the recommendation regarding nomination of women/co-option on the ground that it was 'Subversion of the Constitution'. They demanded 30 percent reservation for women in panchayats and municipalities 'with due representation for women belonging to Dalit and Tribal communities' but to be filled only by election.

Thus, final version of the Government's NPP recommended reservation for women in panchayats and municipalities, to be filled in by elections. This version was then incorporated in the 64th Constitutional Bill of 1989. The late 1980s and the early 1990s witnessed three changes of government at the national level, with two general elections in 1989 and 1991. The Panchayati Raj Amendment Bill went through successive revisions, and finally emerged as the 73rd and 74th (Constitutional) Amendments in 1992. The response of women to these two measures in the elections that followed in several states, and the political dynamism demonstrated by them persuaded women's organisations into putting forward a joint demand for one-third reservation in state assemblies and Parliament. The plan too like the CSWI did not raise the issue of women's reservation in Parliament and State Assemblies.

The demand was accepted and almost all pre-election party manifestos contained promises to implement 33 per cent reservations for women as well as The Common Minimum Programme. The newly formed coalition government of the United Front which introduced the

81st (Constitutional) Amendment also known as the Women's Reservation Bill. In September 1996, a private member's bill was moved, introducing reservations for women, a day before the closing of the monsoon session. However it was this move that subsequently led to the introduction of the present Reservation Bill. The 81st Constitutional Amendment Bill 1996, seeking to reserve one-third seats for women (including within the two already reserved categories—for Scheduled Castes and Scheduled Tribes) has become a highly debated issue. It is worth noting that none of the arguments that have been brought up against the 81st Amendment Bill came up during the passage of the 73rd and 74th Amendments (1989-92).

The motion for consideration was mooted on May 16, 1997, but it lapsed, following the dissolution of the 11th Lok Sabha. The Bill was again brought before the House during the 12th Lok Sabha on July 14, 1998, as the Constitution (84th Amendment) Bill, 1998, when the Union minister sought leave of the House to introduce the Bill. Permission for this was granted only on December 14, 1998. The Bill did not reach the consideration stage and therefore lapsed, following the dissolution of the 12th Lok Sabha. Then, the Constitution (85th Amendment) Bill, 1999, popularly known as Women's Reservation Bill was introduced on December 23, 1999. On December 22nd, 2000, it was once again shelved. On May 5, 2003, during the Budget Session of Lok Sabha that the Women's Reservation Bill was last resisted amidst loud protests from many opposition parties and some sections of the ruling NDA alliance. The house was forced to adjourn and when it returned after an hour and a half, the speaker of the Lok Sabha announced that he would call for an all-party meeting to generate unanimity/consensus on the Bill in order that the house may agree to its smooth passage.

The 81st, 84th and 85th Constitutional Amendment Bills providing for reservation for women in Parliament and State Legislatures has not been passed for not having reservations within reservation for women on the basis of caste. The Bill was referred to the Joint Select Committee, headed by the late Geeta Mukherjee, who presented their report to the House on December 9, 1996. The Joint Select Committee accepted two provisions of the 81st Amendment Bill. They are: one third of the seats in the Lok Sabha and Legislative Assemblies must be reserved for women; and there will be no reservation for States with less than three seats for the Lok Sabha for a period of fifteen years (for three elections). Amendments that were not accepted included reservation for women of other backward classes (OBC). This committee also recommended the following: the Bill be passed with out delay; the OBC reservation for women be considered by the government; and a modus operandi for reservation of seats for women in the Rajya Sabha and Legislative Councils be introduced.

In the discussion with the Select Committee of Parliament, the delegation of the national women's organisations countered all charges of elitism for not recommending reservations for women of 'other backward classes', they point out that (a) they had requested the quota within the sections which already enjoyed reservation within the Constitution; and (b) they saw the need for a Constitutional amendment to force all political parties to undertake the much needed reforms within their own structures. This is because little had been achieved in more than two decades since the CSWI's recommendations to the political parties and resolutions made by many political parties themselves. The women's delegation emphasised the crisis facing India's democracy with increasing political instability and growth of irresponsibility, fragmentation and criminalisation. Despite their efforts, the Bill was not passed due to the lack of a majority in the parliament, and strong opposition from members across parties. In this context, the lapse of the women's reservation bill, seeking one-third of the parliamentary and legislative seats is extremely distressing.

The most recent dialogue regarding reservation for women is now suggesting an amendment to the People's Representation Act. The new formula suggested seeks to reserve 33 per cent tickets for women. This could be achieved by an amendment to the People's Representation Act, enjoining political parties to allocate 33 per cent tickets to women candidates. This reveals that women will continue to be under-represented, unheard and excluded from decision making processes. In the almost total absence of a conducive environment for women to enter into politics and lack of empathy by the larger society and the mainstream political culture, the government must take immediate action to ensure that the Bill be passed immediately.

It is for the women's movement to demonstrate their political responsibility, not merely through the politics of protests, but also through direct intervention in the tasks of governance. And this is not possible unless larger numbers of women are present in all these bodies to collectively engender politics.

Even after more than 50 years of democratic governance, it is distressing that the government and the policy makers are lulled into complacency, by not translating de jure rights to de facto rights, to effect changes in the society. History reveals that women have had no space in the political arena and even in the political parties as decision-making partners. Further, it also shows that other formal institutions have not validated or recognised the participation or contribution of women.

Women's role in the sphere of decision-making has so far been insignificant to have any kind of multiplier effect. Their numbers in formal decision-making bodies have not increased over the years. Statistical records show that there has been only a marginal increase in the last few decades in the number of women candidates fielded during the elections. The number of women parliamentarians has never exceeded 15 per cent of all seats. At the state level, their membership in the legislatures is abysmally low, lower than their numbers in the parliament, with the highest being 7.1 per cent in the state of Delhi. Articles 325 and 326 of the Indian Constitution guarantee political equality to all, yet women have not benefited from this right.

The political climate as it exists today continues to be male centered and is therefore perceived to be conducive to male participation. Women are not treated as a political entity in their own right. They have been treated by political parties and other power groups as a means to further their own interests and gains. This is evinced by the declining number of women candidates fielded during the elections, despite promises made by political parties in their manifestoes to provide reservation of seats for women.

Across parties, the trend is to treat women as decorative pieces, relegated to women's wings, with not much importance given to them in mainstream activities. Even the few women who are elected are sidelined and often allotted 'soft portfolios' such as, welfare, education etc. In both cases women lack access and control over apex bodies where decisions and policies are formulated. Women's participation in political processes is impeded due to various social, economic, historical, geographical, political and cultural factors, thereby resulting in their minimal participation and even their exclusion. Illiteracy, women's triple burden, patriarchal values, lack of access and control over income and other resources, restrictions to public spaces and insensitive legal systems continue to impair their effective political participation. This is compounded by the absence/inadequate availability of infrastructural facilities and support services to facilitate their participation. There are no specific laws or policies so far, that can strengthen the grounds for political and economic empowerment of women.

The Government has attempted to empower women politically through affirmative action by providing for one-third reservation for women in local bodies, to ensure their participation at the local and district levels of governance. While these initiatives have created the political space for women, they have not been able to guarantee a non-discriminative or conducive environment for women to participate. However, even this legislative intervention in higher political bodies i.e., State Assemblies and parliament is absent.

The mechanisms to facilitate and protect women in political participation are not in place, such as a strong supportive constituency particularly for women, increased awareness of their rights and responsibilities as elected members, training and information dissemination on governance processes, gender sensitisation of the male elected members, and so on. In the absence of these mechanisms, women would become subject to negative experiences like no-confidence motions moved against women presidents and at times coercion. In the process, women may experience a backlash, which may act as an overall deterrent to their future career prospects and re-entry into politics.

The effectiveness of women's participation continues to be evaluated against indicators that have been defined by men from a male dominant perspective that is non-gendered. While disadvantages continue to impede women's participation, the disparities between the sexes get widened because of the manner in which women's participation is perceived. For example, while the women's agenda prioritises issues like health, education, safe drinking water, etc., which have long-term benefits and returns, the men's agenda primarily comprises of issues related to infrastructure that have immediate and tangible returns. Further, the resources that men give importance to are mostly financial in nature while women, because of their inability to mobilise financial resources often resort to human (women) resource mobilisation. Thus, while women may have participated in the political field their participation often remains invisible. This comes out clearly in the analysis of the available gender insensitive data on political participation of women.

The 33 per cent reservation quota provided for women in the local self governing bodies have enabled several women, who had never been in power and even those illiterate, to enter politics. Historically Indian women, who have risen to power, have done so as a result of familial or other elite connections and rarely because of the voting decision or power of a female constituency. As such these women have typically been more accountable to those who helped them get into power, i.e. their families, caste, or political party connections rather than to their constituencies.

Thirty three per cent as a number denies them their voting majority on issues of concern to women and leaves them without the power to make the changes expected of them. This would mean that even after an historic democratic experiment of such magnitude, a million women would not necessarily have the majority in any given decision making body to actually make a difference. They need to gain the confidence and capabilities for contesting elections to the local bodies against the unreserved categories, thus increasing their overall representation. However, at the levels of the higher political bodies, the absence of reservation of seats for women has led to an increase in their powerlessness due to their representation being very low.

Finally, there is a legitimate concern that electoral quotas do not really have a long-term solution. An environment should be created wherein women choose to come into power bereft of their men's support, but on their own right, on their own terms and in a position to build and sustain their constituencies.

7.1. Disadvantages Faced by Women

The following main areas have been identified and presented as the disadvantages faced by women leading to their low levels of political participation:

— Access to Resources and Information;
— Awareness;
— Control over Resources and Information;
— Personal/Familial Support;
— Socio-Economic Factors;
— Organisational Infrastructure;
— Cultural Barriers and Law and Policies.

7.1.1. Access to Resources and Information

7.1.1.1. Access to Information

Unequal access to information and other economic and non-economic resources is a barrier to women's political participation. Most information on governance is written in a language that is inaccessible to women. Because of the high rate of illiteracy and low levels of education among women they are deprived of information. Women's mobility being restricted they do not have the exposure to public life, thus limiting the scope of their interaction with others and the acquisition of information.

7.1.1.2. Access to Economic Resources

Women are concentrated in the informal economy, the subsistence sector, where many are engaged in low wage or unpaid, low skilled or unskilled labour. Much of their work remains invisible, unrecognised and devalued and is therefore unprotected by laws and legislations. The incomes they earn, however meagre are still seen by them and their families as an income to be spent on the family. This compounded by the fact that 34 per cent of households are female-headed, places the burden of providing for the family primarily lies on women. Women get entangled in the web of oppression right from childhood. It is the girl child who is the first to be drawn out of the school to contribute to wage earning or to assist in sharing women's domestic chores in the household or to be surrogate mother to her siblings.

Batliwala et al. show that "if we go by male reporting of land ownership we see that over 82 per cent of land of all types is owned by men... In contrast, less than 2 per cent of the female respondents owned land in their own names, 10 per cent is held by other women relatives, a little over 6 per cent is held jointly and the 1 per cent is held by other male relatives. In sum, only 12 per cent of all land is owned exclusively by women, 6 per cent jointly by men and women and as high as 82 per cent by men only. Six per cent of land is held jointly. This study further demonstrates that first, very few women own land and second even when they do they are unaware of their ownership.

According to Batliwala et al male respondents reported that 80.4 per cent of the houses owned belonged to men and only 14.3 per cent are owned by women and the rest is owned jointly. Thus, women's access to shelter is highly dependent on the male members in the family.

Similar results were found when access to credit by men was assessed wherein, "47 per cent or nearly half of all male respondents had accessed credit from different sources," while 21 per cent of all female respondents had done so.

There is a strong relationship between access to economic resources and participation in the political sphere.

The lack of access to economic resources results in low representation of women as elected members at all levels of governance. The number of elected representatives is directly proportionate to the economic resources that women have access to. Gram panchayat members coming from the lower socio-economic strata have to forego their daily wages and also incur additional expenditure for fulfilling their role as elected representatives.

Elected representatives incur expenditures, both overt and hidden, to meet the community demands. Building and sustaining a constituency requires economic resources over which, men have greater entitlement, access and control. Generally men are advantageously positioned as they are engaged in economic activities with higher incomes, own assets and are able to access credit from financial institutions.

The strength and the effectiveness of women's participation in political parties and other network such as, trade unions, cooperatives and the like is directly correlated to their economic status.

The low turnover of women voters especially among the poor and those working in informal and the unorganised sector is due to the loss of wages they incur in order to exercise their franchise. This nullifies the right of women to exercise their vote.

7.1.1.3. Access to Government Officials

Access to government officials determines GP members access to government resources. In a study conducted in two districts of Karnataka, respondents in Tumkur perceived local government officials as approachable. Swain and Mahapatra in their study of women leaders in Orissa found that 92.5 per cent said that they either did not interact with or were frustrated with the quality and quantity of interaction with government officials.

7.1.1.4. Access to Informational Resources

Information or knowledge is a key input towards enabling women in the GP to function effectively. Several studies confirm that the lack of access to information, results in women members not being taken seriously. The most effective way to provide women with information is through training and capacity building.

7.1.1.5. Access to Media

Media, both print and visual, is an effective source for gathering and disseminating information. But for women political leaders, family and male party members seem to be the primary source of information. In West Bengal, interviews with 50 GP women members revealed that only ten women (20 per cent) had access to information via media such as newspapers, radio and television. Only two women were made aware of the Constitutional Amendments on reservation through the radio. Party men informed the other women and also encouraged women's husbands to motivate them to stand for the elections.

7.1.1.6. Access to Decision Making Arenas

In the formal political arena, it is observed that women have very low voting percentages and their representation in local, state, national governments and political parties is not proportionate to their population. Describing the situation in 1994, Ramchandran states that, "at the national level there is only one senior minister and six states ministers in a cabinet of 74. There is only one woman governor and two chief ministers out of 30 in the country." Where we do see some real change in the formal political arena as a direct consequence of the 73rd and 74th constitutional amendments is in local government. In a majority of Indian States women now constitute at least 33 per cent of the total number of seats. Furthermore, according to Ramchandran, "entrance of women in rural leadership role through constitutional reforms has its own impact upon a) the linkages of village politics with the political parties b) determination of issues and priorities in rural power dynamics, and c) role of women in the political community."

While women's participation in formal decision making arenas has been less visible, their participation in grassroots democracy and social movements is very high. While this participation is not directly in the traditionally "male" political arenas such as party and parliamentary politics, it is vital for women's issues to gain the legitimacy and the visibility for women parliamentarians and politicians to even raise women-specific issues in the formal political spheres.

7.1.1.7. Access to Organisational Membership

A study of the background of political leaders revealed that most men have had past experiences as leaders in trade unions, co-operatives and societies. These organisations have been a training ground which prepare men as leaders in politics. The trade union and co-operative movements have been male dominated and women's participation in them has been negligible. The co-operative movement has facilitated women to establish independent all women societies, which does not enable women to gain experience to participate in mainstream political activities.

While the majority of newly elected officials may not have had any prior political experience, some women officials have had prior exposure to public life and have strong social networks even while not directly in the political arena. For instance, Mogra Devi is a newly elected panchayat member. Though this is the first time she has been in a political role, she has been a public figure for over a decade and was a teacher for more than five years. She does not see any contradiction between her domestic and political roles, which may be because she had led a public life. Because of her activities she was able to make a range of contacts in the village. Her social networks helped her win the elections. Furthermore, her children and her family support her work as a panchayat member. This is possibly because her family was already used to the woman of the household having activities that took her outside it and probably saw her GP involvement as an extension of this role.

Recent experiences have demonstrated that the activities of social networks like self-help groups have expanded to provide women specific skills in building the women's constituency and promoting leadership. But the experience gained by them is not adequate to function in formal political structures that are largely male dominated.

7.1.1.8. Mobility

The cultural norms operate both as a restriction on a woman's mobility as well as an impediment for her participation in the public sphere.

The location of polling booths and their relative distances from their homes and workplace often deter women from exercising their right as voters. The demands on contestants right from filling nominations to canvassing for elections, requires them to be mobile.

The inconvenient timings, location, distance and the lack of escort are impediments for women elected representatives to attend meetings. Often there are situations when emergency meetings are called at inconvenient timings (late night, early mornings) preventing women's attendance and thus excluding them from the decision-making processes at large.

Women face additional logistical problems in accessing decision-making spheres, which are rarely taken into account by other members of the GP. These logistics include distance and meeting timings. Timings have to take into account women's dual roles in the home and at work and that they do not feel safe after dark. In Himachal Pradesh, some women GP officials did not attend meetings as they found that the meeting timings were not convenient. The combination of timing and distance made meetings doubly hard for women to attend. Therefore getting access to decision-making fora become difficult for women when timings and mobility have not been taken into consideration when GP meetings are held.

7.1.1.9. Awareness

The lack of knowledge and awareness of elections and electoral processes among women is a major barrier in participating in elections. Also, the low level of literacy among the majority of the women prevent them from accessing information about the various political candidates, parties, party manifestos and the debates that preceed elections that are critical for making an informed choice of the most appropriate candidate. For the elected women representatives who are relatively new in the political field the lack of knowledge of the roles and responsibilities associated with political institutions impedes their effective participation in decision-making processes of governance including that of financial management.

7.1.1.10. Awareness of Roles and Responsibilities

Though women are elected to the panchayats evidence indicates that most are not aware of the roles associated with becoming an elected official. One pilot study on GP Members in Kerala, found that women political leaders were still not clear about the exact roles they were expected to play in this new system or why a reservation bill had been set for women representatives. Swain and Mahapatra claim that 49 per cent of women leaders said they were not aware of the role of PRIs, 12.5 per cent thought their role was to attend GP meetings, while only 17.5 per cent thought their role was to solve people's problems. Only 20 per cent were aware that the GP could sponsor people's development projects through a governmental programme.

Furthermore this showed that women GP members were not aware of where the resources lay for them to be able to meet the needs of their constituencies. In Karnataka and Gujarat, Asha Ramesh and Bharati Ali analysed the performance of GP women members. They found that while most women attended GP meetings, not many supervised work and few handled work outside the village. Here although the women knew what their roles were, most of them did not go beyond attending meetings. Furthermore, the range of responsibilities of GP members need to undertake, from planning to monitoring and finally to implementation, are rarely spelled out as part of their duties.

In a study conducted by Stephen and Rajasekaran, the women members of the Rajoor panchayat were not aware of their roles and responsibilities. Though women were seven as against five male members, they were unable to influence the decisions made in the Gram Panchayat.

7.1.1.11. Awareness of Electoral Processes

In a recent study done in Karnataka and Gujarat it was found that there was a greater number of women representatives in Karnataka who were aware of the electoral process and had participated in their own election campaign than the women in Gujarat. It is heartening to note that most of the women were elected through proper elections and were not co-opted and that quite a few of the women knew the number of votes that they got and what their winning margin was.

In Karnataka, which has a prior history of women involved in the GPs due to reservation has even more positive indicators of women's political participation. For example, more women in Karnataka became elected through proper election, participated in their election campaigns, and knew how to file their nomination papers. Furthermore, women elected representatives in Karnataka also are probably more accountable as only 3 per cent became GP members without going through an election as opposed to 13.3 per cent of elected members in Gujarat.

7.1.1.12. Lack of Access to Information

Studies conducted in Orissa and in Himachal Pradesh found that women elected representatives were not adequately informed about GP finances. Even fewer were able to shape the budgets of their GPs.

In Himachal, out of 70 women GP members, 38 had some financial knowledge, while 29 said they had no idea about finances. In both places, at least a third of the members were completely unaware of financial matters of the GP.

In Karnataka, most GP representatives were unable to explain how the funds were allocated to a GP. Though they knew the time for allocation was from three months to one and a half years they complained that there were delays in the allocation of funds. As to how budgets are made, they said initially there is a council meeting with GP members and a list is prepared on the work that is pending, based on this an estimate is drawn up. This indicates that while the Amendments require a financial devolution in reality this has not yet taken place. In Karnataka and Gujarat, very few women members had complete knowledge about the financial aspects of the GPs. In Karnataka out of 12 GP women members none of them had complete knowledge of GP finances, seven had partial knowledge and five had no knowledge at all.

In Karnataka, only 11 per cent (7) of the women had complete knowledge, the majority or 55 per cent had partial knowledge and a third or 21 women had no knowledge. In Gujarat, 16 per cent had complete knowledge while 41 per cent had partial knowledge and 43 per cent had no knowledge at all.

The above data shows that most women members have only partial knowledge about the financial aspects of the panchayat. While training is essential to improve their knowledge base, a comparative analysis between women and male GP members is lacking.

7.1.2. Control Over Resources and Information

7.1.2.1. Control Over Earnings

According to the definition of control over income used by Batliwala et. al., "control over income is asserted or lost right from the point after receiving one's wages/earnings in hand; if it is customary to hand over one's earnings as soon as one is paid…" By this definition, they found that 30 per cent of wage earning women do not hand over their wages to their husbands, 60 per cent do hand over their incomes and the remaining 10 per cent hand over their wages to other relatives.

7.1.2.2. Control over GP Funds

Based on the Karnataka experience Vyasulu has tried to outline the funds available to each GP namely:

1) Rs. 1,00,000 per annum.
2) Funds from JRY, which are tied, conditional, and difficult to utilise.

3) Taxes on local markets, property fines, leasing of fruit trees, etc, which amount to very little.
4) Expenditure from government schemes through the line departments which is tied and where there is no flexibility with reference to local conditions.
5) Funds with the MLAs or MPs to their constituency development schemes, which has some freedom.

Vyasulu uses the World Bank indicator, "availability of untied funds" to suggest that "our panchayats are not very free" and that there is "little by way of untied funds." On the other hand, he points out that this lack of untied funds has not pre-empted the implementation of locally important projects. The result was the "Education Guarantee Scheme was initiated under which 17,000 schools were set up in 35 districts." This represents an experiment "where local needs were identified" and responded to via the GP.

Typically, most new entrants to the PRIs are unaware about how to exert control over the financial matters of the GP and how to make these matters more transparent to the community. In a study done in 2 districts in Karnataka on GP members many respondents were vague about the finances of the GPs. Many respondents were not aware that they could demand complete transparency and accountability in financial matters.

7.1.2.3. Control over Decisions in Elected Bodies

When elected as proxies, control over the decision making process is much lower than when elections are contested and won by a woman elected representative in her individual capacity. In a pilot study conducted on Panchayat members in Kerala, when women panchayat members were spoken to what emerged clearly was that the existing women members were mere proxies. Women GP members had no training in decision-making and were dominated by male members, especially the male president. Women members were not entrusted with money.

7.1.3. Personal/Familial Support

The primary area of subordination is the family, where the patriarchal values are enforced, and where the control over women's person-hood is rarely questioned. Women in the family are viewed as liabilities because of which gender-based discrimination in all dimensions of their lives prevail. This is reflected in the alarming proportions of violence against women within thc family female foeticide, infanticide, malnourishment, school dropouts, neglect and deprivation through limited access to resources, dowry violence and torture, etc. This control takes the form of families only supporting women to get elected in order to keep the position in control of the family but then refuse to help her participate in the daily tasks of the political processes. Women having young children in the family do not have the support system that can free them to participate in activities outside the home. Younger women and unmarried women have more restrictions placed on their participation because of the control exercised on their sexuality.

At the personal level, due to the socialisation process, reinforcing her subordinate position, private and public dichotomy results in the lack of self-esteem and confidence in women and the internalisation of these value systems. This is one of the biggest barriers to their development and participation in public life and activities. Because of this, women have not been able to mobilise and strengthen their constituencies, who could support them in articulating their interests.

When the family of the women members is already involved in politics, it helps provide the necessary exposure and even entry for women into the political arena. When a woman comes from a family with political affiliations she typically has more confidence and feels she needs less training than one without any familial ties with political parties. For example, Sajabai Katkar is a GP member in Maharashtra. She is literate and studied up to the third standard. Her father was active in politics and she followed his example by standing for a general seat in the GP. She won the support of both opposing panels who wanted to co-opt her as she was already actively involved in welfare work related to the village prior to elections. After serving for ten years she decided to withdraw from politics because it had become so debased.

Similarly, Samuben is the scheduled caste corporator of the Ahmedabad Municipal Corporation. She comes from a political family where both she and her father have been active Congress workers.

When she stood for elections she was aware of the election procedures. She has been able to fulfil most of the promises she made during elections and has helped people get the benefits of several employment-related schemes. She also has sufficient knowledge of the financial resources of the corporation. As she has had immense political exposure she does not feel the need for training.

Uttam Bai is a panch from Karebor in Madhya Pradesh. She comes from a schedule caste background, called Satnami. Though this is the first time she has taken a political role, as a traditional Satnami singer she has moved in public spaces. Her family is supportive of her political role and her husband and uncle have been elected representative in the Karebor panchayat before.

Women receive minimal support from their families. The nature of this support tends to be in the form of encouragement to run for elections but rarely does it extend to helping them fulfil their responsibilities as elected representatives by taking the burden of domestic work off them. Usually women elected officials get help from their husbands in the form of their initial contacts and encouragement to join politics.

Resistance from in-laws proves to be another major detriment for women participating in political activities. In fact, their work in the GP often proves to be a source of tension once they assume office. One female Panchayat member suffered intense opposition from her mother-in-law with regard to her GP involvement. Although she did not neglect her household work, her mother-in-law was never satisfied and put pressure on her son to remove his wife from the panchayat.

Sometimes, support from in-laws is purely for the women getting elected but not to carry out her duties. The primary motivation in supporting her getting elected is to ensure that the seat does not go elsewhere and to retain power within the family/party. Dali Begum is the daughter-in law of a prosperous tobacco merchant in Murshidabad. The political party, to which her father-in-law was a member of, nominated her for the panchayat election because they were sure that she would maintain their seat for them.

7.1.3.1. Community Support

In West Bengal, 50 GP women members were questioned on the

receptivity of the communities to their political involvement and how conducive was the social environment for their participation. 32 of them stated that party men and male members of their families took the initiative to enter their nomination papers during elections. Only 3 women entered their nomination papers on their own initiative. Only some women from Birbhum could specify concretely that they expected that direct participation in politics would enable them to improve their villages and improve the lives of the women there. Only 2 women were actively involved in women's organisations and were aware of issues relevant to women's empowerment. Nine women knew of the existence of such organisations in their vicinity.

Community support is an important factor in promoting women's participation in the panchayats. For example, Kalpana Ghosh was opposed by a section of elderly men belonging to a political party who did not like the idea of women participating in the panchayat. They incited the women of the area against Kalpana who began to attack all her actions.

7.1.4. Socio-Economic Factors

7.1.4.1. Triple Role of Women

Women typically are forced to play a triple role when they enter politics, namely they have to work at home, in their jobs and in the political institutions. Since, it is hard for a woman to sustain this triple burden, it can pose as a barrier to her political work or her political work can interfere with her work at home or in her vocation.

There are no mechanisms to reduce the burden of women in fulfilling their domestic responsibilities. In particular, poor women who are engaged in long hours of non-waged productive activities like collection of water, fuel, fodder, grazing cattle, childcare, etc the absence of support services to free women to participate in political activity limits their participation.

Badali Soren is a gram panchayat pradhan and represents a typical case of having to perform in several capacities. She earns a daily wage by working in the fields.

A more common case is of Rebathi Das where she was not able to sustain all three roles. She is the pradhan of West Bengal's first all women panchayat. She is unmarried and lives with her brothers. Due to the volume of her panchayat responsibilities Rebathi was forced to sell her market stall, that was a personal financial loss. Worse still three of her brother's children fell very sick and two of them died while she was engaged in very urgent panchayat work thereby unable to attend to them. Another pradhan of a GP in West Bengal also had to put in a lot of time in the GP and was unable to spend time with her children as a result. She goes to her office six days a week for 4-5 hours per day as well as conducts visits outside the office. The result is limited time at home and a tremendous amount of guilt regarding this matter. While the experience of men in public life may be the same in terms of time spent with the family, because of the value system and traditional roles conferred on women and the expectations of family members and society, women have felt and are made to feel guilty about the time they are away from home while the same is accepted from men.

Sometimes, women can cope with the "triple burden" if they have some one at home who can help them. This could be a grown up daughter, a daughter-in-law or in rare instances, even her mother-in-law. In his study on 70 GP members in Himachal Pradesh found that 17 have at least one daughter in law and 26 have a daughter who is 12 years or older who is a school drop out to help them. In other words, 43 women (61.4 per cent) have some female member at home, who can take over their domestic responsibilities. Even in the economic arena, Rasheeda Bhagat states that, "Women who are working full time at decent salaried jobs in offices, manage to do so because their responsibilities at home are taken over by other women."

Yet evidence shows that even when women are supported they still find it difficult to take on this triple burden. Indrani Bai is a sarpanch from the schedule tribes in Madhya Pradesh. She contested the elections on the advice of her friends, in spite of having no prior experience in politics. Even though she loses her daily wage, she attends all the panchayat meetings. Her family members are supportive of her work but she still does find it difficult coping with her roles as wage earner, homemaker and a panchayat member. There is a tremendous amount of financial sacrifice required of GP members as they are not in paid positions.

7.1.4.2. Marital Status

Generally, unmarried women are less represented in the GPs. In a study done in four districts in West Bengal on 50 GP women members four of these women were widows and four were unmarried, while 42 (84 per cent) were married.

Given the fact that women wield less power within the family and in the institution of marriage, representation of "married women" need not necessarily indicate their real participation since in most cases the men are the actual decision makers. Though marital status is not a bar for participation in politics, in practice acceptance of married women contesting elections is more accepted.

7.1.4.3. Number of Children

The number of children a woman has, has no direct impact on her right and ability to participate in political activities. But certain policies adopted by the State as a family planning measure has indirectly affected women's potential to participate in political activities. The number of children that a citizen has can impede his/her participation in elections. This is especially true for women. The average age at which women get married (19) is lower than that of men (21). By the time they stand for election they already have two or more children, and therefore are not qualified to contest election. Though this policy is meant to help control population, it can act as a direct impediment to women's participation in the panchayats.

7.1.4.4. Caste

Caste has played an instrumental role in raising issues related to the more marginalised among women. In a highly hierarchical society, women belonging to the lower castes have lesser access to public fora, which is compounded by their gender.

Social divisions on the basis of caste often limit the potential for gender solidarity between women, thereby thwarting attempts at developing a common political agenda. As a result of reservation, women of all castes now sit together sharing a common space and power, which can create conflicts. Mohanty questions the inclination of lower caste women to oppose upper caste women. Women of different ages and castes participating in the GPs may upset existing behaviour patterns of the family. Furthermore, she emphasises the role of caste panchayats who may oppose women of their castes coming out in public particularly if this challenges traditional norms.

Caste has posed to be a more difficult barrier than gender in electoral politics. In Rajasthan, two different caste groups had their women candidates running for a GP seat reserved for women. The jats tried to persuade the harijans to withdraw their candidate as it become an issue of prestige for them. The harijans were forced to withdraw their candidate and were given monetary compensation for doing so. In another case Vidya Nasar, the daughter of a night watchman, stood for election against a former Pradhan who was very angry that a woman of low caste would be contesting against him. Only when none of his actions succeeded he decided to change his constituency. In general, upper castes historically dominate the GP polity. This is true even when looking at women's representation as well.

Despite reservation, caste dynamics in elections still pose barriers for participation. At the parliamentary level, caste is one of the reasons why the 84th Amendment never got passed in the Lok Sabha. At the lower levels where reservation has been put in place caste politics takes other forms.

7.1.4.5. Class/Income

While there is a large variation across class in women's political participation, within every class, women of that class have lesser access to the political realm than do the men of the same. This is because women do not have access to or where they do have access lack control over economic resources.

The number of women gainfully employed are less. According to the Labour Ministry statistics, there are 244 million men and only 90 million women in the total workforce. While 18 per cent of the men are in regular salaried jobs, only 8.3 per cent of the women belong to this group. There is little consensus on whether being gainfully employed, helped women perform better in the GP or not. On the one hand, women with jobs feel more secure and confident of themselves. However, they have to contend with the triple burden of economic, political and domestic work.

Women constitute only 15.4 per cent (4.23 million) of the organised sector (public and private) till March 31 1995. The public sector employs 62 per cent of the women in the organised sector. But 57 per cent of the women in the public sector are in soft areas such as community, personnel and social services.

Women members when questioned on whether having a job and personal income helped ease the financial burden on them from their GP work, had mixed responses. Some felt that while it may help financially it created a burden on their time. In West Bengal 14 out of 50 GP women members felt that women with a personal income were capable of being active members of the panchayat.

At the municipal level most of the women were unpaid family workers. There were a few women who had a small business, and others did not work at all. Income plays a major role in deterring women from contesting elections as campaign expenditure is a major problem for any potential candidate.

This class bias is reflected in a study done by Mohapatra, in five districts in Orissa with a sample of 32 women elected representatives, where he found that all of them belonged to the landed classes. Furthermore, he found that those belonging to the upper tiers of the PRIs such as the ZP were generally from higher income groups.

Women with independent income have a clear advantage, in that they are not dependent on the men for money. If they get enough (more than what is given as of now, which is Rs. 20 around US $ 0.40 per sitting) remuneration for their panchayat work then, this advantage that arose out of having an income could be substituted by the sitting fees.

7.1.4.6. Class and Caste Nexus

The lower the caste, and the poorer the woman, the lower the chances she has of being elected on a general seat or of being accorded her full due as a political representative when elected. Though higher castes are associated with higher positions with more access to economic resources, women in this category are subjected to more social controls in accessing these resources.

Women are victims of triple discrimination, i.e. caste, class and gender which has the effect of limiting their potential for solidarity, thereby hindering efforts towards developing a common political agenda. At an individual level, women suffer discrimination and subjugation.

A combined effect of these factors adversely impact on women as a political entity and a leader. It has been observed that powerful men in the community field candidates who are inarticulate and inexperienced thereby defeating the very purpose of the reservation policy for women.

7.1.4.7. Literacy

Literacy on the one hand is linked to women's socio-economic status and on the other, her status as a woman has an independent and equally strong implication for her access to this realm. The world's largest number of illiterate women are in India. According to the 2001 census, there is rampant illiteracy among women, it being around 46 per cent as against 24 per cent for men. Among the Scheduled Castes and Scheduled Tribes women's illiteracy is as high as 76 per cent and 81 per cent respectively. Illiteracy rates of women vary widely by region. Due to the preference accorded to the education of the male child, drop out and absentee rates among female children tend to be higher thus contributing to female illiteracy.

One cause of women's lack of access to information is illiteracy. In India, only 65.38 per cent of the population are literate. The breakdown by gender is 75.96 per cent of men are literate while only 54.28 per cent of women are literate.

There are wide disparities in literacy rates among men and women across state. The highest literacy rates in general are seen in Kerala with women also at a high level of 87.86 per cent. The states/ union territories that follow closely with high literacy rates for women include Mizoram, Lakshadweep and Chandigarh. On the opposite side of the spectrum lie states like Bihar, Jharkhand Uttar Pradesh and Rajasthan with 44.34 per cent.

At the municipal level, literacy rates of elected officials are higher. In Karnataka and Gujarat, it was found that there were only one or two illiterate women representatives in the urban municipality. Most had gone through primary education.

At a lowest tier of the PRIs a profile of the educational status of the GP representatives shows that there is a wide gap between men and women. While 40 per cent of the women representatives were illiterate only 2.6 per cent of the male representatives were illiterate.

Literacy has a strong impact on women's capacity to perform in the political institutions. Illiteracy can result in women being unable to identify misappropriation of funds and thereby take action. For example, Manavva from Beldadi village, Gadag Taluk, Karnataka State, was elected to the position of GP president, which was reserved for Scheduled Tribe women. Because she was aware and articulate, her family encouraged her to stand for elections. Manavva was unaware that the secretary was appropriating funds. In time, Manavva became suspicious and reported the secretary's action, which were investigated and resulted in the secretary's replacement.

Illiteracy can also act as a barrier towards getting elected. Very often literate women are given preference in being selected for nominations and elections. These women are typically from the more privileged backgrounds. This results in both poor women not being able to represent their communities but furthermore in them not even being able to relate easily to the more privileged women who are in power. Here one woman, a graduate, was elected as president of the panchayat but is unpopular among the other women representatives. She is seen as having a superior attitude and reluctant to involve herself in the actual work of the panchayat or in training.

Even when illiterate women come into power they lack confidence. Shyam Bai makes her living through seasonal wage labour. She lives alone and subsists on her wages alone. She makes it a point to attend the monthly meetings although it would mean a loss of a day's income. She feels a sense of achievement through her work as a sarpanch. She, however, feels a sense of inadequacy because of her illiteracy. She has participated in training programmes, but feels the need for further and continuous training for her to be able to perform her role more effectively.

7.1.5. Organisational Infrastructure and Barriers

7.1.5.1. Political Party Support

A national debate on the role political parties should play in supporting women is emerging. Currently, indicating the complete lack of support to women, Kishwar states, "In our country, even the best of women parliamentarians feel sidelined and powerless within the party. The few women leaders have not been able to facilitate the entry of greater number of women in electoral and party politics, and so remain an ineffective minority" and recommends that in allocating tickets for elections, parties should be compelled to give at least one third of their tickets to women through amending the Representation of People Act.

In a study done in Karnataka, when representatives were questioned about their political party support or affiliation, 47.8 per cent said that they did not support or affiliate to any political party. Those with affiliation said that they neither allowed themselves to be pressurised by the parties nor did they allow the parties to dominate PRI proceedings. In general women elected officials do not have much party support and their source of support is more from their families and community members. The families of 11 women urged them to stand for elections. Most women learnt about the elections from members in their community (56 women or 80 per cent).

Patriarchal norms are encoded in myriad ways within institutional structures. At every step women encounter resistance by men in general and those occupying positions of power.

The lack of experience in working or heading organisations can prove to be an impediment in their leadership capabilities once in power. There is the lack of commitment and political will of parties to foster women's leadership. This manifests itself in:

1) fewer women members in the parties holding positions of power;
2) fewer women are allowed to participate in decision-making;
3) fewer women candidates being fielded for elections;
4) fewer being given positions of power in the political institutions and finally
5) in the lack of support that is rendered for women's issues/agendas.

Issues raised by women, especially when they are in the minority, are devalued by male counterparts. When the issues are those concerning women, they are valued even less by the larger polity. Finally, in areas where a vibrant civil society is not forthcoming, women representatives lack the support to assert themselves and the mechanisms for the female electorate to field candidates are fewer.

7.1.5.2. Criminalisation of Politics and Corruption

Another deterrent for women to enter politics is the very nature of politicking. Money and muscle power are used to threaten opponents and the voters; and impose their decisions on the electorate and to raise the kinds of funds required to get into and stay in power. Violating women's dignity is an integral part of politics instilling fear in women, thereby restraining their entry into politics. In addition corruption is also insitutionalised systematically. Once in power they are unable to withstand these forces and their attempts in the political activities are frustrated.

7.1.5.3. Communalisation of Politics

The nexus of religion with politics often becomes a convenient tool to divide the women's constituency. Women by and large are religious in nature and hence by injecting the venom of communalism they are unable to transcend their religious identity. There are examples where women have resorted to promoting violence like the "Durga Vahini" that played a major role in the communal riots of Bombay and Gujarat. On the one hand while women supported communal riots, it was again women who were the main victims of such communal violence.

7.1.5.4. Backlash to Entry into Politics

Women who have entered the political process are faced with a lot of resistance. There are many instances where they have been subjected to physical violence, threats and intimidation. This has especially occurred when elected women representatives aspired to be articulate, assertive and effective in discharging their responsibilities.

7.1.5.5. Character Assassination

Patriarchal values relegate women to the home. By the very nature of this value system, any woman bold enough to come out in the open and into politics is viewed with suspicion. It is natural that she is particularly targeted for slander and character assassination. It is always her sexuality that is first questioned.

7.1.5.6. Party Interference

Women's decision-making is prevented due to party interference. This inhibits them from fully exercising their leadership. Political parties do not want to transfer control to women and are reluctant to invest in women as candidates fearing that they do not have the capacity to draw votes, and finally they do not see women as having financial credibility to compete with male contestants.

7.1.5.7. Lack of Interaction

Women have entered the political arena in large numbers at the level of local self-governance through the enactment of the 73rd and 74th Constitutional Amendments. Sharing of experiences and struggles of elected women is lacking between themselves and among those at the different tiers. This is due to division on party lines and on caste/class identities. Therefore the bonding and solidarity building is almost non-existent. The absence of elected women's interaction both horizontally and vertically reduces their unity in representing the women's agenda.

7.1.6. Law and Policy

7.1.6.1. Reservation

Women must be in crucial decision-making positions if they are to impact on the course to change and transform the lives of women and the society to uphold the principles of 'Equality'. There is no affirmative legislation to enable women to participate in the higher levels of political governance at the State and Central levels.

So far women have only been provided reservations not less than 33 per cent of the total seats in local governance. However, this reservation quota is misinterpreted to imply that women can contest only 33 per cent seats and not against the general seats.

The policy of rotation in reservation of the constituencies for women and other reserved categories in local self-governance has proved to be detrimental to the enjoyment of their right to political participation. Women who have been given the opportunity to enjoy this right are faced with the situation of being denied the opportunity to nurture their constituencies, which is important for their effective political participation, as their constituencies keep changing for every election term.

7.1.6.2. Traditional Caste/Community Panchayats

At the village level traditional caste/community Panchayats have been in existence, since several decades much, prior to introduction of elected Panchayats. These Panchayats are male dominated, feudal, and patriarchal. Such Panchayats interfere with the elected Panchayats and continue to impede women's political participation.

7.1.6.3. Lack of Women's Quorum in Gram Sabhas

The gram sabha is the entire village level constituency that is expected to meet not less than twice a year. The purpose of the sabha is to share with the community members the activities undertaken by the elected representatives for their improvement and development. It also provides the fora for the community and the panchayat representatives of the village to discuss, plan and develop a village agenda and the resource allocations received, spent and required. The whole process focuses on the importance of accountability and transparency on the part of the members through people's participation. Women continue to be traditionally kept out of this process.

Inspite of the legislation inducting 33 per cent women into the local bodies, due to the pressure exerted by family members and other male members of the local self governance bodies, women are either prevented or excluded from attending and participating in the gram sabhas. Therefore, only those women who are beneficiaries attend the gram sabhas. As such they constitute a small number and therefore do not voice the demands of the women's constituency or participate in these meetings.

While the policy of legislation providing for Grama Sabhas is laudable the implementation has been ineffective in ensuring women's participation in the Grama Sabhas, which is a space provided to voice concerns and problems.

Impact: The lack of a vibrant civil society that includes women in large number acts as a deterrent for women's participation in public life. It prevents women from uniting and forming a pressure group that can promote women's interest and ensure that the elected representatives fulfil their roles and responsibilities. Absence of an active civil society also deprives elected representatives particularly women the much required support mechanism which impact on their performance.

7.1.6.4. Civil Society and Organisational Support

The primary strategy employed by civil society institutions to increase political participation of women is to organise grassroots constituencies.

Nagar found that 68.5 per cent of GP representatives in Himachal Pradesh.had not participated in nor had any exposure to any social movement. This is indicative of the fact that women who accept patriarchy are preferred to those who challenge it through their participation in social movements NGOs have a long history of successful and not so successful initiatives to get women into politics. Madhu Kishwar in her discussion of women candidates from Shetkari Sanghathana in Maharashtra showed that they did not get elected despite a very enthusiastic election campaign where the organisation was able to play a supportive role. She claimed this outcome was because "money and muscle power play a crucial role in determining the outcome of those [panchayat and Zilla Parishad] elections." Here, civil society initiatives were not strong enough to counter the local anti-social elements and power politics.

Mahila Samakhya (MS) organised women into sanghas (women's collectives) and "a significant number of grassroots women in the villages selected by MS were members of Taluka and Zilla Panchayats. "…. it was quite natural that many women Panchayat Raj Institution members became active in the emerging Mahila Sanghas. It soon became evident to MS staff that a majority of these women had been forced to contest elections by their male relatives and kin." MS surfaced problem areas in women's political participation and then organised a series of mixed workshops for SC/ST mandal panchayat members and for women specifically across caste. The workshops resulted in increased gender solidarity and identifying and training women for the next elections for both reserved and open seats. MS trained women in a variety of areas, ranging from functional literacy and numeracy; dominant political culture, structures, institutions and strategies for change; nature, powers and functioning of PRIs, state assembly and national legislature; problems faced by women and the lower castes; and bras tacks of panchayat functioning such as meeting notices, sitting fees, framing resolutions, minute keeping, procedures and so on. As a result of these efforts out of 200 sangha women who contested the panchayat elections in 2000, 135 won and of them 2 won against the general category. One reason for their success was the active support of the sanghas.

Civil society institutions utilise their community-based organisations (CBOs) to help put up candidates for elections and build their vote banks and support. They also work in the reverse order of utilising GP leadership to organise their CBOs. The vital roles played by sanghas and other CBOs in generating genuine leadership for the PRI cannot be overestimated. According to Batliwala, "Sangha women who have become GP members have not only been found to be consistently more articulate, aware, assertive and effective as GP members, but appear to be challenging and bringing some change in the conduct and culture of the GP as a whole."

7.1.6.5. Training

It is another source of information for the women. However, there are several barriers for them to participate in the training imparted to them. Due to the restrictions imposed on their mobility, the distance of the training centre to the residence, the number of days of training involved, non-availability of transport facility, the opportunity cost of training in terms of the wages lost, non-availability of support from family members to take care of the household chores and children, lack of support services, etc. impede the participation of women in training programmes organised for them.

While, the content of the training does impart information on the roles and responsibilities of elected members, it does not impart information on important issues like budgets, accountability to constituencies, rights and so on, which inhibits their effective participation. Further, at the higher levels of political participation the women do not have access even to training. Training is an essential input in ensuring that women leaders who do not have prior experience in politics are imparted information on the rules, procedures, functions, finances and responsibilities of the GP. Training encompasses the dissemination of information, skill development, confidence building, role clarification and raising gender awareness. It has been found in studies in Karnataka that often women are not taken seriously, not because of their lack of experience, but because of their lack of knowledge.

The areas where information is lacking are: the Constitutional Amendments (their powers and duties), GP jurisdiction, financial matters, benefits and disadvantages of taking loans, a broad understanding of the working of banks and other relevant institutions and governmental bodies and so on.To keep the GP representatives well informed, there has to be a constant updating and transferring of information. This can be done through local resource centers such as literacy classes. As macro level perspectives clarify issues at the micro level, national and state resource centers should keep local level resource centers updated.

GP members also need to develop skills in planning, analysis, collective action and lobbying, management of problems and leadership. This is especially true for women where these skills have been traditionally seen as masculine. Developing skills is time consuming and quite often goes against the traditional norms and values of the family or community. Training has to be complemented with confidence building with local support groups.

Representatives of gram panchayats in the Dharwad district of Karnataka, were asked whether they thought training was needed for GP members. While 82 per cent of the representatives said that was very much needed, 1.4 per cent said that it was not needed and 17.4 per cent had no answer. Asked whether there was skill enhancement with training 81.2 per cent said that training would help in skill enhancement while 1.4 per cent answered in the negative. Around 17 per cent did not answer Representatives when asked about the kind of training they should receive, 23.2 per cent stated that they should receive training about the acts and rules, 18.8 per cent on responsibilities as members, 29 per cent on how to work with officials, 8.7 per cent in other areas and 18.8 per cent did not respond.This survey explains clearly the areas that the representatives expressed the need for training in.

The number of representatives who received training was 21.7 per cent, out of which 46.7 per cent were men and 53.3 per cent were women. The reason why there are more women receiving training than men is because men have a negative attitude towards training, and it could also be because women from the majority who lack education and exposure. But it is disheartening that there is still a large majority (both men and women) who did not receive training.

For instance according to a study done by Stree Adhar Kendra "The Maharashtra government states that 22 organisations are active in decision making training for women. According to Aalochana, a women's organisation only 8-10 organisations are actually conducting such training programmes." There are, on the other hand, some nongovernmental organisations that have spent a fairly large amount of time refining their training tools and modules on local government, such as SEARCH and Mahila Samakhya in Karnataka and Swayam Shikshan Prayog in Maharashtra. These are the exceptions rather than the rule. Most women elected officials do not get easy access to training. Asha Ramesh and Bharati Ali found that "women at the ZP level have had more opportunity to attend training programmes compared to those at the other levels. At the urban level there has been virtually no training." This is because most of the NGOs work with rural women and very few with urban women.

So far training has focused on the village level panchayat presidents and the vicepresidents largely. "To ensure that information reaches out to all levels it is necessary to have training for all three tiers both vertically and horizontally, which will facilitate interaction and experience sharing of the members. Such interactions would also provide a platform to clarify the roles and responsibilities of each tier of governance."While conducting training some factors need to be taken into consideration such as mobility and duration of the programmes. Most women are not allowed to travel far on their own, so the programmes should either be near their residence or they should be allowed to bring escorts. The women also feel that the programmes should not be for more than three days at a time and if necessary, there could be periodic sessions to update their knowledge. The above table shows that in the PRIs the percentage of women invited is substantively higher than the urban municipalities. For example, out of 12 TMC members only one was invited to the training while at the ZP level all members were invited. Even when invited, a fourth to a third did not attend training sessions.

Training is provided by both government and non- governmental institutions. While government training covers functions that pertain to governance of the GP and other PRI levels, NGO training raises awareness of the issues relating to good governance, relationship between governance and community participation, gender awareness, etc. Training is necessary for governance to be transformed, for women to become effective and for the necessary attitudinal changes.

Training has to be a continuous effort that addresses all members of the panchayat, as only then can the whole PRI be strengthened. And finally, only networking and coordination of efforts in training will strengthen the Panchayat institutions.

7.1.6.6. Gender Sensitisation

Bureaucrats and government functionaries lack sensitivity in their interaction with elected women representatives. Women elected into political positions are required to closely interact with the state administration. This is particularly the case with those elected at the local levels of governance where women face a lot of resistance and indifference from government officials. This becomes a major impediment in discharging her responsibilities as a political representative.

Therefore, it is necessary that the state administration personnel at all levels are gender sensitised. It is important that they view women as important political entities capable of shouldering the responsibilities they have been entrusted with. Also there is the need to recognise that due to the social discrimination women are subjected to, they lack the information and knowledge and are therefore not equally equipped as their male counterpart. They need the assistance from the machinery to keep them informed of the developments on the one hand and on the since they work closely with the representatives as secretary of the local institution, they can be instrumental by providing a conducive environment for the women. Women in state and national level politics also face resistance from administrators and officials, thus limiting the scope of their work.

7.1.6.7. Media Insensitivity

The media being largely male-dominant has not been favourable in depicting a positive image of women and more so of women's political participation. When they do report on women in politics, they tend to highlight women's deficiencies and ineffectiveness in functioning. Further the highlights largely are in relation to the kind of devaluation and violence meted out to elected women representatives who question, articulate and act against the dictates of the dominant sections. Success stories of women who have been able to overcome resistances and have proved their governing abilities are rarely reported. Media is an image building institution and any sort of negative portrayal tends to reinforce the stereotypical role of women as being best suited in home keeping and not for public life. In the absence of a sensitive women-friendly media policy with focus on affirmative action for women in the country, the encouragement required for political participation will be lacking.

7.1.7. Cultural Barriers

The age-old patriarchal system gives primacy to males and perpetuates deep rooted values within society that discriminate against women of all ages, classes, castes and religions. Men are privileged as a result and this privilege extends to several spheres including privileged access to the economic, educational, political and social spheres. Patriarchal norms typically relegate women to the private sphere, place restrictions on her mobility, perpetuate the view that the girl child is an economic liability, and place the responsibility of reproduction squarely on the shoulders of women. Further beliefs, traditions and customs endorse practices that are derogatory to women's dignity and perpetuate stereotype images strengthening the dichotomy of the private being the domain of women and public for men. This in turn restrains the development of selfconfidence and esteem among women. The culture of silence is practiced and perpetuated. When women do build the confidence to articulate their needs and demands, their voices often go unheard, or they become targets for further violence and terrorised into silence and invisibility. The unequal gender-based power relations impose restrictions on women's mobility to participate in the political processes. Impact: The cultural framework of values and religious beliefs, men's failure to share the household tasks and child rearing activities and lack of support services inhibits women from participating in public life and political activities. Liberating women from some of the burden of the domestic work would allow them to engage more fully in the life of their community.

7.2. Effects of Women's Low Political Participation

The government has acknowledged the need to increase the number of women in decision-making processes at all levels, as early as in 1976. As a first step to facilitate women's participation in politics, in 1993, it introduced 33 percent reservation for women in institutions of local governance through the 73and 74Constitutional Amendments. It has also provided one-third reservation for women to the posts of Presidents and Vice Presidents in these institutions. While the government has succeeded in facilitating women's participation by providing for reservation at the lower levels of governance, it has failed to do so in passing the reservation Bill for women in the higher echelons of political institutions i.e., in the State Assemblies and the Parliament. The effects on women's political participation have been examined in this study at two levels:

i) Representation of women in political institutions at all levels.

ii) Inadequate number of women as elected representatives.

The Constitution of India, no doubt guarantees equal rights to participate in political activities and adult franchise. However, the prevailing value system, the private-public dichotomy and male dominance in political institutions restricts women from exercising and enjoying their rights.

The lack of representation of women in decision-making positions results in women's agenda not getting reflected and addressed in policies and programmes. The on going research cum action cum advocacy efforts of the Gender Studies Unit at National Institute of Advanced Studies, Bangalore on 'engendering governance' revealed that the priorities of male and female representatives differed. The women prioritised and addressed issues of long term effects such as education, health, violence against women, basic amenities while men took up issues of immediate and visible relevance such as roads, community and commercial centres, tanks, bridges, etc.The visual prioritisation tends to subsume the women's agenda and therefore undervalues the contribution made by women, which is in the larger interest of the community. The government has attempted to introduce reservation for women at the legislature and parliament levels on three occasions in the years 1996, 1999 and 2000, which have lapsed. If there were more women parliamentarians, constituting a significant number, they would have been in a position to consolidate their strength and advocate for the enactment of the Bill, transcending their multiple identities.

Lack of critical numbers of women elected representatives impedes them from negotiating for important portfolios such as finance, home, defence, etc., which are generally termed as key portfolios and primarily controlled by men. It has been observed that women are allotted soft portfolios such as those related to women and children, information and culture, social welfare, etc which are relatively less important and have correspondingly lesser resources both financial and human. As there are few women in positions of power at all levels of governance, they are unable to negotiate for resources to nurture their constituencies. They cannot mobilise the necessary financial resources to meet the demands of their electorate, which facilitates women being accepted as political leaders.

Further, women, being in insignificant numbers, are often pressurised to align with men along their caste, class, religion and ethnic identities rather than on the basis of gender. This has resulted in dividing women on the one hand from centre-staging gender issues and concerns and on the other their solidarity.

Inadequate numbers of women in governance makes them vulnerable and voiceless. Women's self-confidence and esteem is affected in a predominantly male set up, as their male colleagues view them as being weak and ineffective. Cultural inhibitions restrict women in expressing their views and opinions openly in such an intimidating atmosphere. Even when women attempt to express their views, generally it is trivialised and ignored. The presence of women in large numbers would have created an enabling environment, as the mere strength of their numbers would have facilitated their effective participation. It would also encourage them to express their opinions and viewpoints and negotiate on them with their male counterparts.

At the lower levels of governance, (local bodies), despite reservation there is resistance to women participating, particularly when they hold leadership positions such as that of presidents and vice-presidents. The resistance is manifested in the form of 'no confidence' motions being passed against elected women representatives holding these leadership positions. Women contesting such action by the dominant groups also become extremely difficult when they are unable to consolidate their strength across caste, class and religious lines. Further, this division results in the absence of a quorum, thus increasing their vulnerability to those in power.

The prevailing political environment of corruption, criminalisation and communalisation inhibit women from entering politics. In the on going study at NIAS, Bangalore, it was observed that with the entry of women in the Panchayat Raj Institutions, as a result of the reservation policy for women, the overall atmosphere has visibly changed. There has been a considerable reduction in the incidence of corruption, due the pressure exerted by on their male colleagues in relation to transparency and accountability. While the overall use of money and muscle power and criminalisation of politics has reduced, there has been an increase in the incidence of violence against women elected representatives and those in positions of power. This has been more as resistance to their entry into politics and a backlash against particularly articulate and strong women. Violence is used as a weapon to subdue and silence them.

This reveals that the entry of women into political institutions have changed the atmosphere more positively and has made it more transparent and accountable. If affirmative action has a positive influence on the environment at the PRI level, it is all the more reason that the same would happen at the higher levels of governance. Though the government's initiative of introducing reservation for women in local governance is laudable, the policy of reserving the constituency for women through a policy of rotation has had a negative impact by restricting their chances of getting reelected from the same constituency. This has resulted in the loss of experience gained by the elected women during her tenure. In this regard, the concept of having vasathi sabhas or hamlet-level meetings, is encouraging as it helps women to build their constituencies and overcome the limitation imposed by the rotation system. This is one of the outcomes of the advocacy efforts made by NIAS with the Government of Karnataka. It also helps women to overcome the limitation they face in mobilising resources and nurturing their constituencies to contest subsequent elections.

The policy of 33 per cent reservation for women has been interpreted in such a manner that it restricts the scope for women to contest the elections. Men, who are officials, members of the political parties and the communities, define it to mean that women can contest only against the "reserved constituencies" and not against the constituencies categorised as 'general'. This implies that the 'general' seats are exclusively meant for men. This deprives women of opportunities to contest against the general category despite having the potential and aspiration to do so.

Ms. Lakshmi, an ex-member of an 'all women's gram panchayat' in a district in Karnataka State, reprehended that rotation of reserved seats deprives aspiring women candidates of their chances of contesting elections. During the previous term, she was nominated as a member to represent the reserved constituency for Scheduled Caste (SC) women. If she wanted to contest in the second term she either had to contest under the unreserved category or change her constituency to a reserved one, which would reduce her chances of winnability. Contesting against the dominant communities is difficult because of the lack of financial and human resources available to her. Moving into a new constituency would mean the loss of her previously nurtured constituency and building an entirely new one.

The lack of affirmative action for reservation of seats at the higher levels of governance such as in the legislative and parliament hinders the entry of women from the lower economic strata, those without political familial connections and for those from groups. The absence of reservation perpetuates the entry of only those who are politically connected through family and those belonging to the upper economic strata.

The lack of vibrant and supportive constituencies has adversely affected women's participation in governance in large numbers.

Where the constituency is aware and informed, they are able to influence and change the political climate and quality of governance. For instance, in a village in Uttarakhand, due to an informed and organised constituency, particularly of women, they were able to revert a decision taken by the forest panchayat to destroy a section of the forest for development. The women demanded a re-election in which women en masse voted for women to all the nine positions in the panchayat.

At the lowest level of governance that is at the village level, there is a parallel traditional governing body based on caste called the "jati panchayat", which is exclusively male. The absence of a critical mass of women in the institutionalised PRI system would affect the decisions made by the jati panchayats. They will not be in a position to counter the 'anti-women' pronouncements that are made in these panchayats. Similarly, in the scheduled areas, which are predominantly tribal, the village councils are the decision making institutions in the field of administration, religion, politics, economics, justice and so on. Generally, these councils do not have women members and in cases where there are women, they hold peripheral positions. For instance, in Nagaland, during an interaction on 'Women's Political Participation' with the National Commission for Women in 1998 on the issue of reservation at the higher levels of governance, the Naga women's response was divided. They did not feel the need for reservation for women at the higher levels of governance, especially in the absence of women in the village councils. They expressed that it was crucial for women to be represented in these councils first, where decisions affecting their lives were taken.

References

Batliwalla, Srilatha. "Transforming of Political Culture" *Economic and Political Weekly*, XXXI, Number 21, p.1248-251. *Women and Political Leadership*

Institute of Social Studies Trust. Strengthening the Participation of Women in Local Governance, (Uma Project), Bangalore. 1995.

Kishwar, Madhu. "Women and Politics: Beyond Quotas" *Economic and Political Weekly*, XXXI, Number 43, p.2871. 1996.

Pamela Philipose (ed.) "The Political Agenda. Issues Towards Beijing", Coordination Unit, New Delhi. 1998.

8

From Reservation to Participation

The 73rd and 74th Amendments to the Constitution of India provide the legal basis for direct democracy at the local-level, both in rural and urban areas. The amendments stress the need to bring people belonging to marginalized groups into the political process by reserving seats for women and for people belonging to the Scheduled Castes (SC)and Scheduled Tribes (ST). It is envisaged that by mandating not less than one-third of the seats for women in local government bodies, the governance process at the local government level will reflect the voices of women and the concerns and issues that confront them. This has resulted in 247,115 elected *Panchayats* (locally elected self government bodies) in the country, which contain more than 2.8 million elected representatives. Of these elected representatives, more than 1 million are women.

However, this aggregate figure tells only part of the story. While *representation* is adequate (as per the norm of one-third of all seats) *participation* is less than adequate. While it is relatively easy to legislate representation, it is more difficult to create conditions suitable for participation. Experience indicates that representation does not automatically lead to participation.

A number of factors limit the active engagement of women in the political sphere. First, deeply entrenched stereotypical norms relegate women to the domestic space, with severely restricted engagement in public affairs, an area largely dominated by men. Second, caste and class restrictions and the patriarchal system and mindset pervades the political space provided to women. Women are still not recognized as political entities and their perspective is seldom seen as integral to the design and delivery of services. The third factor is the lack of exposure of women themselves to politics and the absence of any experience in exercising their political responsibilities. Low literacy levels, absence of education and limited or no exposure, all lead to a lack of confidence and many women are unable to comprehend the true spirit of decentralization and recognize the opportunities that it provides.

Factors such as these, that deter the effective participation of women, led to the initiation of the project *Capacity Building of Elected Women Representatives and Functionaries of Panchayati Raj Institutions* by the Ministry of Panchayati Raj (MoPR), Government of India and United Nations Development Programme (UNDP) India, from 2003 -2008. One district each of the10 selected states (Bihar, Chhattisgarh, Jharkhand, Haryana, Madhya Pradesh, Maharashtra, Orissa, Rajasthan, Uttarakhand and Uttar Pradesh) was chosen. Specifically, the project aimed to:

— Build capacities of Elected Women Representatives (EWRs) for effective functioning and setting of women's agenda.
— Institutionalize mechanisms to strengthen capacity building of EWRs to better understand and perform their functions.
— Mobilize community and strengthen processes of constituency building to enable women to articulate their voices and participate in the electoral process.

The project activities were implemented through Civil Society Organizations (CSOs) to harness their expertise in mobilizing women and creating awareness of issues at the grassroots level. For each of the 10 states, one CSO was identified based on the demonstrated work experience on local governance issues in that area.

The capacity-building project focused on EWRs and *panchayat* functionaries. One district in each of the 10 states was chosen by the respective organizations as the unit of intervention. In some states, the entire district was covered through a combination of intensive (covering the entire block by conducting a range of activities) and extensive (covering the district through dissemination of information and educational material) methods, while in others only a few specific blocks were covered.

The following partner organizations were identified to carry out activities in the project districts.

Table 1. CSO partners in project districts

	State	District	CSO Partner
1	Bihar	Muzzafarpur	CENCORED
2	Chhattisgarh	Rajnandgaon	Participatory Action for Tribal Heritage (PATH) 3 Haryana Rewari Social Centre for Rural Initiative and Advancement (SCRIA)
4	Jharkhand	Palamu	Integrated Development Foundation (IDF)
5	Madhya Pradesh	Dewas	Samavesh
6	Maharashtra	Gadchiroli	Aalochana
7	Orissa	Anugul	Institute for Socio Economic Development (ISED)
8	Rajasthan	Jodhpur	Unnati
9	Uttarakhand	Tehri Garhwal	Shri Bhuvneshwari Mahila Ashram (SBMA)
10	Uttar Pradesh	Ghazipur	Sahbhagi Shikshan Kendra (SSK)

In addition, Society for Participatory Research In Asia (PRIA, Delhi) and Mahila Chetna Manch (MCM, Bhopal) were identified to provide handholding support to the partners.

8.1. Strategies for Capacity Building

The overall project strategy was designed to bring women into political structures and support their participation in politics, by organizing campaigns and training programmes to prepare women to discharge multiple roles, enabling them to link local priorities to the planning process.

The CSOs adopted a multi–track approach to achieve the project objectives. They were tasked with facilitating women's participation, inspiring them to lead the process of change in the district, strengthening the existing collectives and networking with them at different levels. Within the overall objectives and the framework of the project, different organizations were mobilized to assist in the implementation. In Madhya Pradesh, the *Sakhi Manch* and Self Help Groups (SHGs) were pivotal to the programme, in Rajasthan, the Panchayat Resource Centres (PRCs) and community based units were critical, in Chhattisgarh, SHGs and community volunteer groups were extensively used and in Uttar Pradesh, local Non Governmental Organizations (NGOs) were engaged in project execution.

The key interventions for building capacities of EWRs and other *panchayat* functionaries were:

(1) environment building through the campaign approach;
(2) building capacities of EWRs and other women leaders;
(3) strengthening women's collectives and building networks;
(4) activating the *gram sabhas* and
(5) strengthening information dissemination mechanisms.

8.1.1. Environment-building

The design of the project activities in each state envisaged implementation over the five-year electoral cycle. Consequently, activities commenced with a Pre-Election Voters Awareness Campaign (PEVAC), which was followed by capacity-building interventions.

A campaign-based approach was adopted to influence peoples' perspectives on *panchayats* and local governance and to encourage them to participate in *gram sabha* meetings. In the pre-election period, campaigns were devised to motivate people to participate constructively in the elections, both as voters and/or candidates.

PEVACs, carried out both in intensive and extensive modes, sought to promote an enabling environment for free and fair elections, encourage increased participation of women and people belonging to marginalized groups (as voters and candidates), generate awareness among voters about the importance of exercising their right to franchise and encourage them to vote for women candidates. In the intensive mode, an entire block was covered through a range of activities; while in the extensive mode, blocks were covered largely through the dissemination of information and educational material. PEVACs adopted innovative approaches to ensure that the message reaches the people, irrespective of literacy levels. Approaches were designed in a manner that was sensitive to the local ethos, work culture and differences in literacy levels.

Some elements of the campaign approach were:

i) Awareness generation and perspective building: These campaigns focused on the importance of people's participation in governance, the features of the 73rd Constitution Amendment Act and the role of women in governance. Posters, pamphlets, handbills, inspirational songs, *nukkad nataks* (street plays) and *mashaal jaloos* (torch light processions) were organized in Haryana, Jharkhand, Madhya Pradesh, Orissa and Uttarakhand. Graffiti, posters, pamphlets, and handbills also served to widen and diversify the process of dissemination. Women were encouraged to contest elections, vote for women candidates and explained the significance of participation.

ii) Support in filing nominations and mock polling exercises: In many states 'nomination camps' were set up to offer support to aspiring candidates, especially women. These camps provided information regarding filing of nominations, assisted in filling nomination formsand encouraged women to contest from unreserved seats. As a consequence, there were relatively few instances of invalid nominations being filed and an increase in the number of women who contested from unreserved seats. Mock polling exercises undertaken in Bihar and Jharkhandserved to generate awareness among voters and make them familiar with the polling process. After the elections, in Madhya Pradesh, Maharashtra, and Uttar Pradesh, the partner institutions organized felicitation functions for the newly EWRs. This helped to create a positive impact, especially on the women who had won the elections.

iii) Mobilizing people to participate in *gram sabha* meetings: Mobilization campaigns were conducted in Chhattisgarh, Haryana and Uttarakhand, in an effort to increase people's participation in *gram sabha* meetings. Printed material, highlighting the importance of *gram sabhas*, the role, powers and functions of the members, was distributed to create awareness.

8.1.2. Building Capacities of EWRs

The basic premise of this exercise is the idea that informed and welltrained EWRs and leaders will be equipped to handle their roles and responsibilities independently and will be in a better position to participate effectively in *panchayat* affairs. Capacity-building approaches sought to enhance the understanding of women representatives and leaders about their role and responsibilities, the procedures and mechanisms associated with decentralized governance and the schematic interventions of the Government. Gender sensitization was taken up in some areas; activities included training programmes, perspective-building meetings, exposure visits, strengthening women's collectives and developing information dissemination mechanisms.

Several innovative and successful actions were taken under this subcomponent of the project. Most states arranged exposure visits for the EWRs to other states, where the project was underway. In Rajasthan, information kiosks were established in the Panchayat Resource Centres (PRCs). In Madhya Pradesh workshops for women *panchayat* representatives and *mahila sammelans* (womens' gathering) facilitated dialogue and better coordination. In Haryana, the campaign involved street corner meetings, street plays and thematic songs.

A series of six *nagrik samvads* (citizen dialogues) was organized on the issue of self and inclusive governance. In Chhattisgarh, Haryana and Madhya Pradesh, gender sensitization training initiatives were organized specifically for elected male *panchayat* members.

In Maharashtra and Orissa, the partner institutions' main strategy was to consciously include men in the training, wherever possible. The orientation programmes, which were organized for both men and women in Orissa, led to a district-level convention of women on *Panchayati Raj*. The convention led to capacity-building of EWRs and the emergence of a district-level women's forum. In Chhattisgarh, gender sensitization training programmes were held for EWRs; in addition, PATH also organized leadership training for EWRs and SHG members, training camps for the purpose of networking among elected women, SHG leaders and members of CBOs and refresher training to consolidate the knowledge and capacities of EWRs. A

Pratinidhi Pati Sammelan (a gathering of husbands of EWRs) was organized by SBMA the partner organization in Uttarakhand.

Personality, Perspective and Performance (the three Ps) were the core elements that were stressed in the structured training programmes conducted by UNDP's partner institution (SSK) in Uttar Pradesh. In addition, interfacing and handholding were other aspects of the capacity building approaches. *Samman samarohs* (felicitation ceremonies) of EWRs helped to defuse the political polarization within the village and build up the confidence of the members. Similarly the organization of *amna samna* (interface) meets between EWRs and the community enabled regular interaction to discuss local issues, the provisioning of services etc.

In Uttarakhand, elected women members were given training as master trainers. This enabled them to mobilize other women ward members on issues of governance. The partner institution in Madhya Pradesh produced training modules for the training of *saathins*, (village level professional women workers), *manch leaders* and EWRs. Training of trainers, orientation workshops, refresher workshops, exposure visits and the formation of an association of EWRs were the major capacity-building initiatives in Rajasthan.

8.1.3. Strengthening Women's Collectives

The interplay of several factors prevents women's voices from being heard, their needs being addressed and their active engagement in governance processes. The culture of continued subordination has rendered many women less than confident to exercise their public responsibilities. Coupled with the fear of being ridiculed and sidelined, this has been a major constraint to the active participation of women in governance. The linkages between EWRs and women's groups or movements are limited. Recently there have been some efforts at building networks of women, though these have been limited.

Under the project, partner organizations facilitated the formation of women's forums and networks that developed a sense of solidarity amongst the women. In some places, new forums and networks were formed by bringing together various self help groups/ women's groups and EWRs, while in other places existing networks were expanded and strengthened. The basic focus was on building the capacities of traditional and local associations of women and making them aware of governance issues. Such networks were federated at the block, district and state levels.

These networks have helped women gain collective strength and solidarity, a common platform to share experiences, increased recognition and voice and enabled dialogue and the sharing of experiences. A lot of ground work and a mix of interventions such as perspective building, training programmes and informal meetings was required to motivate women to form networks. In certain areas the partner organizations had to deal with additional constraints of caste and class in the formation of networks, particularly in eastern Uttar Pradesh.

In Bihar, the idea for the formation of a network emerged at a function organized by CENCORED, the partner institution for newly EWRs, to provide a platform to share experiences and build confidence. The network was called the *Mahila Jan Chetna Manch*. Similarly, the partner institution in Chhattisgarh utilized the leadership training programme that they had organized to plan for cluster/network meetings, to work out strategies for establishing a platform for collective action. Block-level forum meetings were organized to develop bye-laws, discuss women's issues and build the level of coordination required to make the network sustainable.

These networkswere instrumental in performing a wide variety of functions. In Uttar Pradesh the networks acted as pressure groups and enabled women to raise their issues at various forums. Initiatives were taken through the networks to combat issues of alcoholism, women's health and related issues including violence against women. It was useful in monitoring the Janani Suraksha (women's safety) scheme (under which pregnant women are encouraged to visit the closest hospital for their deliveries), the work of Accredited Social Health Activists (ASHA) and *anganwadi* workers, the Midday Meal Scheme (MDMS) and the Public Distribution System (PDS). The network has played an active role in convening *gram sabhas* to take up issues such as encroachment of public land; in some areas these networks succeeded in reclaiming the land and redistributed it among landless people. Another notable achievement of the network has been to ensure the provision of basic education for girls in rural areas.

Women were instrumental in ensuring better and more accessible education for girl children – an initiative that was commended by the Union Ministry of Panchayati Raj. A district level forum of women leaders called *Shakti Parishad,* formed by SCRIAthe partner institution in Haryana—was actively involved in cases of violence against women. The members of this forum assisted women who were victims of domestic violence, social intolerance and economic injustice. In many instances, this network acted as a pressure group and lobbied with the relevant administrative bodies, legal offices, social and political institutions. The network was also active on issues of poverty reduction and access to information; along with other villagers, it was instrumental in rectifying the Below Poverty Line (BPL) list. Due to pressure exerted by the group and the village community, a special *gram sabha* was convened by the *panchayat* and the villagers were instrumental in rectifying the BPL list.

In Maharashtra, the network focused on women's issues and ensured that at least 10 percent of the revenue of the *panchayats* was earmarked for women's welfare. The network also organized a campaign called *Tanta Mukti Abhiyan* (freedom from violence) to build up pressure against domestic violence.

In Jharkhand, where *panchayat* elections have not been held, a federation of women SHGs has been formed and it plays a significant role as a pressure group to ensure the enforcement of the provisions related to women at the village level. Similarly, existing networks were strengthened by partner institutions in Madhya Pradesh and Chhattisgrah as well.

In Uttarakhand, existing networks of women were encouraged to organize themselves into forums at the block level, so that they can participate effectively in the governance process. Here also the process of forming a network involved identification of active EWRs by the block level volunteers; door to door campaigns, regular meetings and field visits by volunteers to motivate women to participate in activities related to political processes. Once the forum started to take shape; block level workshops were organized to formulate the Constitution, formalize the forum, debate the agenda and discuss the need to provide a supporting role to the forum until a natural leadership emerged from within the forum.

In Orissa, women's forums were created at the cluster, block and district level and covered the entire district/ project area. The district-level forum formed the apex body, the block-level forums the middle level, and the cluster-level forums were at the bottom of the pyramid. Each cluster consisted of members from seven *gram panchayats* and this ensured maximum participation. It was envisaged that each and every woman would be a part of the forum, if not directly, at least in the decentralized system, consisting of the village, block and district level. To strengthen the women's forum, periodic district-level conventions were organized by the partner organization. Nearly 500 women from different *panchayats* of Anugul district gathered at the *Anugul sabhaghar* (community hall) to review the progress, interact with government functionaries and plan the future course of action. The fact that these women took out the time to attend the convention is an indication that they realize the importance of participation. The network has helped women interface with government officials and build cohesion among community organizations.

8.1.4. Activating the Gram Sabhas

Empowering the community to enable people to participate proactively in the governance process was another aspect of the role undertaken by the *partner institutions across states. Unless regular* gram sabhas *are convened,* with the active participation of the villagers, the objective of decentralized governance cannot be achieved. A special effort must be made to ensure that women and people belonging to the disadvantaged sections feel empowered and motivated, so that they can voice their concerns and ensure that these are placed on the agenda and discussed. In the absence of such motivation, very few people attend or participate effectively in *gram sabha* meetings.

Awareness generation programmes, community mobilization activities and perspective-building programmes were organized by almost all partner organizations. Substantive educational programmes were adopted. For instance, in Rajasthan, a 15 minute radio programme in the local language was broadcast every week, covering subjects like the role of *panchayats* in providing basic services and their monitoring, planning and budgeting, identification and verification of the BPL list, micro-planning, the significance of participation in the *gram sabha* and the ward *sabha*, domestic violence, legal provisions relating to the rights and protection of women, social practices and their impact on women.

In Rajasthan, the broadcasts encouraged people to share their experiences and provide feed back through telephone helplines and postcard responses. At the end of each episode, listeners were asked a question that sought their opinion on a particular issue or on some information provided during the episode. Prizes were awarded to the best responses. The issues which were identified then fed into the training needs assessment, which was taken up subsequently as part of the capacity-building initiatives. Similar tele-help lines were also used quite successfully in Haryana.

Since *panchayat* elections were indefinitely postponed in Jharkhand, it was decided to use the capacity building exercise to strengthen people's understanding and participation in National Rural Employment Guarantee Scheme (NREGS). *Nukkad nataks* were organized to clarify a number of technical points regarding the National Rural Employment Guarantee Act (NREGA). The main features of NREGA were communicated to the people and aspects such as how to write an application for a job, whom to address and the value of compensation if employment is not provided within the specified time, were covered.

Once again, the *nukkad nataks* were followed by feedback sessions, where queries were addressed. Street plays were also used in Madhya Pradesh to familiarize women with the procedures and conduct of the *gram sabha* and to encourage them to participate effectively in the *gram sabha*. Using the play format, women were asked to identify five problems on a priority basis. They were then asked to put this in the form of a proposal and given tips as to how to present it in the *gram sabha*. One woman was made the *sarpanch*, another woman the *patel* of the village and two others played the role of secretary and *gram sabha prabari* respectively. The play format was a very effective way of illustrating the functioning of PRIs to people.

A *yatra* (rally) was undertaken in Orissa, to familiarize people in the more remote areas with the features of NREGA. Audio presentations with the main features of NREGP were prepared in the local dialect, so as to be able to reach the widest possible audience.

A series of model *gram sabhas* were organized in Chhattisgarh to build awareness about the *gram sabha* and encourage more participation. These 'mock *sabhas'* demonstrated the methods and procedures of conducting a *gram sabha* meeting and helped to mobilize villagers to identify an issue which could be placed before the *gram sabha*. Door-to-door visits made in the pre-preparatory stage were followed by the organization of ward-level and group-level sub-groups to motivate villagers to participate in *gram sabha* meetings. Special focus was given to SHGs, *panchayat* members, traditional village leaders and leaders of CBOs.

The holding of mock *palli sabhas* (assemblies at the level of a revenue village) and *gram sabhas* in Orissa by the partner organization helped women become more familiar with conducting meetings, noting proceedings and maintaining records. Women were also familiarized with government policies and circulars. In Bihar, *kishore* and *kishori groups* (groups of young boys and girls respectively) comprising of adolescents in the age group of 14 to19 years, were formed and these were used to motivate villagers to participate in the *gram sabha* meetings. The objective was to encourage young people to become aware of the democratic process and encourage them to participate in *gram sabha* meetings in the future.

In Maharashtra, special focus was given to strengthening the *mahila gram sabhas* (women's village assemblies). SHG members were motivated to actively participate in the *mahila gram sabhas*.

8.1.5. Information Dissemination Mechanisms

Information dissemination strategies that were adopted included formation of information centres, information *melas*, radio programmes and the establishment of PRCs. Information centres were set up in Jharkhand, Chhattisgarh, Maharashtra, Rajasthan and Orissa. At these centres materials and posters on *Panchayati Raj* and government schemes were displayed. Thirteen *panchayat*-level centres were set up in Jharkhand; each centre was provided with a radio to enable discussions on issues of current importance. Centres in Maharashtra were equipped with contact details of key government functionaries, literature on women's rights, and material on government programmes, especially on the Right to Information (RTI) and the NREGA. Computers installed in the information centres in Orissa encouraged and facilitated computer literacy amongst women. In Rajasthan also, the PRCs functioned as information and dissemination hubs. In addition to posters, pamphlets and calendars, a weekly 15 minute radio programme provided useful and interesting information to a large audience. A fictional character, *Paanchu Panchi* (a mythical bird), was used to carry the message of self-governance on posters and calendars and in short films. The PRCs facilitated training programmes and functioned as an interface between government departments and *panchayat* functionaries.

Information *melas* (fairs) in Haryana and Jharkhand provided another mode of dissemination of information and brought a range of stakeholders including elected *panchayat* representatives, teachers, government officials, SHGs and the media to a common platform. Information, Education and Communication (IEC) materials were prepared in Uttar Pradesh, in the local dialect with large fonts and pictures. These were very effective in meeting the information needs of neo-literate and semi-literate audiences.

Even as partner institutions followed a common strategy and approach, they developed tools, modalities and mechanisms that were specific to the local context and requirements. As a consequence, the project has been successful in building capacities, confidence and skills amongst EWRs and women's groups and has exerted a positive and catalytic influence on the local governance process. It has strengthened existing networks of women and helped to establish new networks. The magnitude and scale of building and sustaining the effort required for participatory government is daunting. Equally daunting are the challenges faced by the local governance systems and by patriarchal social systems. These are compounded by practical everyday challenges faced by the teams in the implementation of these projects, everywhere.

8.2. Stories of Success

8.2.1. Women Assert their Rights

Capacity building exercises and the strengthening of women's networks were critical elements in the transformation of many EWRs from passive, non-participating members to confident, active and responsible members of the community. In Orissa, women who had so far been largely silent in public began to share and voice their concerns. Acknowledging this trend and the importance of womens' participation, block-level officials provided forum members with space in the block office to conduct their meetings.

In Rajasthan, in several *gram panchayats*, women *sarpanchs* who had been denied their legitimate right to chair *gram sabha* and *panchayat* meetings were enabled to do so. In fact inspite of the feudal, conservative and paternalistic environment that prevails in the state, *dalit*women have been enabled to participate in PRIs, which is a remarkable success.

In Maharashtra, women organized successful campaigns to implement the State Government's avowed policy of registration of houses in the joint names of husband and wife and the inclusion of the name of the mother in all official documents pertaining to children. The women also succeeded in asserting their right to influence the utilization of 10 percent of the *panchayat* funds, earmarked for them.

The most significant impact has been the solidarity established amongst women through the networks and forums. In a path-breaking instance in Orissa, a no-confidence motion was sought to be passed against the woman chairperson of the *panchayat samiti*. She was also the chairperson of the district *mahila manch* and the members of the *mahila manch* united crossing party lines, to ensure that the motion was defeated.

When women in Karond village, Bandi *Panchayat*, of Madhya Pradesh, realized that women wage labourers were being paid less than their male counterparts on the construction site of a dam, they took up the matter in the women's forum. They then raised it with the *sarpanch* and the secretary of the *panchayat*, who asked them to approach the concerned authorities, which they did. Though the work stopped for a few days, when it was finally resumed, equal wages were paid to both women and men.

These and a number of other instances from various project areas show that the capacity-building project has helped to empower women to demand their rights.

8.2.2. Engagement of Women in Panchayats

A key outcome of the project has been the increased recognition by women, both elected members and *gram sabha* members, of the importance of their participation and engagement. In Maharashtra, a 75 percent increase in attendance of women was recorded in the *gram sabhas* of several villages. In more than half the *panchayats* in Rewari in Haryana, 65 percent of the EWRs participated in *panchayat* meetings, a 20 percent increase from 2004, the year when the projectwas initiated. Similar increases in participation have been reported from the other states as well.

An interesting case was reported in Basala *gram panchayat*, in Anugul block of Orissa, where the Block Development Officer (BDO) refused to acknowledge a *palli sabha* because only women were present at the meeting. When he was questioned, he claimed that the *panchayat* manual does not recognize a *palli sabha*, where only women are present. However the *sarpanch* with the help of the forum members protested against this stand and lodged a complaint with the Collector, who intervened and decided in their favour.

8.2.3. Incorporating Women's Issues in Panchayat Meetings

Efforts to bring women's issues to the forefront of the agenda of *gram sabhas* and *panchayat* meetings have been successful. For instance, in Rewari district of Haryana, which is noted for its adverse sex ratio, 15 percent of the issues raised in *panchayat* meetings related to female foeticide, dowry and domestic violence. Similarly, 25 percent of the issues raised in the *gram sabha* were related to women. In most villages, an average of four proposals in each *gram sabha* were proposed by women and taken up for action.

8.2.4. Monitoring of Basic Services

Reflecting increased confidence and awareness, elected women members and network members have begun to monitor the functioning of *panchayats* and the departments within the purview of the *panchayat*s, as well as the implementation of government schemes. Some areas where the women have been active include monitoring of the Public Distribution System (PDS), the running of the Integrated

Child Development Services (ICDS), the Mid-day meal scheme (MDMS), identification of BPL families, ensuring attendance of teachers in schools and the provisioning of services like water and roads etc.

Between 30 to 35 percent of the EWRs in Ghazipur district, Uttar Pradesh, visited government departments and discussed their concerns and grievances with the concerned officials. They have also built pressure on *panchayat* secretaries to ensure that schemes are effectively implemented. In Rajasthan, elected women members monitored 36 schools in 12 *gram panchayats* and 93 *anganwadi kendras* (creches) in 25 gram *panchayats*. Participatory monitoring was undertaken in 62 *gram panchayats* in eight blocks of Jodhpur district.

In Jharkhand, village level meetings were held to discuss the different Government sponsored schemes. Before the *aam sabha* (general assembly) called by government officials to identify beneficiaries under different schemes like Dindayal Awas Yojana, Indira Awas Yojana (IAY – housing scheme for the poor), Annapurna Yojana (food security initiative), efforts were made to organize village meetings so that names of the beneficiaries were decided by consensus among the villagers. Such meetings improved the efficiency of service delivery by the Government.

Even though elections have not been held in Jharkhand, the members of the women's forum have been active in monitoring the programmes and schemes of the government. They identified areas where these schemes were not being implemented correctly and where they suspected that corruption was prevalent. The women brought this to the attention of the Member of the Legislative Assembly (MLA), who agreed that the corruption had to be stopped. However, the persons against whom the women had complained took them to court; and the case is still on. The women maintain that they are fighting for their rights and they will continue to do so, regardless of how much money they have to spend or the threats they receive, a vindication of their new confidence.

8.2.5. Women Entering the Political Arena

The PEVACs enabled voters to make informed choices. Their success is reflected in the fact that there was a perceptible decline in the number of dummy candidates, and in the rejection of nominations. There was increased voter participation and a larger number of women contested elections on reserved seats, as well as from general seats. Women's collectives were instrumental in identifying potential women candidates and in helping them to file their nominations.

8.3. The Way Forward

It is clear that the collaboration of partner organizations with SHGs, women's groups, trained citizen leaders and the people themselves, as part of the strategy of design and implementation, has added value to the project. Greater partnership between the government, stakeholders and NGOs can therefore make for effective interventions.

Training has been a valuable and core element of this capacity building project. Training must be seen as an ongoing process and should not be a onetime intervention. It is important to identify mechanisms that will support and strengthen the training process in the future. For example *Panchayat*i *Raj* training institutions at the state level should involve experienced NGOs in their training programmes, especially for the training of EWRs.

Most of the partner institutions focused their interventions on women and only a few institutions directed their efforts towards gender sensitization programmes. While such interventions are needed on a continued basis, gender sensitization training programmes need to be provided on an even larger scale to both women and men. In general, men were not targeted in the interventions and this is a serious gap that needs to be addressed in subsequent initiatives.

Experience sharing of EWRs needs to be actively encouraged, wider publicity to success stories and greater exposure for women's groups though visits and *sammelans* is required. Documentation and record keeping are additional areas that require attention. Another major component that needs to be strengthened is the interventions that are specifically targeted at women belonging to marginalized sections (*dalits* and tribals). While some partner organizations did organize an interface with other *panchayat* functionaries at the block and district level and tried to reach out to academics and media persons, this aspect too needs much more attention.

While the women's networks have played a very important role in developing individual and collective leadership, sustained efforts are needed to consolidate and stabilize these networks and they need to be given formal recognition. Many of the concerns identified at the beginning of the project remain, since the project duration was too short to develop institutional mechanisms that can take into consideration factors like caste and class divides, patriarchal forces and the heterogeneous nature of the groups. Yet, the interventions have contributed significantly towards building capacities and developing institutional mechanisms. Such interventions at the grassroots level, on such a scale can best be done by NGOs in the field. These interventions will need support in the near future, as more and more women candidates enter the political arena. To equip them to work constructively, an informed and sustainable framework needs to be created.

Building the capacities of women collectives has contributed immensely in developing leadership qualities among women. While the focus of most of the interventions was on building the capacities of EWRs, interventions also need to be scaled up to develop the capacities and skills of women's collectives and women leaders. This will ensure that the collectives form a support structure for EWRs and contribute to women's agency and their participation in governance structures.

8.4. Cases Studies

8.4.1. Muzzafarpur District, Bihar

Bihar is a landlocked state, located in the eastern part of the country. Bihar lies between West Bengal in the east and Uttar Pradesh in the west; to its north is Nepal, while Jharkhand lies to its south. The Bihar plain is bisected by the river Ganga, which flows through the state from west to east. The state has an area of 94,163 square kilometres and a population of 83 million. The population density is extremely high (880 people per square kilometre), compared to the average density of 324 people per square kilometre (2001), in the country as a whole.

Bihar is part of the fertile alluvial plain of the Gangetic valley and is well endowed with water resources due to the Ganga and its numerous tributaries. It is also rich in mineral resources and the main minerals that occur here are steatite, pyrite, quartzite, mica and limestone. The state has the lowest literacy rate in the country and the gap between the literacy rate for men and women is more than 25 percentage points. Only one in three women is literate and this reflects the limited access that women have to education and opportunities for growth.

Muzaffarpur district, with 4.5 percent of the population of Bihar, was chosen for the project intervention, and CENCORED was identified as the partner agency. The district has 16 blocks, Aurai, Bandra, Bochahan, Giaghat, Kanti, Katra, Kurhani, Marwan, Minapur, Motipur, Muraul, Mushari, Paroo, Sahebganj, Sakra and Saraiya and all these blocks were covered through extensive partnership with local NGOs.

8.4.1.1. Challenges

In the 2006 elections, 50 percent of the seats in Bihar were reserved for women candidates. Awareness amongst the people about the *Panchayati Raj* system and its benefits was low and there was lack of knowledge amongst them about the election process in general and about the reservation for women in particular. In the past, money and muscle power, caste and religion have played a major role in elections. Many *mukhiyas* created trouble during the election; they 'put up' their wives as front candidates and tried to mobilize support based on caste. Compounding the many problems in Muzaffarpur district were poverty and illiteracy.

In the perspective building phase, getting women to come out of their houses was quite difficult. Even after the election, many of the EWRs were unable to comprehend that they had become leaders and carried certain responsibilities and accountabilities.

Finding a substantial number of local level volunteers and ensuring that they stayed through the duration of the project was another challenge.

8.4.1.2. Strategies Adopted

The involvement of grass roots NGOs, who were familiar with village politics and dynamics, helped in implementation of the programme.

Formation of groups of young boys and girls: Soon after the project began, it became clear that the engagement of the family and the husband in particular, was critical to the participation of women in the programme. Children played an important role in building the confidence of the women, by encouraging and assisting them. Groups of young boys and girls (called *kishore* and *kishori* respectively) were formed, in a bid to encourage participation of the parents at *gram sabha* meetings.

Pre Election Voters Awareness Campaign (PEVAC): It was necessary to give prospective candidates and voters the opportunity to utilize their right to franchise freely and without fear. PEVACfacilitated the filing of nomination papers, persuaded people to exercise their franchise and upheld the enforcement of a model code of conduct. Incidents of violence and disturbances were fewer during the *Panchayati Raj* elections as compared to the Parliamentary and Assembly elections in Bihar. Felicitation ceremonies were held in Bihar, once the elections were completed. The occasion was used to congratulate the newly elected women representatives and publicly acknowledge their new status.

Networking and creation of forums: Networking between EWRs was attempted but was at a very preliminary stage and requires assistance to be sustainable in the long run. The EWRs needed support in their day to day activities and local resource persons played an important role in this regard. The programme has shown that capacity building of EWRs should be a continuous process, requiring regular inputs, continuous monitoring and follow-up. Therefore the duration of such projects should be a minimum of five years or the project should have a provision for extension.

8.4.2. Rajnandgaon District, Chhattisgarh

Chhattisgarh was carved out of the north-eastern part of Madhya Pradesh and became a separate state in November 2000. Located in the heart of India, Chhattisgarh's shares its borders with six states of the country; Uttar Pradesh to the north, Jharkhand to the north-east, Orissa to the east, Madhya Pradesh to the west and north-west, Maharashtra to the south-west and Andhra Pradesh to the south-east. The geographical area of the state covers 135,000 square kilometres and the total population in 2001 was 20.8 million people (2001 Census). Richly endowed with resources like forests and minerals (diamonds, gold, iron-ore, coal, corundum, bauxite, dolomite, lime, tin and granite), the people hold the earth and its forests in high regard and esteem.

The state has 16 districts and an urbanization rate of 20 percent, (less than the all-India urbanization rate of 27 percent). Chhattisgarh is one of nine states of the Union of India that falls under Schedule V of the Constitution, due to the high proportion of Scheduled Tribes (STs) in the population. The ST population is as high as 31.8 percent (2001 Census)—the highest in any state in the central Indian tribal belt. About 90 percent of the population is dependent on agriculture for their livelihood.

Mining has become the fastest growing sector of the economy and accounts for 13 percent of the Gross Domestic Product (GDP) of the state. A fall out of extractive industries like mining has meant the destruction of large tracts of land and forests and has led to unrest in the tribal heartland. Large parts of the state have seen conflict between the armed 'Maoists' and Naxals and the state armed militia of the Salwa Judum programme. The district of Rajnandgaon was

selected for the project and the partner agency identified was Participatory Action for Tribal Heritage (PATH). The district has nine blocks and 696 *gram panchayats*. Of the nine blocks, the project covered four blocks—Rajnandgaon, Dongargaon, Mohla and Ambagarh Chowki (Chowki). The first two blocks are situated closer to the district headquarters, while the other two are located in the interior of the district and are under Naxalite influence. These districts are under PESA (Panchayat Extension to Scheduled Areas). About 60 percent of the district is forested and collection of minor forest produce is an important occupation for the tribal communities.

8.4.2.1. Challenges

At the commencement of the project, the major challenge was to persuade the EWRs to assume greater responsibility and play a pro-active role in the affairs of their *panchayats*. It was essential to explain to male family members and to male representatives on the *panchayats* that the participation of the EWRs would facilitate discussions on pivotal issues that affected the well-being of the community as a whole.

Organizing trainings and ensuring participation was a difficult task, because EWRs and other women had to be encouraged and persuaded to give up their domestic and *panchayat* duties to attend the training sessions, outside their villages.

In a number of *panchayats*, elected members were content to simply implement Government schemes and showed little interest in making their own plans or taking any developmental initiatives. Raising local issues as part of the *gram sabha* agenda was often a major problem, as the agenda is pre-set by government officials and valuable time is lost in explaining government schemes and proposals, with little time left to discuss important local issues. The announcement of government initiated programmes and new schemes sometimes impacts the conduct of project activities and distracts the attention of participants from the training and capacity building programmes under the project.

Chowki and Mohla Blocks of Rajnandgaon district are Naxalite-affected; intimidation and threats prevented the villagers from participating in *gram sabhas* and *panchayat* activities. As a consequence, the PATH team faced stiff resistance and hurdles in their efforts to organize meetings, monitor *gram sabhas* and strengthen PRIs in these areas. This made the conduct of trainings both difficult and dangerous.

8.4.2.2. Strategies Adopted

Three broad areas were the focus of the programme: to enhance the capacity of EWRs, strengthen the PRI institutions and to achieve gender equity. Volunteers were used in each *panchayat*, as contact persons between PATH and *panchayat* representatives. The main strategies that were used to build the capacity of EWRs and women's groups were:

Training and capacity building programmes: A training needs survey was carried out in all the four blocks and PATH identified the factors responsible for the poor participation of women in public affairs. Subsequently, several types of training programmes were initiated during the course of the project. In addition to leadership skill development trainings and gender sensitization workshops, three-day residential trainings were organized to provide intensive training and sensitization to EWRs. These capacity building and training programmes have enabled women with low levels of literacy to function more effectively in their *panchayats* and understand their roles and responsibilities. Most women representatives in the programme have begun to manage *panchayat* affairs without help from their husbands, making the *sarpanch pati* (husband of the *sarpanch*) redundant in the targeted project areas.

Formation of networks and clusters: Networks of EWRs and cluster groups were created and these have enabled women to gradually enlarge the scope of their activities; in some villages they handle the Food for Work and National Rural Employment Guarantee Programme (NREGP). In other villages, the issue of encroachment of land has been taken up by women representatives. Women's groups have been instrumental in stopping the sale of liquor and have also taken up the issue of males acting as 'proxies' for women *sarpanch*s, and announced that male *panchayat* representatives cannot take decisions on behalf of the EWRs.

Setting up a Panchayat Information Centre: A district level Panchayat Information Centre was set up to provide information on *panchayat* matters and guidance to the community and to young people to enable them to strengthen local self governnment in their areas. The main learnings from the Rajnandgaon awareness campaign are:

— Basic training on the role and functioning of PRI is instrumental in bringing women out of their assigned roles and spaces and helping them claim their rights and function effectively. Training should be a continuous and on-going process. Experience sharing, information dissemination and exposure visits and *sammelans* (large gathering) must be an important component of any exercise that seeks to empower EWRs.

— Women's networks are an important medium of empowerment and change and they should be given formal recognition. EWRs can play an important role in monitoring basic services in their villages, a role that they should be encouraged to pursue.

— Better record-keeping and documentation methods are required, so that programmes can be adequately evaluated and shortcomings addressed.

8.4.3. Rewari District, Haryana

Haryana became a separate state of India on 1 November, 1966. It has 1.37 percent of the geographical area of the country (44,212 square kilometres) and less than 2 percent of India's population. Haryana has grown and developed rapidly in the past three decades. Both agriculture and industry have seen high rates of growth and Haryana enjoys the unique distinction of having provided electricity, tarred roads and potable drinking water to all its villages. It is among the most prosperous states in India, with one of the highest per-capita incomes.

Lying as it does on the northern trade route linking the Gangetic plain to Kabul and beyond, Haryana's embattled past has moulded the traditional institutions of its dominant groups. Despite the outward modernity and signs of the globalizing economy, its rural societies remain locked in a rigid social framework, in which caste and inter-caste *panchayats* control social relations, meting out punishment for violations of customary law and the caste hierarchy. Women and Scheduled Castes (19.3 percent of the population) have remained oppressed, *purdah*is prevalent in many parts and persecution of boys and girls attempting to break the caste divide is common.

The low status of women is reflected in the highly adverse sex ratio in the state (861 women for every 1,000 men). Haryana is one of the four states of the country where the child sex ratio (0-6 year age group) has declined drastically in the last two decades. Gender inequity is apparent in the gap in the literacy rate (a difference of over 20 percentage points) and in the enrolment of girls in school (24.2 percent of girls were never enrolled in school as opposed to 6.9 percent of the boys).

Although women are important contributors to the farm economy, particularly in livestock rearing and dairying, the workforce participation rate is only 28 percent. In the political sphere, representation at the state and national level is low but in the *panchayats*, women and women belonging to the SC community, both occupy more seats than those reserved for them. Rewari district was selected for the programme. The partner agency was Social Centre for Rural Initiative and Advancement (SCRIA). Rewari district borders Gurgaon to its east and north east, Rohtak on the north, Mahendragarh district to its west and Alwar district (Rajasthan) to the south east. The district is spread over 1,559 square kilometres and has two sub-divisions, Rewari and Kosli. It has five development blocks-Jatusana, Khol, Rewari, Nahar and Bawalwhich were all covered. There were 398 villages and 348 *gram panchayats* in the project area.

8.4.3.1. Challenges

As the project commenced, the primary hurdle to be contended with was the lack of interest in the training courses amongst the EWRs.The highly patriarchal society in which the women live makes it difficult for them to find time for anything outside their domestic sphere. Household chores, including caring for the family and animals—fetching water, cooking and cleaning, health care, gathering fodder, take up considerable time and energy. In the few instances when EWRs were keen to attend the trainings, the men in their families strongly opposed their participation in the entire process. There was indifference among male PRI representatives to issues like inclusive governance and gender sensitization. They were only willing to participate in programmes that brought funds to the *panchayat* or schemes that involve substantial financial dealings.

The pre-election campaign in Rewari faced several challenges and uncertainties. *Panchayat* elections were declared at short notice, which made the filing of nominations a hurried affair, especially for newcomers. When the elections were announced harvesting was in full swing, a busy time for everyone. An 'atmosphere of uncertainty' was created when the Government brought about sudden amendments to the *Panchayat* Act of the state, to prepone the elections. The non cooperation of Government officials in the interface dialogues, which were organized to foster multi—stakeholder partnerships was another indication of the lack of commitment to decentralized government.

Low literacy levels and the educational attainments of the EWRswere a constraint that limited access to information, particularly from government sources. Many EWRs were forced to rely on male relatives for information and interpretation which meant they were unable to function independently.

8.4.3.2. Strategies Adopted

Intensive staff training and continuous feedback on strategy implementation: Field campaigns covered hundreds of villages in Haryana. Prior to the campaigns, a three-day pre-campaign workshop was organized with the resource persons, where objectives of the programme, logistics, events/schedule, implementation details, role of concerned resource persons, expected outcomes along with participants' profile were discussed. Post campaign, a one-day feedback workshop was organized. Programmes were reviewed on a weekly basis. Every alternate week an issue of concern was taken up for a two hour open discussion session with the team leaders. At every stage of the training, a training of trainers (TOT) programme was conducted and at the end of the training there was a feedback session. Internal reviews and planning for future initiatives were done on a fortnightly basis.

Continuous impact assessment enabled mid-term course correction: The partner agency demonstrated flexibility in implementing strategies that did not draw a response from key members of the target groups. The reluctance of EWRs to attend trainings specially convened for them and the lack of response on the part of elected men representatives (EMRs) on the issue of 'inclusive and accountable governance' led to a decision to change the strategy from direct training to awareness campaigns and 'hands on' practical trainings. Similarly, after a desultory attempt to organize gender sensitization trainings for male representatives in October 2005, the effort was dropped and work deferred.

Reliance on people's institutions – the Sangathans: Older *sangathans* (women's groups) set up by the partner institution SCRIA earlier, were among the most active promoters of the project's goals. They quickly understood the issues and were able to draw new recruits into their fold, to further project activities. These sangathans and their federations were able to make decisions and take action independently, with minimal support from the PIA.

Community participation: One of the innovative strategies adopted by SCRIA was the use of a tele-helplineto connect EWRs and members of SHGs. This provided SHG members with direct and immediateaccess to EWRs and enabled them to raise issues of concern to them. This idea needs to be scaled-up and the use of technology to make information accessible to the people is one that needs to be pursued. The use of a wide range of volunteers from the project area provided a cadre of social workers, who could be relied on to sustain interest in the activities without personal gain or benefit. They were an invaluable aid to SCRIA teams which worked for three years to cover the entire district of Rewari.

The first phase of the programme focused on awareness creation. In the future, more in-depth information needs to be provided to EWRs on the functioning of local governments and their role in them. Technical expertise and information, village level planning, checking accounts and learning book keeping procedures should be part of the second level training.

Continued hand-holding is required by the EWRs, particularly in their interaction with district level functionaries. The networks *and* sangathans *that were an important* part of the strategy in Rewari need to be made sustainable. A common sangathan comprising of PRI representatives across districts is another idea that needs to be discussed and explored further. New strategies and methods need to be employed to deal with the resistance shown by EWRs in participating in trainings. The State Training Institutes need to involve CSOs in training activities.

The plummeting child sex ratio in Rewari is an area of concern and the EWRs can be motivated and mobilized to monitor this by ensuring proper records of pregnancies, abortions, births and deaths. Better record keeping in all future activities is required, so that better analysis of data can be undertaken.

8.4.4. Palamu District, Jharkhand

One of the youngest states in the country, Jharkhand came into being on 15 November, 2000. It is known for its mineral resources, including uranium, mica, bauxite, gold, silver, magnite, dolomite, fireclay, quartz, feldspar, coal, iron and copper. It is also rich in forest resources and has a forest cover of more than 29 percent.

Jharkhand has a difficult geographical terrain and insufficient infrastructure; only 8,464 of its 32,620 villages are connected by road and only 14,667 villages have electricity. The per-capita income is low and the literacy rate is 54 percent. About 26 percent of the people belong to the Scheduled Tribes and another 12 percent belong to the

Scheduled Castes. The Jharkhand *Panchayati Raj* Act was passed in March, 2001. The first ever *panchayat* polls in Jharkhand were scheduled to be held in 2006, but they have still not been held as there is a case pending in the Supreme Court.

Five blocks of Palamu district (Daltonganj, Chainpur, Satbarwa, Patan and Lesliganj) were chosen for the project. The partner agency that implemented the project was the Integrated Development Foundation (IDF).

8.4.4.1. Challenges

In Jharkhand the *panchayati raj* system is largely non existent. In this context, the implementation of government schemes is one of the biggest challenges for the state. In the absence of any elections and the consequent setting up of *panchayati raj* systems, it is no surprise that in Jharkhand people's participation in local government is extremely limited.

The main challenge faced by the project was that the people were not aware of their role. Women were unaware of the reservation for them in local government and the male members of the community were reluctant to allow women to participate in *gram sabhas*. They were not open to the idea of women contesting the elections. The absence of a functioning *panchayati raj* system has resulted in the emergence of 'middlemen' between the people and the government, who facilitate the implementation of government programmes. This has often led to incorrect selection of beneficiaries and corruption in the implementation of programmes.

Participation at the *gram sabha* has been weak and the project tried to focus on increased participation at the *gram sabha* level. In many places, only the *gram pradhans* were identified. However they did not have any formal orders and as a result most of them did not have the power to take decisions. At the block level, the key person is the BDO and he/she is responsible for the implementation of schemes and programmes. However in the absence of the *panchayati raj* functionaries, participation of the people in development activities continued to be limited. Some guidance and handholding by local NGOs played an important role in furthering the required coordination between the government and the people.

The project aimed at sensitization of the community towards women's participation and the empowerment of women, so that they can participate meaningfully in decentralized governance systems, as and when they become a reality. The uncertainty regarding the holding of the elections meant that the project was largely limited to creating awareness and preparing the ground for subsequent effective participation of women. Creating awareness of NREGA and RTI were amongst the activities undertaken towards the later part of the project.

8.4.4.2. Strategies Adopted

It was essential to create a gender sensitive environment to encourage women to function effectively in public spaces. Systems were created that helped to equip women and women's groups, so that they are able to better negotiate their entitlements from PRI resources and participate in decisionmaking. Several activities were carried out to create a favourable environment in villages, so that the community, particularly the women, can internalize the concept of PRI.

Training and capacity building initiatives and awareness creation: Trainings and workshops were undertaken for the *gram pradhans*, SHG and cluster members and programme functionaries. Some of the other activities undertaken for environment building were: *nukkad nataks* explaining the various features of NREGA, mock polling exercises to familiarize people with the electoral process, broadcasting of radio programmes focusing on PRI and the importance of women's participation in PRI, the creation and distribution of relevant IEC material.

Village level meetings were held to discuss different government sponsored schemes. Preceding the aam sabha (general assembly) to identify beneficiaries under schemes like Dindayal Awas Yojana, Indira Awas Yojana, Annapurna Yojana, efforts were made to organize village meetings so that names of the deserving persons could be decided by consensus. The villagers themselves decided who should be benefited under specific schemes; middlemen were discouraged. Such meetings were important to bring people together on the issues that concern the development of their village and to thwart the practice of middlemen that has emerged in the state. The meetings helped to improve the access to government schemes and the efficiency of service delivery system.

Strengthening SHGs and formation of clusters and forums: In many villages in the project area, SHGs were in existence. Efforts were made to strengthen these SHGs so that they can act as pressure group at the *gram sabha* level. The SHGs were in turn consolidated under a larger institution called a cluster, which could emerge as a pressure group at the *panchayat* level. As a result of rigorous input towards strengthening of women's clusters, women gained recognition at the *panchayat* level. Since women had no recognition or voice at the block level, efforts were made to consolidate the clusters at the block level as well. Women's forums were established and the representatives of women's forum were selected unanimously. Monthly meetings of women's forums at the block level were initiated.

Information Centres: In order to disseminate information regarding *panchayati raj*, recent development schemes and news of local importance, Information Centres were established at the *panchayat* level. Awareness regarding the importance of *gram sabhas* has increased and there is an increase in the presence of women in *gram sabhas* and *aam sabhas*. Several initiatives at the village level have been taken by women and the women have built up the confidence to contest the *panchayat* elections when they are held. The environment building exercises have created an environment that is supportive of women's participation at the *gram sabha* meetings.

8.4.5. Dewas District, Madhya Pradesh

Despite the carving out of Chhattisgarh in 2000, Madhya Pradesh continues to be the second largest state in the country in area (308,000 square kilometres). With a population of 60.34 million people, the population density is 196 people per square kilometre, substantially less than that for the country (324 people per square kilometre). Agriculture is the mainstay of the economy and 74.73 percent of the people live in the rural areas. Foodgrains (rice and wheat) and oilseeds (soyabean) are the main crops, but sugarcane and cotton are also grown. The state is rich in minerals like iron ore, manganese ore, bauxite, copper, dolomite, diamonds and limestone.

Dewas district, located in the western part of Madhya Pradesh, was chosen for the capacity building of (EWRs) programme. Samavesh was identified as the partner agency.

The name of the programme, *Sakhi Pehal*, emerged from discussions amongst the participating women. *Sakhi Pehal* was initiated in June 2004, in three blocks of Dewas district—Khategaon, Sonkach and Tonk Khurd. Samavesh was the partner agency in Khategaon block and two other NGOs Jansahas and Dewas Gauri Mahila Samiti were responsible for Sonkach block and Tonk Khurd block respectively. There is a high proportion of people belonging to the SC community in Sonkach and Tonk Khurd blocks and a high proportion of STs in Khategaon block.

8.4.5.1. Challenges

Deeply entrenched social prejudices and caste-based discrimination were major factors that inhibited the implementation of the project in Dewas, particularly in the early stages. The project area was located in a remote area, inhabited largely by people belonging to the SC and ST communities, with very low levels of literacy. Initially it was decided that girls who had completed Class X11 should be recruited as *saathins* (village level professional women workers) to enable smooth functioning of the programme, but since girls with this level of education were not available, it was decided to recruit girls with education up to Class VIII if necessary, who were then trained during the course of the project. There was stiff resistance and occasionally hostility from the elected male representatives.

The *saathins* faced a number of difficulties in their work. Concerns of security made women reluctant to travel out of their village. Some women dropped out of the programme because of opposition from their families; others dropped out because of the domestic constraints and workloads. These factors made the task of empowering the *gram sabhas* more difficult.

Among the early challenges was how to identify an approach that would motivate and involve the women in the programme, encouraging them to take ownership and participate at each step.

Another challenge that the programme encountered was that information was often withheld from the EWRs or not made available to them on time. Women did not get prior information about *panchayat* meetings and sometimes issues raised by women were not recorded in the minutes of the *panchayats*.

8.4.5.2. Strategies Adopted

This programme was called *Sakhi Pehal* by the women themselves; this gave the women a sense of ownership of the programme.A number of strategies were adopted under this programme, some of which are detailed here.

Common Platforms: Under the *Sakhi Pehal* programme, collectives were formed at different levels, as women tried to create pressure groups that focused attention on issues relevant to women's development. Learning from the experiences of other groups and the partner agencies, it was decided to facilitate the formation of village platforms, where women could participate actively to learn, debate and take their struggle forward at their own pace. Women who were active in SHGs, women's representatives and women leaders in the villages were encouraged to come together on a common platform, to form *sakhi manchs*. These *sakhi manchs* were critical to the strategy that was adopted. To support this strategy and provide the *manchs* with maximum local support, the women leaders created a team of *saathins*, drawn from the young women in the villages. The training and capacity-building of the *saathins* was the responsibility of the partner agency team.

Existing SHGs were strengthened and new SHGs were formed in Dewas, to act as a base for developing bigger forums. The block-level *sakhi manch*, the cluster *manch* and village *manch* trained their members for community mobilization, monitoring and support and prepared them for active participation in the process of governance. As a result, these networks (*manchs*) generated interest, confidence, initiative and a sense of self-esteem in the women. In the initial stages, male members were not allowed to attend the *sakhi manch* meetings, but gradually, male members were allowed in the *Sakhi Pehal* meetings, in an attempt towards gender mainstreaming. Provision of larger common platforms in the form of annual seminars at the block level brought more women together and gave them a feeling of collective strength. *Mahila sammelans* (women's forums) were organized in all the blocks (Sonkach, Khategaon and Tonk Khurd) in March 2006 and were attended by over 1,500 people. Another *mahila sammelan* was organized in March 2007, which was attended by over 2,300 women. A *sammelan* is also organized every year in March on the occasion of International Women's Day. Such activities have helped to bring about a positive change in the attitude of men, who extended logistic and moral support to the women. A youth *sammelan* was organized at Khategaon block headquarters, in September, 2007 to encourage the younger generation to engage in the development of the village; this *sammelan* was attended by 325 boys and girls from 66 villages, who enthusiastically shared their experiences and views.

Contact based training: The contact-based training for capacity building faced several constraints. The lack of cooperation from male associates and domestic prioritiesprecluded the participation of many women, leading to low attendance by EWRs. To counter this problem of poor participation, a mid-course strategy correction was made, and the *saathins* were encouraged to visit the EWRs at home, at least once a fortnight. They discussed issues of concern, provided information about ongoing programmes and developments and motivated the EWRs towards better participation. They also interacted with their families, in an effort to influence them and elicit their cooperation.

Planning and review meetings: Regular meetings were held with stakeholders of the capacity building programme to plan and review developments constructively, and prepare for further capacity building. Preparatory meetings were organized by the respective *sakhi manchs* to identify and discuss issues, as well as to explain procedures for making applications and raising matters in the *gram sabhas*. A review of the earlier *gram sabha* meetings to analyse and discuss the pending issues helped to plan for their satisfactory resolution.

Recognizing that the panchayat can be effective only when *gram sabhas* function smoothly, special attention was given to gram *sabha* mobilization. Efforts were made to convey information regarding the meeting to all villagers, by talking to the *panchayat* secretary and the *sarpanch*, before the date of the *gram sabha*.

Committee meetings were held periodically to review the programme and its functioning. Attempts were also made to hold meetings with several important district and state-level *panchayat* functionaries such as the *Zilla Panchayat* President, the District Collector and the Commissioner of Panchayats and Social Justice (Madhya Pradesh), which proved very useful in assessing the progress and sorting out small administrative matters. The empowering effect of these meetings encouraged the women to take greater interest in village issues and build up pressure on the concerned functionaries to hold *gram sabha* meetings regularly. The *sarpanch* began to provide opportunities to women to raise and discuss issues. The women utilized the procedural knowledge that they had acquired to good effect and were able to discuss their problems with the local MLA with confidence and full conviction.

Learning visits: Exposure visits facilitated experiential learning *for the women. In addition to visits to* anganwadis *and midday meal centres,* manch *leaders participated in a Science and* Culture Mela, visited the Women and Child Development Department in Dewas and obtained information on the various *schemes of the distict* panchayat. *These visits gave them* confidence, experience and information, which they shared with *their co-workers in* manch *meetings. An exciting and moraleboosting* experience was the visit to the All India Radio (AIR) *station in Bhopal by the EWRs and* manch *leaders, where they* recorded their experiences. The women visited Jaipur (Rajasthan) and attended a *panch mahotsav* (a convention of elected women representatives) along with several *panchayat* leaders from Madhya Pradesh, Maharashtra and Rajasthan, as well as other women leaders. Women *panch*, *sarpanch*, *sakhi manch* leaders, *saathins* and cluster coordinators from Khategaon, Tonk Khurd and Sonkach blocks visited Gadchiroli village in Maharashtra and interacted with organizations like Aalochana and Aamhi Amachya Arogya Sathi, that implement similar programmes in these areas. They were inspired by the level of cleanliness in the villages of Maharashtra and learnt of the total sanitation project as well about the special *gram sabhas*that are mandatory and unique to Maharashtra.

The confidence and learning gained from visiting other panchayats resulted in the demand for exclusive women's *gram sabha* meetings in their own villages. This allowed women to openly discuss their issues without the restricting presence of the older men of the village and the consequent need for *purdah*.

Communication tools: Video documentation of the main activities of the programme (*gram sabhas, manch* meetings, *mahila sammelans*, workshops and interviews) was very valuable in preparing short films for capacity-building trainings. The preparation of booklets on *panchayati raj* issues also proved helpful.

The publication of '*Apni Paati*' – the programme newsletter (from March 2006 onwards) has helped to bring the activities of the *Sakhi Manch* and their views into the public domain. One of the main learnings from the programme was that capacity building of women can be done effectively only by bringing them together on a common platform. These platforms increase women's confidence and courage and bring about changes in the way they think. Some *saathins* argued that unless women had some pressing issues they would not come forward to join the *manch*. Yet, when women from some SHGs started meeting regularly to discuss social and economic issues, they themselves began defining their demands. Thus they began moving towards the formation of a *manch* on their own. Once the *Sakhi Manch* was formed in one village, it had a snow-balling effect. Women raised their issues on their own initiative in the *gram sabha* (although they were not familiar with the rules and procedures of the *sabha*). Soon women's groups were formed in all villages and the SHGs were the main stay of these groups.

8.4.6. Gadchiroli District, Maharashtra

Maharashtra, located on the west coast of India is the second most populous state and the third largest in area. It extends over an area of 307,713 square kilometres and the population is 96.87 million people (2001 Census). One of the richer states of the country, its per capita income is 40 percent higher than the all-India average. Maharashtra's income is derived largely from the secondary and tertiary sectors.

Agriculture has not made the state self-sufficient in food grains but commercial crops have given rise to a vibrant agro-processing industry.Maharashtra has a 720 km long coastline stretching from Daman in the north to Goa in the south and the state is encircled by the states of Gujarat, Madhya Pradesh, Chhattisgarh, Andhra Pradesh and Karnataka. Maharashtra has the country's second largest urban population, about 43 persons out of every 100 live in towns and cities. It also has a large migrant population. Gadchiroli (the block chosen for the project) is about 960 kms from Pune. Aalochana was the partner agency for the project and it in turn collaborated with a local NGO, Aamhi Aamchya Arogya Sathi (AAAS), for the execution of the project.Gadchiroli is a primarily tribal region.

Eight of the 12 blocks and some villages from the four other blocks fall within the purview of the Tribal Self-Governance Act. The Gond, Madia, Kanwar and Pardhan are the major tribes that inhabit this region. Of the 12 blocks, five blocks were selected for implementation of the project. Out of these, three blocks.

Gadchiroli, Kurkheda and Armori were selected for intensive work and formed the main project area, while Korchi and Dhanora were selected as extended project areas. Five *gram panchayats* were selected from each of the three blocks- Gadchiroli, Kurkheda and Armori.

In all, 15 *gram panchayats*, that also include group *gram panchayats*, were the focus of the intensive activity. The number of villages covered under a *gram panchayat* was sometimes three to four villages. The villages comprised of small *tolas* and *padas* (clusters of houses). The primary occupation in the area is agriculture and paddy is the main crop. Besides this, forests are a major source of livelihood and the people are dependent on minor forest produce.

8.4.6.1. Challenges

The challenging political situation in Gadchiroli prevented many people from participating in the programmes. A number of *bandhs* (strikes) were called by the Naxalites, when public transport came to a standstill. Poor communication systems, especially in the interior, discouraged women from attending training programmes, as they had to walk miles to get to the training venue. Most EWRs belonged to the younger age group and they were doubly burdened with child-care and household chores, which made it difficult for them to attend training camps that were often of three to four days duration. In some cases, family members opposed their participation in activities, which were located outside the village. Widespread and acute poverty inhibited the participation of people, in particular of women, in the programme. This also affected the planning of the events, as participation rates varied by season.

The gender gap in literacy remains high in Gadchiroli. Over 50 percent of the women are illiterate. This affects their status, efficiency and independence, both at home and in local government and business.

Absence of trained social activists and trainers created pressure on the few trainers that were available in the region. Trained staff was not easily available at the local level. Among field workers, the drop out rate of ST volunteers was high; a majority of the field workers were from OBCs. Male colleagues opposed the demand of the EWRs that 10 percent of the budget be spent on the women's component plan. Even *gram sevaks* and *sachivs* opposed the EWRs, as the money which should have been earmarked for women and child welfare had so far been diverted by them for other purposes.

Few elected women completed the full round of training. The partner agencies felt that it is only when women realized that their participation can change their situation that they were willing to attend the trainings. This was a challenge which the partner agency tried to address. Government officials were often ill-informed about *panchayat* matters and on many occasions unhelpful. Moreover, government officials keep changing and this required constant liaison with new officials. The absence of caste certificates prevented many women belonging to the SC and ST communities from standing for elections, even for reserved seats. This was a major problem encountered by the project partners in promoting women candidates for reserved posts especially during the PEVAC phase. Most women had never contested an election before and the need for such certificates had therefore not arisen earlier. The procedure for acquiring these certificates was cumbersome and involved going back to the parental village in most cases. In many instances, the certificates could not be procured in time to allow filing of nominations.

8.4.6.2. Strategies Adopted

A number of initiatives were taken as part of the capacity building programme in Maharashtra among which the specific focus was to bring EWRs and women from the community together for trainings, in an attempt to bridge the barriers between them. An attempt was made to include men in the trainings wherever possible, to sensitize them to gender issues and issues of participation and minimize intra-family conflict.

Training for EWRs and SHGs: Past experience showed that EWRs often faced opposition from their families and seldom got any cooperation from them or from the men in the village or even from the *gram panchayats*. Support usually comes from women's groups or mahila mandals, women's SHGs or *bachat ghats* extend both moral and physical support. Training programmes therefore included EWRs as well as women from the SHGs in the villages. This strategy was successful in almost all the villages where it was adopted. The partner agency, AAAS provided a base for the execution of the project through its network of SHGs. Since the major objective was to prepare women to enter the political arena and participate effectively in politics, work was focused largely on capacity building programmes, creating the right resource materials (which should be easily accessible), setting up of resource centres, holding networking programmes to bring the women together, building up their confidence and enabling them to speak out.

A participatory methodology was adopted for training. Resource persons who were well-versed with village administration processes, rules and regulations, who had worked at the village level and had an understanding of women's issues, were selected as trainers. Every issue was analysed through the gender-lens. This helped women to make connections between their real life situations and their powerlessness in the *panchayats*. Training programmes have led to information transmission and a campaign was started across the project area to encourage women to assert their right over the resources assigned for them. The process of this assertion of women's rights over the funds earmarked for them has been empowering in itself.

Gender sensitization for men: Male representatives and youth groups were included in the project, to facilitate interaction between men and women representatives, to impart gender sensitization to the men and to create a supportive environment for the programme. The project envisioned capacity building of government functionaries to make them gender sensitive and to enable them to work in cooperation with the women. One of the obstacles in the effective functioning of the EWRs is the non-cooperative attitude of *gram sevaks* and BDOs. The project provided for *gram sevak* training and helped them to look at the problems women face more sensitively and to extend their cooperation. Creating such a gender sensitive environment at the *gram panchayat* level was an outcome of the project.

Mobilizing the gram sabhas: Since 63 percent of the SC and 58.5 percent of ST households in the district were in the BPL category, they were eligible for inclusion in poverty alleviation schemes like IAY, NREGS and the Maharashtra Rural Employment Guarantee Scheme (MREGS). The official lists required revision urgently, as they were incomplete. These communities could be mobilized through the *gram sabhas* with the support of the *gram panchayat* and women's groups to ensure inclusion of all genuine BPL families in the lists. This required the cooperation of block/*tehsil* level functionaries to overcome stone-walling by vested interests. The opposition came from the dominant castes and non tribals, who often benefited by giving false certificates and accessing the resources under these schemes. A strategic alliance between EWRs and SHG members led to a fruitful co-operation between the two groups.

The project has established the need to support NGOs in training and awareness-raising activities for EWRs as well as for the wider community, particularly in remote areas with poor communication links. The state's 11 *Panchayati Raj* training institutes and the Yashwant Rao Chavan Academy of Development Administration (YASHADA) provide training to about 26,660 elected *panchayat* representatives annually, covering about 130,000 representatives in a five year term. There are approximately 230,000 elected representatives and therefore there are roughly 100,000 representatives (including 34,000 women), who are not able to access the training offered by government institutes. Thus it is important that the non-governmental sector be involved in *Panchayati Raj* training, particularly for women, at the village and block levels.

8.4.7. Anugul District, Orissa

Orissa with a population of 36.71 million people is located on the eastern coast, bounded by the Bay of Bengal in the east, West Bengal in the north-east, Bihar in the north, Madhya Pradesh in the west and Andhra Pradesh in the south. The state has the third lowest population density (236 persons per square kilometre in 2001) among the major states of India, ahead of only Rajasthan and Madhya Pradesh. There is significant inter-district variation; Khurda has a population density of 666 persons per square kilometre while Kandhamal has a population density of only 81 persons per square kilometre. There is therefore spatial concentration of the population; for example, coastal Orissa has 52 percent of the population and 25 percent of the area. The rate of urbanization in Orissa (at 14.91 percent) is one of the lowest among the major states of India. The sex ratio in Orissa was 972 in 2001, the third highest among major Indian states, lower than only Tamil Nadu (986) and Kerala (1058). About 22 percent of the population belongs to tribal communities. They are largely concentrated in the north-western and south-western part of the state. They depend heavily on forests for their livelihood. People belonging to the Scheduled Castes account for about 17 percent of the population. They are mostly concentrated in the four (undivided) coastal districts of Balasore, Cuttack, Ganjam and Puri.

Anugul district, carved out of the erstwhile Dhenkanal district in 1992, was selected for the capacity building programme in Orissa. The Institute for Socio-Economic Development (ISED) was selected as the partner agency to execute the programme. The blocks where the project was implemented were Anugul, Banarpal, Talcher, Kaniha, Pallahara, Chhendipada, Athamallik and Kishorenagar.

8.4.7.1. Challenges

Since the passing of the 73rd Amendment to the Constitution, three *Panchayat* elections have been held in Orissa; in each election more than 35,000 women have been elected to positions in the *Panchayat*. The visibility and impact of most EWRs has tended to be extremely limited. Many of them do not see the need to attend *palli sabha*and *gram sabha* meetings and often remain silent participants at *panchayat* meetings. Given the constraints that women operate under and their own perceptions, long term plans and strategies are required to enable women to use the available opportunities for their own advancement as well as to assist them in influencing the processes of development in their favour. Specific support was required (beyond technical training), so that women could come together and linkages between women's organizations and elected bodies could be established. Facilitation was required for the creation of forums of EWRs at various levels. These forums enabled them to share their experiences and build up a supportive peer network. These networks also enabled the EWRs to achieve unity and consensus on common concerns and helped them to function as pressure groups. Many EWRs were dependent on the support of their husbands and other family members. The challenge was to involve *anganwadi* workers, leaders of SHGs, teachers and other women who were active and played a prominent role in the affairs of local government, in this initiative. In addition, key government functionaries at the district and block level associated with *panchayati raj* were engaged in the effort.

8.4.7.2. Strategies Adopted

In Anugul district, linkages between SHG members, *anganwadi* workers, EWRs and women have been instrumental in effecting changes at the *panchayat* level. There has been a continuous process of empowerment and awareness building, which is evident in the high representation that women enjoy in the *panchayats* in the district (40 percent of the seats in PRIs are represented by women).

Mahila Manch Panchayat Nirvachan Abhiyan: Enthusiasm for decentralized governance among the people and members of the forum (a informal association of EWR, SHG members and *anganwadi* workers) was created by continuous interaction among the members, initiatives for leadership building and providing access to information through learning materials. A decision was taken to contest all key positions in the PRI elections held in February/March 2007. This initiative was called the '*Mahila Manch Panchayat Nirvachan Abhiyan*', a campaign for *panchayat* elections by the womens' forum.

While 33 percent of the seats in PRI are reserved for women, in Anugul district, women contested elections in 42 percent of the seats and were elected to 40 percent of the seats. The *Abhiyan* concentrated on mobilizing participation at cluster meetings as well as participation at all tiers of the *panchayat* system. As cluster meetings began to focus on social issues such as domestic violence, harassment for dowry, opening of liquor shops, the participation rate of women increased. Women put pressure to ensure enumeration of beneficiaries under social security schemes such as the old age and the widows' pension schemes, IAY (housing scheme for the rural poor), Annapurnaand Antyodaya Anna Yojana. At several meetings, men vehemently opposed the participation of women. In some *palli sabha* meetings (at Basala, Budhapanka and Badakera), women were not allowed to participate; forum members complained to the concerned authorities and the *palli sabhas* were re-convened, to ensure the participation of women. The clusters grew in confidence, as they were entrusted with a variety of tasks. For example, the clusters in Sankhapur, Kanjara, Jokub were entrusted the task of running the mid-day meal programme in their schools.

Similarly CF members in Badakera *panchayat* were asked to supply packed food to *anganwadi* centres. In many villages, cluster members ran the PDS system successfully. Training under various programmes: Forty SHG members belonging to the forum were given training under the district sanitation programme. They have since played an active role in implementing the programme. Forum members became members of Parent-Teachers Associations and Mother-Teachers Associations in a number of villages, which has led to a perceptible improvement in the quality of education in these villages. About 200 women were given computer training and seven computers were installed, two each in Anugul and Banarpal blocks and three in Talcher block.

Building communication and mobilizing resources: Forum members brought out a bi-monthly bulletin called *Mahila Samarthya* which documents the various issues and success stories that dot the road to women's empowerment. Three forum members participated in a *Gramsat*programme on Women's Empowerment and *Panchayat* Finance. The *Gramsat* team interviewed Pratima Behera and Tulsi Nayak, identifying them as empowered *panchayat* representatives, for their programme. These examples illustrate the confidence that many of the EWRs display, when they are given appropriate opportunities.

Women members have been active in mobilizing resources from the National Aluminium Company Pvt. Ltd. (NALCO), and through income generation activities like dairy, poultry and pisciculture, all reflective of their enhanced confidence and zeal. Today, women PRI members have become more articulate and assertive in the *gram panchayat* meetings and some of the *sarpanchs* are particularly eloquent. The *sarpanchs* of Gobra, Basantapur, Batisuan, Pedipathar and Jamudoli have set examples for other women representatives to emulate.

Thus the experience in Anugul district has been extremely positive, even though there was some initial resistance, but much remains to be done before women can claim their rightful place in governance.

8.4.8. Jodhpur District, Rajasthan

Rajasthan has a geographical area of 342,239 square kilometres, and is India's largest state. Fifty six million people live in the state (2001 Census) and the population density is 165 persons per square kilometre. There is diverse physiography, ranging from the desert and semi-arid regions of western Rajasthan to the greener belt east of the Aravallis and the hilly tracts of the southeast. More than 60 percent of the state's area is desert, with sparsely distributed population. Rajasthan is deficient in water (surface and ground). Ground water at many places is unfit for human and livestock consumption. Literacy levels, especially for girls, are among the lowest in the country.

Jodhpur district was selected for the project intervention and the partner institution was Unnati –Organization for Development Education. The project was imple-mented in nine blocksof which five blocks (Mandore, Balesar, Bhopalgarh, Shergarh and Osian were covered by Unnati, while the other four blocks (Phalodi, Baap, Luni and Bilada) were covered by local NGOs, that had a long association with Unnati.

8.4.8.1. Challenges

In Rajasthan, women were actively prevented from participating in *panchayat* activities by male family members and other members of the *panchayats* itself. The male members often insisted on attending meetings in place of EWRs. Male *panchayat* members took advantage of the low levels of literacy and lack of knowledge and experience to take decisions in the absence of EWRs and tried to keep them out of important meetings. The practical realities of poor rural women's daily existence also kept them out of the *gram panchayats*. Burdened with housework and child care responsibilities and sometimes also employment prevented many EWRs from active participation in the activities of their *gram panchayats*. The low self-confidence and poor self-image also kept many women away.

To enable women to participate and function effectively at every stage, capacity building support was needed from the beginning of the election process and through the tenure of the elected representatives. An enabling environment was required for the recognition of women as leaders and the elimination of proxy candidates. Continued hand-holding support to EWRs was required throughout their tenures.

8.4.8.2. Strategies Adopted

The capacity building was not limited to structured training programmes. The EWRs were assisted on a range of practical and day-to-day issues and aspects, including gram sabha mobilization, interaction between officials and EWRs on finalization of the BPL list, campaigns on health issues, girl child school enrolment, voter awareness, monitoring of drought relief work, mid-day-meal programme and the functioning of *anganwadis*.

The objective was to make grass-roots democracy effective and to strengthen the community and their representatives. While the capacity building of the PRI representatives was a major focus, the wider community also needed to be enabled and empowered. All of this required continuous sharing, learning, reviewing and planning during the course of the project. Among the most successful initiatives in Rajasthan were the setting of Panchayat Resource Centres and the use of radio for awareness creation among the common people on developmental issues and PRI functioning.

Setting up Panchayat Resource Centres and Local Resource Groups: Panchayat Resource Centres (PRCs) were located on the premises of the Intermediate *panchayats*. They were staffed on a rotational basis by men and women functionaries and provided cost effective support to the EWRs, and to *panchayats* headed by women. The PRCs provided training and helped mobilize and catalyze participation in the *gram sabhas*. Local Resource Groups (LRGs) were also set up and served as a link between the PRC and the EWRs. They facilitated the exchange of information, interacted with EWRs on issues of concern and relevance to them, and assisted PRIs in the monitoring of basic services. In the *Panchayat* election of 2005, the LRGshelped women to file their nominations. The objective was to improve the delivery of services and ensure that marginalized sections—particularly women and those belonging to the *dalit* communities were covered by the schemes.

Training, capacity building and training of trainers: From the commencement of the project, Unnati emphasized a bottom-up approach. On the job and residential trainings/workshops/seminars were held to orient the newly elected representatives on the functioning of PRIs and on how to manage everyday affairs. Orientation training was provided to the resource group; these trainingscovered the Panchayati Raj Act, basic services, leadership and PEVAC. These groups provided support to the EWRs. Unnati utilized its network of associated NGOs to cover additional areas and used the training of trainers (TOT) component to build a grassroots level team of trainers. Developing the reading skills of the EWRs was an important component of the training imparted to PRC staff and to the LRGs.

Radio as a tool for awareness creation and feedback: The radio was used effectively to communicate to reach out to the people. Special radio programmes, each of 15 minutes duration were broadcast every week, to create awareness about the decentralized mechanisms of governance and the role of EWRs. To attract listeners, drama and quiz formats were utilized. At the end of each programme, a dedicated telephone line allowed listeners to call in with their queries. Unnati received 3,349 postcards and 1,242 phone calls as a result of this popular programme. The PRC has played an important role in bridging the gap between the EWRs, local government officials and the community. An effort was made to form networks (nine such networks were formed) of EWRs and bring them on common platforms to promote collective action. The project has led to a greater understanding amongst the people, especially women, of the importance of participating in *gram sabha* meetings, as well as of the role and responsibilities of EWRs. People belonging to Scheduled Castes, marginalized families and vulnerable groups were the most important beneficiaries of this process.

8.4.9. Tehri Garhwal District, Uttarakhand

Uttarakhand (formerly Uttaranchal) became the 27th state of the Republic of India on 9 November, 2000. Uttarakhand borders China in the north and Nepal to the east. To the west, Himachal Pradesh is its neighbour and to the south lies Uttar Pradesh (the state of which it was a part, before 2000). The state is spread over an area of 55,845 square kilometres and has a population of 8.5 million, with an average density of 159 persons per square kilometre.

The provisional capital of Uttarakhand is Dehradun, a rail-head and the largest city. The state comprises of two regions, the western half is Garhwal and the eastern half covers the Kumaon region. The district of Tehri Garhwal was selected for the project. The district stretches from the snow clad Himalayan peaks of Thalaiya Sagar and Jonli to the foothills near Rishikesh. The Bhagirathi river divides the district into two. The neighbouring districts are Uttarkashi, Chamoli, Pauri, Rudraprayag and Dehradun. A large part of the area of the district is under forests, which occupy a place of importance not only in the ecology but also in the economy of the district.

The partner agency engaged in this project was Shri Bhuvneshwari Mahila Ashram (SBMA); and a three year pilot project called Women in Governance (WIG) was launched in 2004. The blocks covered under the programme were Bhilangana, Chamba, Devprayag, Jaunpur, Janknidhar, Kirtinagar, Narendranagar, Pratapgarh and Thauldar in Tehri Garhwal. Five additional blocks from three other districts were also covered under the project, these were—Almora in Almora district, Ghat and Gairsain in Uttarkashi district and Bhatwari and Dunda in Chamoli district. The first *panchayat* elections after the formation of the state of Uttarakhand were held in 2003. Like other states, Uttarakhand has a threetier *panchayat* structure with 13 *zilla* parishads, 95 kshetra panchayats, and 7,055 gram panchayats. Challenges

Uttarakhand is regarded as a progressive state in many ways but it still has a male dominated society, where women play a subservient role. Nevertheless there are a few dynamic women who are assertive and are striding towards effective participation and decision-making. In general, there is a dual pressure on the EWRs active in the political arena, since they have to attend to household chores and responsibilties as well as participate in meetings and discharge their functions in the *panchayats*. In the elections held in March 2003, 42 percent of the seats in local government bodies in the Garhwal area of Uttarakhand were won by women, a figure substantially higher than the 33 percent seats reserved for them. There are however social, cultural and economic factors that impede the functioning of women as effective panchayat functionaries. The heavy workload on women, family constraints, difficult geographical conditions, economic compulsions and discrimination are some of them. community members as well as the forums is a challenge. Organizing women into forums is a slow process and requires a lot of patience both on behalf of the community and the organization. The State Steering Committee had not been formed (till 2007) and there was only peripheral involvement of the State Government.

8.4.9.1. Strategies Adopted

The WIG programme aimed at promoting good governance in rural areas by building the capacity of female *panchayat* members and facilitating effective participation of EWRs, the program sought to build an enabling environment for women's empowerment and ensure gender equity in democratic governance.

Capacity building and training: The WIG programme worked to build capacities amongst *Mahila* Forums and to identify and articulate the strengths, problems and needs of women in public life. The nine forums that operated in Tehri addressed issues of health and education and provided information on government schemes (for instance pensions for widows). WIG has worked to empower women *panchayat* leaders to be effective in the work that they do as representatives of the people. The women have acquired leadership skills that enable them to manage and lead the forum and to take on responsibilities. There are visible successes – women who rarely left their villages now visit the block office frequently and those who found it difficult to speak to the leadership of their village now boldly present issues before senior Government functionaries.

Creation of forums and leadership trainings: EWRs are encouraged to organize themselves into forums at the block level, so that they are able to address issues of social justice and participate meaningfully in local governance and emerge as effective leaders. Forum members have become more confident. They no longer require to be escorted by a male relative to meetings; some women have even spent a night away from their homes to attend block-level (*kshetra panchayat*) meetings. Women attended structured trainings on leadership, gender, financial management and data collection and have become familiar with the *Panchayati Raj* system. Inter-forum meetings have enabled the women to share ideas and experiences with the other groups. *Mahila* forums have organized events such as International Women's Day and Annual Day celebrations, indicative of their organizational capabilities and confidence.

Exposure visits and expansion of training: Exposure visits have opened new worlds and provided fresh perspectives. In March 2005, 15 EWRs went on a 10-day exposure visit to Himachal Pradesh to study the *Panchayat Raj* system. In an expansion of scope, women trained by the WIG program in Tehri are helping to train EWRs in the districts of Almora, Chamoli, and Uttarkashi.

Mobilization of support from male members: Mobilizing support from male members to create a positive environment for the empowerment process was seen as an essential requirement of the programme. For this SBMA had organized a '*Pratinidhi Pati Sammelan*' (a gathering for spouses of the EWRs), which was very useful to mobilize male support to take up issues at the village and district The forum members are taking a lead in addressing gender stereotype roles, for example many forum members delegate their responsibilities to their male counterparts and come out for meetings and sometimes the members stay out of their homes at night to plan for the block level events and activities.

Documentation and record keeping: The empowerment process is being documented (for example the events records maintained by forums and block volunteers, calendars, Annual Reports and video documentation of programmes)—the successes and failures, problems and strategies and will provide valuable inputs to the empowerment process elsewhere in the state. The programme has had considerable impact in Tehri Garhwal. Women are emerging as vocal and powerful leaders, comfortable in talking with male government officials and are working towards empowering themselves and their communities. A major indicator of success of the programme is that although, SBMA had initially restricted its interventions to Tehri Garhwal district, women from Uttarkashi and Chamoli enthused by the success of the forums in Tehri Garhwal have come forth to form their own forums.

SBMA received requests from Bhatwari in Uttarkashi and Gairisain and Ghat in Chamoli to help them establish women's forums there and the forums are functioning in these districts as well. The women's forum at the district level needs to be further strengthened and there is a need to establish a women's forum at the state level.

8.4.10. Ghazipur District, Uttar Pradesh

Uttar Pradesh is a large state, bordered by as many as seven states (Bihar, Madhya Pradesh, Rajasthan, Delhi, Himachal Pradesh, Haryana and Uttarakhand) and by one country, Nepal, to its north. With an area of 236,286 square kilometres, it is the fourth largest state of the country. It is the most populated state, accounting for 16.7 percent of India's billion plus population and has a population density of 689 people per square kilometre.

Uttar Pradesh has one of the most fertile land masses for agriculture with the Ganges, Yamuna, Ramganga, Gomati and Ghaghra rivers flowing through the state. It is largest producer of foodgrains (particularly wheat), sugarcane, pulses and potatoes in the country.

The state has the largest SC population in the country (there are 66 SC communities) accounting for about 21.1 percent of the population. The five ST communities of the state constitute only 0.1 percent of the population.

Women and people belonging to the SC communities are among the most marginalized in the state. The literacy rate for women is only 42.20 percent and the sex ratio is 898 women for every 1,000 men: reflective of their status in society. Ghazipur district, which falls in the Varanasi division and borders Bihar was selected for the project. The district has 16 blocks of which seven blocks – Sadat, Jakhnia, Saidpur, Karanda, Mardah, Muhammdabad and Sadar – were covered under the project. The partner agency identified was Sahbhagi Shiksha Kendra (SSK).

8.4.10.1. Challenges

Initially, the project had to contend with a lack of interest in its activities and objectives amongst the women. The women were burdened by household responsibilities and social pressures and restrictions added to their inhibitions and reluctance to come out of their homes. The established dominance of their male associates on the PRIs and the opposition of vested interests led to poor participation by EWRs. The idea of women as leaders is not easily accepted at the community level or indeed even by government officials.

Many of the female *pradhans* had male secretaries. This led to a problem; the conservative mores of society made it difficult for the women *pradhans* to talk to their male secretaries, let alone guide and instruct them. In many cases, the problem was resolved in a most unsatisfactory manner, with male relatives acting on behalf of the women *pradhans*.

There were other challenges at the organizational level, and the lack of a strong and committed cadre at the inception of the project hampered the capacity building programme. Lack of support from government officials and the inability to form the State level and District Steering Committees placed the programme at a further disadvantage.

Implementation was especially difficult in the case of marginal groups like *dalits* and SCs, as the external environment was very unsupportive. The local NGOs involved in implementation of programme, also had limitations with regard to project implementation (particularly in management and documentation), and there was a high turnover and dropout of coordinators, which impacted on the project.

8.4.10.2. Strategies Adopted

A combination of the following strategies was used to bring EWRs to the mainstream and facilitate their empowerment.

Sensitization and awareness: A pivotal and facilitating component of the project was sensitization and perspective building for the stakeholders, at various stages of the program. *Panchayat Rath Yatras* (rallies to create awareness on *panchayats*) during the PEVAC and *Panchayat Soochana Raths* (information vans) in the Panchayati Raj Jan Abhiyan (PRaJA) were modes used for mass mobilization. Decorated rickshaws or bicycles with posters, pictures and slogans attracted attention. Announcements made through songs in the local dialect, using the voices of film stars were used to draw the attention of the rural populace. In the second stage, interactive activities, puppet shows, street plays and cultural programmes generated awareness on *panchayati raj* issues. Oneday sensitization trainings, organized at the cluster level, helped in environment building and raising awareness. Informal meetings (with both men and women) were organized to mobilize and strengthen perspectives of EWRs.

Sensitization of government officials at block and district levels, through orientations and workshops explaining the objectives and concept of the capacity building program of EWRs facilitated their understanding of work-related needs and the problems faced by EWRs. Sensitizing male associates and male family members of EWRs was another useful initiative. Widespread illiteracy made the EWRs dependent on the more literate male members of the family. Orienting male associates enlisted their support and encouragement.

Trainings and experiential learning: Newly EWRs often lacked knowledge and skills. Residential trainings provided an opportunity to these women to express their views and concerns, to share experiences and gain confidence and skills. Exposure visits to other projects sites/ areas helped EWRs to learn from each others experiences. The visits also facilitated the process of networking amongst the EWRs and led to the formation of district level networks.

Enabling environment: Various campaigns were adopted to create an enabling environment for the EWRs. Mobilization of the gram sabha and its empowerment was a part of mainstreaming of EWRs. Open meetings of gram sabhas were organized and the identification of issues, setting of agendas and displaying the same, were taken up.

For many first timers, who belonged to disadvantaged social backgrounds, sudden exposure to government programmes was quite intimidating. Confidence building *Samman Samarohs* (felicitation ceremonies) held after the elections provided recognition and inculcated a feeling of togetherness between the stakeholders and the EWRs. An extremely important initiative was the setting up of information dissemination mechanisms. Updated information and learning materials were provided. Special attention was paid to those EWRs who were not able to read, by preparing suitable information and communication materials like posters, pictures, audio cassettes and films. Radio programmes were effectively used for information and knowledge dissemination and provided a platform to EWRs to reach out to the community. These were aired by AIR Varanasi, in five districts of eastern UP.

Support and backup: Sensitization exercises, trainings and interface meetings, were followed by providing continuous support. EWRs were assisted in the writing and filing of applications (for example under the RTI), giving them the confidence to manage issues and problems. Household visits by field level workers and informal meetings were undertaken to facilitate the movement of women outside their homes.

Women Citizen Leadersprovided support to EWRs in organizing *gram sabha* meetings, accompanied them to block and district offices and created a favourable atmosphere for them to carry out their functions. In this process, they gained visibility and a platform to build their own leadership skills. The 56 Panchayat Information Centres (PICs) evolved as hubs for activities and for the dissemination of information. Through visits to the PIC, EWRs acquired information and confidence. The PIC also provided a platform for EWRs to come together, share views and discuss issues related to the *panchayats*.

Strong networks: The strengthening of existing womens' collectives and the facilitation of new platforms was intended to counter the traditional male dominated structures. These networks created an enabling environment, to promote gender sensitive policies in the PRIs and advocated increased accountability of the structures of local government.

EWR collectives were formed at the block and district levels. The district level network (*pradhan sangh*) consisted of the all the pradhans whereas the *Mahila Panchayat Pratinidi Sangh* (MPPS) included the women *panchs* only. Eight MPPSs were formed in the eight intensely covered blocks and one *pradhan sangh* was formed at the district level. These helped to raise women's issues at various forums, provided a voice and platform to EWRs and allowed them to play a more active role. The realization of their collective strength, in turn, gave the EWRs the confidence to take up initiatives and their successes led to the acceptance of the forums.

References

Beneria, L. *Gender, Development, and Globalization*. New York: Routledge. 2003.

Brown, D. S. Democracy and gender inequality in education: a cross-national examination, *British Journal of Political Science* 34 (1). 2004.

Desai, Neera. 'Indian March Towards Equity – A Review of a Decade and half of Action and Policy on Women, *Janata : A Journal of Democratic Socialism*, Vol. 45, Nos. 36 - 40, Jan 6, 1991, pg.9 – 16. 1991.

Patel, Vibhuti. *Getting a foothold in Politics, Reading in Women's Studies Series* : RCUES, SNDT, Bombay. 1986.

Friedrich Ebert Stiftung (FES). *Women in Politics: Forms and Processes.* 1992.

Katro, Jeta. *Women in Development Association*. Phone Interview. February 27, 2009.

Towns, Ann E. *Norms and Inequality in International Society: Global Politics of Women and the State*. Ph.D. Diss. University of Minnesota. 2004.

Valiente, Celia. "The Women's Movement, Gender Equality Agencies and Central- State Debates on Political Representation in Spain." Pp. 174-194 in *State Feminism and Political Representation*, ed. Joni Lovenduski. New York: Cambridge University Press. 2005.

Bibliography

Araújo, Clara. 2003. "Quotas for Women in the Brazilian Legislative System." Paper presented at the International IDEA Workshop "The Implementation of Quotas: Latin American Experiences," Lima, Peru, February 23-24.

Ashworth, Georgina, 1996, *Gendered Governance: An Agenda for Change, Gender* in Development Monograph Series, Number 3, UNDP, New York

Bacchi, C. L. *Women, Policy and Politics. The Construction of Policy Problems*. London: Sage. 1999.

Badie, B. and Birnbaum P. *La logique de l'Etat*. Paris. Hachette. 1982

Balch, Jeff, Tendair Bare and Frances Gardiner. 1998. *Achieving the Advancement of Women in the Post-Beijing Era*. Cape Town and Amsterdam: AWEPA/ African-European Institute.

Baldez, Lisa. 2004. "Elected Bodies: The Gender Quota Law for Legislative Candidates in Mexico." *Legislative Studies Quarterly* 24, no. 2: 231-258.

Barry, Trudie, Sneha Palnitkar . 1996. *Women and Local Politics in Mumbai and London : The quota Innovation*' Third IIAS International Conference (International Institute of Administrative Sciences) – Beijing, China 8 – 11, October, 1996.

Barry, Trudie, Sneha Palnitkar. 1996. *Women and Local Politics in Mumbai and London : The quota Innovation*' Third IIAS International Conference (International Institute of Administrative Sciences) – Beijing, China 8 – 11, October, 1996.

Bataille, P. and Gaspard, F. *Comment les femmes changent la politique et pourquoi les hommes résistent*. Paris : La Découverte. 1999.

Batliwalla, Srilatha. "Transforming of Political Culture" *Economic and Political Weekly*, XXXI, Number 21, p.1248-251. *Women and Political Leadership*

Beall, Jo, 1996, *Urban Governance: Why Gender Matters, Gender* in Development Monograph Series, Number 1, UNDP, New York.

Beckwith, Karen. 1992. "Comparative Research and Electoral Systems: Lessons from France and Italy." *Women and Politics* 12, no. 1: 1-33

Beneria, L. *Gender, Development, and Globalization*. New York: Routledge. 2003.

Bjorkman, James W. 1987. "India: Party, Personality and Dynasty", in Alan Ware. ed. *Political Parties*. Oxford: Blackwell.

Brill, Alida. Ed. 1995. *A Rising Public Voice: Women in Politics Worldwide*. New York: The Feminist Press.

Brown, D. S. Democracy and gender inequality in education: a cross-national examination, *British Journal of Political Science* 34 (1). 2004.

Buckley, Mary and Malcolm Anderson, eds. 1988. *Women, Equality and Europe*. London: Macmillan

Chattopadhyaya, Kamaladevi. 1983. *Indian Women's Battle for Freedom*. New Delhi: Abhinav Press.

CWDS. 1995. *Towards Beijing: A Perspective from the Indian Women's Movement*. New Delhi.

Dahlerup, Drude ed., *Women Quotas and Politics*. London and New York: Routledge, 2006.

Dahlerup, Drude. 1988. "From a Small to a Large Minority: Theory of Critical Mass", *Scandinavian Political Studies*. Vol. 11. No. 4. pp. 275–298.

Davidson, Alastair. 1989. "The Italian women's movement and the Italian Communist Party." Pp. 156-187 in *Politics of the future*, ed. ?. South Melbourne: ?.

Debbie Budlender & UNIFEM. 2004. *Budgeting to Fulfil International Gender and Human Rights Commitments*, Frontline Electronic Publishing Ltd, Harare.

Desai, Neera. 'Indian March Towards Equity – A Review of a Decade and half of Action and Policy on Women, *Janata : A Journal of Democratic Socialism*, Vol. 45, Nos. 36 - 40, Jan 6, 1991, pg.9 – 16. 1991.

Dodson, Debra L. 1991. *Gender and Policy Making: Studies of Women in Office*. New Jersey: Centre for the American Woman and Politics, Eagleton Institute, Rutgers University.

Drèze, Jean and Amartya Sen, "Gender Inequality and Women's Agency", in Class, Caste, Gender, ed. Manoranjan Mohanty. New Delhi: Sage, 2004.

Drude Dahlerup (ed.), *Women Quotas and Politics*, Routledge, 2007.

Folasade Ayorinde. 2005*Local Government Budget & Gender, A Guide Analysis of Kuje Area Council Budget, Abuja, Case Study of the Education & Health sectors*, Nigeria Gender Budget Network.

Folasade Ayorinde. 2005*Local Government Budget & Gender, A Guide Analysis of Kuje Area Council Budget, Abuja, Case Study of the Education & Health sectors*, Nigeria Gender Budget Network.

Friedrich Ebert Stiftung (FES). *Women in Politics: Forms and Processes.* 1992 .

Gaspard, Françoise, ed. 1997. *Les femmes dans la prise de décision en France et en Europe* (Women in decision-making in France and Europe). Paris: L'Harmattan

Golandaz, H.M., 1996, *Human Resource Development for Better Cities with special reference to India*, Bombay, 1996

Haque, Syeda Obaida, 1996, *Urban Livelihood for Women*, Shakti Foundation, Bangladesh

Hoskyns, C. and S. Rai. 1996. "Gender, Class and Representation: India and the European Union", Paper presented at the 1996 Political Studies Association Conference. Glasgow, 10 April.

Institute of Social Studies Trust. Strengthening the Participation of Women in Local Governance, (Uma Project), Bangalore. 1995.

International Union of Local Authorities. 1998. *Women in Local Government. Stockholm: IULA.*

Inter-Parliamentary Union. 1997. *Men and Women in Politics: Democracy Still in the Making, A World Comparative Study*. Series Reports and Documents No.28. Geneva: Inter-Parliamentary Union.

Jones, Mark P. 1998. "Gender Quotas, Electoral Laws, and the Election of Women: Lessons from the Argentine Provinces." *Comparative Political Studies* 31, no. 1: 3-21. 13

Joshi, P. 1989. *Gandhi on Women.* New Delhi: Navjivan Press.

Karam, Azza Ed. 1998 *International IDEA Handbook on Women in Parliaments: Beyond Numbers*. Stockholm: International IDEA.

Karl, Marilee. 1995. *Women and Empowerment: Participation and Decision-Making.* London and New Jersey: Zed Books.

Karmhus, (Mayor) Ingebjorg, 1996, *Municipal Planning on Women's Terms*, Experiences from the Project, Leksvik Municipality, Norway

Karvonen L. and Per Selle. eds. 1995. *Women in Nordic Politics: Closing the Gap.* London: Dartmouth Press. Inter-Parliamentary Union. 1997. *Men and Women in Politics: Democracy Still in the Making*. Geneva.

Katro, Jeta. *Women in Development Association*. Phone Interview. February 27, 2009.

Kishwar, Madhu. "Women and Politics: Beyond Quotas" *Economic and Political Weekly*, XXXI, Number 43, p.2871. 1996.

Knapp, A. and Wrigh, V. *The Government and Politics of France*. London/ New York: Routledge, 4th ed . 2001.

Krook, Mona Lena, "Competing Claims: Quotas for Women and Minorities in India and France". Presented at the European Consortium for Political Research, Budapest, September 8-10th 2005.

Krook, Mona Lena. 2006a. "Gender Quotas, Norms, and Politics." *Politics & Gender* 2, no. 1: 110-118.

Kumari, Ranjana and Anju Dubey, 1994, *Women Parliamentarians: A Study in the Indian Context*, Har-Anand Publications, New Delhi

Leijenaar, Monique. 1996. *How to Create a Gender Balance in Political Decision Making*. Brussels: European Commission.

Liddle, J. and R. Joshi. 1986. *Daughters of Independence*. New Delhi: Kali for Women.

Lovenduski, Joni. 1986. *Women and European Politics: Contemporary Feminism and Public Policy*. Amherst, MA: University of Massachusetts Press.

Madhu Kishwar, The Logic of Quotas, Women's Movement Splits on the Reservation Bill, *Manushi,* Volume No. 107.

Mumtaz, Khawar, "Women's Representation, Effectiveness and Leadership in South Asia". UNIFEM, 2005.

Nelson, Barbara J. and Najma Chowdhury, Eds. 1994. *Women and Politics Worldwide*, New Haven and London: Yale University Press.

Netherlands Ministry of Foreign Affairs 1998. "*Gender and Good Governance*". Conference held in Harare, Zimbabwe (May 1998). The Hague.

Norris, Pippa. Ed. 1997. *Women, Media, and Politics*. New York, USA: Oxford University Press.

Nuss, S.A., 1995, *List of Statistics on Women in Government, Public Sector Employment and Administration*, Judiciary United Nations Agencies and Conferences.

Okojie C.E & Amadi S.I (Eds). 2008*Gender Responsive Budgeting and Parliament: A Handbook for Nigerian Legislators*, a publication of the Centre for Democracy and Development (CDD) and Henrich Boll Foundation (HBF).

Opello, Katherine A. R. 2006. *Gender Quotas, Parity Reform, and Political Parties in France.* Lanham: Lexington.

Pamela Philipose (ed.) "The Political Agenda. Issues Towards Beijing", Coordination Unit, New Delhi. 1998.

Patel, Vibhuti. 1986. *Getting a foothold in Politics. Reading in Women's Studies Series :* RCUES, SNDT, Bombay.

Patel, Vibhuti. *Getting a foothold in Politics, Reading in Women's Studies Series* : RCUES, SNDT, Bombay. 1986.

Pitkin, H. *The Concept of Representation.* Berkeley: University of California Press. 1967.

Rai, S. M. 1995. "Women Negotiating Boundaries: Gender, Law and the Indian State". *Social and Legal Studies*, Vol. 4, No. 3, September.

Ramkumar V. 2008. *Our Money, Our Responsibility, A Citizens' Guide to MonitoringGovernment Expenditures,* The International Budget Project.

Rasheeda, Bhagat, "Getting women into parliament- why the quota system is crucial", The Hindu Business Line, 29 July 2003.

Report of the Joint Committee of Parliament on the Constitution (Eighty-first Amendment) Bill, 1996.

Rule, Wilma and Joseph F. Zimmerman. 1994. Eds. *Electoral Systems in Comparative Perspective: Their Impact on Women and Minorities.* Westport: Greenwood Press.

Sarkar, T. and U. Butalia. eds. 1995. *Women and Right-Wing Movements: Indian Experiences.* London: Zed Press.

Siddiqui, Kamal, (ed.), 1992, *Local Government in South Asia: A Comparative Study*, University Press Limited, Dhaka, Bangladesh

Squires, J. *Gender in political theory.* Cambridge: Polity Press. 1999.

Statistical Reports of Lok Sabha Elections, The Election Commission of India.

Sumita, Ray, Women's Reservation Bill. Advocacy Internet: Vol. 5; Issue No.4; July-Aug 2003; National Centre for Advocacy Studies.

Supporting Gender Mainstreaming, Office of the Special Advisor on Gender Issues and Advancement of Women, United Nations, March, 2001.

Thomson, Suteera, 1995, *Women in Decision-Making Positions: Politics and Administration,* Gender and Development Institute, Bangkok, Thailand

Towns, Ann E. *Norms and Inequality in International Society: Global Politics of Women and the State*. Ph.D. Diss. University of Minnesota. 2004.

UNESCO, 1993. *Women in Politics: Australia, India, Malaysia, Philippines, and Thailand.* (Guest Editor: Latika Padgaonkar). Bangkok.

UNICEF, "Women and Children: The Double Dividend of Gender Equality". 2007.

United Nations. 1991. *Women in Decision-Making: Case-Study on Greece.* New York: United Nations.

Vallance, Elizabeth. 1981. "Women in the House of Commons." *Political Studies* 29, no. 3: 407-414.

Women in Parliament: Beyond Numbers. International Institute for Democracy and Electoral Assistance (IDEA). 2005.

Index